ISSUES IN EDUCATIONAL DRAMA

ISSUES IN EDUCATIONAL DRAMA

Edited by
Christopher Day and John Norman

 **The Falmer Press**

A member of the Taylor & Francis Group
London and New York

First published 1983

ISBN 0 905273 65 6 Limp   OO84O58 X
　　　0 905273 66 4 Cased

125011

3/4.792

DAY

Typeset in Linotron 202 by
Graphicraft Typesetters Limited, Hong Kong

Jacket design by Leonard Williams

Printed by Taylor & Francis (Printers) Ltd
Basingstoke, England
for
The Falmer Press
Falmer House
Barcombe
Lewes, Sussex
BN8 5DL

Contents

Contents

Introduction: Issues in Educational Drama

Christopher Day and John Norman

In the last ten years there have been significant developments in the quest for a deeper understanding of the process we have come to call drama in education. There has been much fruitful exploration of fundamental questions as to the nature of the enactive act, its relationship to art, play, language, thought, feeling and learning and the basic drive to make meaning through symbolic activity. An increasingly coherent account of the meaning and practice of drama in education has begun to emerge through publications such as *Learning through Drama* (1976), *Drama in Primary Schools* (1979) and *Towards a Theory of Drama in Education* (1979). At the same time, publications such as *Drama for Middle and Upper Schools* (1975), *Drama Guidelines* (1976) and *Drama as a Learning Medium* (1977), which have a greater practical emphasis but are of more significance than the many 'tips and hints' books, have attempted to illuminate theory in action. In these descriptions of learning encounters, and through the many journals and courses which are available, teachers of drama have been offered insights into the complex of teaching values, skills and strategies which characterize effective practice.

A noticeable feature of these publications and much of the debate about drama in education is a growing awareness of the need to refer to a variety of other disciplines in the search for a coherent theoretical framework. The literature of drama in education and the idiosyncratic formulations of the pioneers cannot adequately illuminate the underlying meanings and interactions of the drama lesson. Thus drama teachers have begun to draw on sources in social psychology (especially role theory, group work and interaction studies), developmental psychology and the growing body of work which focusses on classroom process and descriptive evaluation. Increasingly we have begun to understand that drama in education represents a view of education *per se* and this has distinctive values, procedural features and implications for the role of the teacher and learner. We have also begun to understand that debate about the drama must be framed in the public language of education, synthesized from the many disciplines which illuminate any educational encounter. It cannot be said, however, that this phenomenal growth in understanding has been translated in real terms into drama posts, children's activity, training courses and support services. Until the mid-1970s there was a parallel growth in provision, but since that time no such claim can be made. If we wish to place drama in the foreground of educational debate, we must perceive ourselves primarily as teachers of children rather than as teachers of drama. There has also been a realization that we must be prepared to enter into the combative, intellectually rigorous exercise of clarification, explanation, synthesis and evaluation which is required to create a public awareness of the significance of drama in the curriculum.

This book was originally conceived when we were both on higher degree courses in education at the University of Sussex. Many fruitful hours of late night discussion and reflection upon our respective views and experience of drama led us to the analysis which forms the basis of this collection. It was essential, we argued, to locate the growing understanding of the drama in education process in the real world of schooling. So many accounts of drama seemed to exist almost in a vacuum and to ignore the constraints and controls which affect all educational activity. By virtue of both its relative immaturity and particular educational philosophy, the practice of drama in education was, we believed, especially vulnerable to attack before it was fully established. We felt, therefore, that it was imperative to identify and understand the many social, economic and ideological factors which would influence the status and development of drama. Only then would it be possible to devise strategies by which drama might become better established. Simply doing the job well, especially when the nature of that job is problematic and unpredictable for many in education, is no guarantee of a future.

Having identified those issues we saw as crucial, we approached various distinguished teachers and thinkers about drama. After many changes, revisions and much reshaping, this collection is now complete. It began as a collection of writings about the development of drama in education. Today, in a world of increasing educational functionalism, it is about the survival of drama in education. The issues which were a challenge then are now more urgent. They are still the same issues but they have been given a new edge and relevance by the political events of the intervening years which have seen the steady erosion of the quality and extent of provision for drama.

Implicit in the individual papers on public attitudes to the arts in education, concepts of drama in education, planning, teaching, evaluation and training is a coherent view of drama in education as a medium for change: change towards a liberating, cooperative, enquiry-centred, non-prescriptive process of education as exemplified in our practice. That view places drama in the front line of the ideological battleground which our schools have become.

This collection is offered in the hope that it will help focus and generate informed debate about the meaning and function of drama in education. It is intended to be a spur to action, both to seek and take radical initiatives and to continue in the development of a secure conceptual framework for drama with special reference to teaching styles and learning outcomes. These initiatives must be concerned with conceiving new contexts for teaching and training, disseminating ideas about drama and seeking credible responses to the economic and political pressures which inhibit the implementation of our vision. Thus the inevitable uncertainties of the eighties could offer a golden opportunity to establish a new position for drama in education. As outmoded educational values and traditions are increasingly questioned, as they will surely be, any curriculum area concerned with personal exploration and expression within a framework of learner-centred values could well come to be seen as offering credible alternatives. There can be no guarantees, except that merely bewailing the plight of drama in education will achieve nothing.

We are indebted to those who have contributed directly to this book and to the many others who have enriched our thinking. May their inspiration continue to guide us all.

1
Overviews of Drama in Education

1   The Status of Drama in Schools

Ken Robinson

The heart of the problem of declining or sporadic curricular and resource provision for drama in secondary schools is its low status. The author argues that prevailing negative attitudes towards drama are largely the result of its association with a perceived progressive, laissez-faire approach to education (no longer acceptable in today's world which has increasingly moved to the political right); its internal divisions – the drama versus theatre arguments that have bedevilled drama over the years; and an increasingly instrumental view of education which has already affected all arts activities. He challenges the increasing moves by many drama teachers towards examinations and separate departments as a means of acquiring more resources and status. He argues that, in doing this, drama is in effect supporting the undue emphasis on vocational preparation through academic work rather than fulfilling its natural function which is to promote social, perceptive, intuitive, aesthetic and creative learning. It is the practice and communication of these kinds of learning which arts teachers need to be pursuing in order that they be better understood and valued. Curriculum strategy in drama should be related to the development within the context of each school of a general policy for the arts.

In placing drama in a well-defined political and social context, Robinson raises general issues of clarity of purpose and practice which are developed in detail in later chapters.

Professional status is related as much if not more to *what* individuals do as to *how* they do it. Solicitors, doctors and architects gain a measure of prestige directly from their professional function. Often this is irrespective of their actual performance in the job. Similarly in schools the status of individual teachers is related as much to their disciplines as to their competence. Partly because of this, many teachers, especially in secondary schools, are preoccupied with the standing and integrity of their own 'subject'. This includes drama teachers for many of whom the status of drama itself is a constant worry. Since it holds the key to resources, facilities and prospects of promotion, some concern with 'subject' status is obviously legitimate and necessary. My argument in this chapter, however, is that some of the efforts to attain or improve it are subverting the basic principles that many drama teachers claim to champion in schools. Moreover, this is at a time when such principles are becoming more, not less, important for children's education. Consequently, there is a need for major revisions in some of the curriculum strategies now being used to elevate drama in schools, and in particular in the use of examinations.

The Status of Drama

It is difficult to be certain of the overall status of drama in contemporary British schools. It varies from one school to another and between one interest group – pupils, parents, teachers, employers – and the next. The indicators of status for any curriculum work are:

1 how much time is allocated to it and when;
2 whether and for how long it is compulsory or optional – and for whom.

An up-to-date national survey of drama provision would undoubtedly show significant regional differences on these measures.[1] But in general we can probably assume in safety that in most schools drama is not well provided for in such terms, that is, its overall status is still low. Why is this and does it matter?

Status is a position in a hierarchy – a rank. It reflects judgments about the importance and value of the thing in question, not just in itself but in relation to others. It refers, that is, not to absolute but to relative importance.

In discussing the status or relative importance of drama in schools, therefore, we need to ask:

1 of relative importance to whom?
2 in relation to what?

We need to consider these separately from the point of view of those who are not involved in teaching drama and of those who are. In doing so we must look first at the general educational context in which drama teachers are now trying to make their way.

The Climate of Education

The status of drama, as of other curriculum work, is always related to prevailing educational priorities. The 1960s are accepted as the boom years for drama in schools. Training courses expanded and specialist departments began to open in the reorganized comprehensive schools.[2] This expansion of drama was not an isolated phenomenon. It took place within a general climate of educational innovation in which two related ideas – those of 'progressive' and of 'liberal' education – became increasingly popular. These ideas are not synonymous but they do converge at a number of points, in, for example:

1   the progressive principle that education should be child-centred;
2   the liberal principle that education should be seen as an end in itself rather than as directed to any instrumental end, for example, vocational qualifications.

A common concern was that schools should provide a broad-based general education for children and young people, and that this should not be distorted or narrowed by a preoccupation with the perceived needs of the labour market beyond the school. Drama teachers were among a growing number to adopt such principles and to claim to practise them. Within drama teaching itself this was associated with a division which many practitioners were keen to promote between drama and theatre and with a growing interest in the uses of improvisation. Developing the individual through creative self-expression – rather than the passing on of received values or of traditional bodies of knowledge – became the key theme.[3] Such ideas sat reasonably well in the mood at the time. The educational climate changed quickly, however, during the late 1960s and into the 1970s. For some time now the political emphasis has been on cutting the cost of education and on accountability. Drama has suffered in this new season of education just as it prospered in the previous one. What lay behind this change and what are the implications for the present and future standing of drama?

Retrenchment and Accountability

Educational accountability is not exclusively nor perhaps even primarily an educational issue. It is economic and political. Nor has the pressure come from a single source. There are four distinct themes to this general chorus.

First, there was from the late 1960s a noticeable disenchantment with some aspects of progressive education. The Black Papers which appeared first in 1969 and then periodically during the 1970s[4] expressed a growing unrest among some politicians and employers with the whole progressive movement. They argued that progressive teaching styles were contributing to a decline in 'basic' skills of literacy and numeracy; to a fall in academic standards; and to an apparent erosion of moral standards among young people. Academic rigour seemed to them to be being replaced with a general attitude of *laissez-faire* in schools. Through association with progressive teaching and 'self-expression', drama teaching was among the many activities to attract such criticisms.

Second, there was during this period a general shift in the political mood. If there was a swing to the liberal and radical left during the 1960s, illustrated in part by the anti-authoritarian, anti-imperialist movements in student politics and exemplified in the events in Paris in 1968, there was during the 1970s and exemplified in the emergence of nationalist and separatist political groups a comparable movement to the liberal and radical right. The pattern of national elections throughout the West has continued this trend into the 1980s. If the Black Papers included nostalgic references to a supposed golden age of academic achievement there also ran through them a turbulent undercurrent of political dissatisfaction with progressivism itself. This came to the surface in the furore over William Tyndale[5] which clearly illustrated that the debate was not simply about methods of teaching. It included fears that the diversity of teaching aims and methods and that progressivism in particular was leading to cultural fragmentation and even political subversion. These charges became associated with criticisms of the whole egalitarian principle of comprehensive education and with calls for a return to the more academic and conservative approaches of the grammar schools. Drama teachers were open to further criticism here through the division of drama and theatre. This appeared to some as an abrogation of their responsibility to pass on the cultural heritage.

A third theme has been the determination to cut the rate of public spending as a general tactic to counter inflation. This has been the policy of successive governments since the Middle East crisis in the early 1970s. This has not only meant less money to spend on education, it has also given further fuel to the debate on educational priorities as a whole.

A fourth factor has been the effects of falling rolls. One of the initial reasons for cutting back on educational spending was a decline in the early 1970s in the overall school population. The downward trend in the birth rate which began in 1964 became a sharp decline by the early 1970s.[6] This has been used to justify some of the spending cuts in education through a reduction in the numbers of teachers and also in the closing of school plant and facilities. Falling rolls have also had significant effects on provision for teacher training.[7]

Education and Employment

A key theme in these changes has been a tendency to associate educational policies with poor industrial and commercial performance and with high levels of unemployment, especially among young people. Consequently, both secondary and tertiary education are now encouraged to relate courses more closely to the needs of the market. This attitude was clearly expressed in *Education and Employment*, published in 1979 by the Association of Chambers of Commerce. No responsible education policy, said the report, can ignore the need to equip school leavers with the qualifications necessary for employment:

> ... The school system has to teach skills essential to modern life. If it fails school leavers will be condemned to unemployment.... This will have serious repercussions on our society. Deprived of sufficient skills, British business will fail to defeat overseas competition and unemployment will continue to rise.[8]

This attitude, widespread among parents, employers, teachers and pupils, creates profound problems for all arts activities because of the associated distinction between work and non-work. On the one hand, those activities which seem most closely related to productive activity are valued above those which are apparently recreational: the one the legitimate province of education, the other not. On the other hand, when employment prospects are bleak or highly competitive, or when, as now, economic stability is threatened, part of the problem is assumed to lie in the schools. As a result vocational and examination pressures on the curriculum intensify. In these terms, the arts are assumed to bear no relation to productive activity and to lie outside mainstream curriculum concerns.

The Current Agenda

These various pressures have combined to change the agenda of contemporary education. My purpose here is not to present the counter-arguments to each of these attitudes – and they do exist[9] – but to register the complexity of the demands for accountability to which, in their search for status, drama teachers must respond. A net result of these changes has been the emergence or re-emergence of public priorities for education which depart some way from the ideal of progressive and liberal teachers. For a good many parents, employers and pupils the status of drama will be judged in relation to these priorities. These are principally an emphasis on:

1 'basic skills' of literacy and numeracy;
2 the development of cognitive/intellectual abilities;
3 instrumental objectives, in particular the preparation for work through academic qualifications.

All activities which make no obvious contribution to these ends have suffered correspondingly. Moreover, since these pressures on the curriculum in secondary schools have been transmitted to a considerable extent through the examination system, those activities which are not examined are even more vulnerable to charges of irrelevance to the mainstream tasks of education. Not surprisingly, many drama teachers have sought to demonstrate the academic rigour of the work and to emphasize its value in vocational preparation. During the past five years there has been a proliferation of drama examinations of all sorts at CSE and GCE level.

This strategy of bending drama to current priorities may be expedient in the short term. It is no basis for developments in the long term. This is because the current public and political priorities are themselves misplaced. Drama teachers and many others began by challenging two related assumptions: first, that education is mainly a process of vocational preparation; second, that academic education is the most urgent priority in schools. It is now more important than ever to maintain this opposition.

Structural unemployment

Unemployment levels are now historically high for all age groups but especially among young people.[10] The causes of this are economic rather than educational. The current rate of unemployment is not the temporary symptom of a passing recession: it results from long-term structural changes in Western economies arising from, among other factors, rapid technological change. Britain is unlikely ever to return to previously accepted levels of full-time employment – certainly in traditional occupations. According to the EEC medium economic policy programme in 1977, for example, it was estimated that:

> to restore even general levels of unemployment to acceptable levels would require an increase of the production of goods and services of at least 25%. The National Institute for Social and Economic Research has similarly commented that GNP must grow at 5% per year for five years before full employment is restored. That figure implies growth of manufacturing industry of about $8\frac{1}{2}$% and a growth of exports of around 16%. A prospect of which it has been said, 'To believe in the impossible and to hope for the unobtainable is no basis for a constructive policy.'[11]

Unemployment is simply not the fault of schools and intensification of examinations is not the way to deal with its effects. There are a number of serious educational objections to competitive public examinations – especially in the arts. We will consider some of these shortly. We should note here that their political and economic value is also seriously flawed – and becoming more so. It is not the lack of qualifications that prevents young people finding jobs – it is lack of jobs. Examinations have a symbolic value, as a negotiating currency in the labour market. Like all paper currencies, they are prone to inflation when too much currency chases too few commodities.[12] As the labour market continues to contract, the intensified race for qualifications is creating an 'academic inflation' in which more and more count for less and less. This may benefit a highly-qualified minority. The majority will be faced with a market in which they have virtually no spending power at all. How will they have benefited? The continuing cut-backs in higher education confirm that the use of examinations to secure the future of young people is an illusion. There is ample evidence to show that more and more young people are coming to the same conclusion.

The Academic Illusion

There is a deep-seated assumption in British education that different curricula need to be provided for different 'types' of child. This has been a major influence in the growth of secondary education. It was a basic tenet of the 1944

Act in providing for three types of pupil in three types of school: grammar, modern and technical. Although the widespread developments in the theory and practice of education since then have done much to modify this view,[13] there are lingering consequences of it. Despite the principle of 'parity of esteem', successful children – 'the more able' – have been persistently associated with an academic curriculum and the 'less able' with practical courses. Significantly, selection at 11+ meant either 'passing' to the grammar school or 'failing' to the secondary modern. This reflects what James Hemmings has called 'the academic illusion', the idea that:

> ... the supreme role of education is the development of the logical, intellectual, analytic aspects of mind and that other aspects – the social, perceptive, intuitive, aesthetic, imaginative and creative aspects – are of minor importance, worth a nod or two here and there but to be valued as nothing beside the glories of academic excellence.[14]

Drama in schools expanded in the 1960s partly as a reaction against academicism. Its proponents saw it, and in many cases continue to see it, as one of the ways of meeting the broader responsibilities of state education by developing, in addition to intellectual abilities, those other equally important qualities and capabilities to which Hemmings refers.

However, the persistent pressures to maintain academic standards fuelled by the political changes we have noted have had direct effects on drama teaching and on its status. First, they have created difficulties for teachers trying to establish drama across the whole age range of secondary schools. Primary schools, being remote from market demands, are relatively free to experiment. Secondary schools, despite the changes we have considered, have never been emancipated in this way. As a result, drama has gained the firmest footing in the lower years of secondary school and only a tenuous hold on the upper years. Nor has the association of drama with non-academic activity brought the hoped-for spread of such activities across the whole ability range. More often it has led to drama being associated with the non-academic child often categorized as 'less able' or 'remedial', for whom, for whatever reason, academic and vocational pressures are relaxed.

Other Constraints

Attempts to develop drama in schools have been closely constrained by these pressures of vocationalism and of academicism. The more these pressures increase, the more important it is to resist them. It is not simply that the status of drama is at risk. There is at issue that broader view of children's capabilities and of educational responsibilities in respect of them which drama and all the arts represent in schools.

Unfortunately, the pressures to conform to the academic curriculum do not come only from outside schools – they also come from within. Some are implicit in the very nature of schools as institutions – others come from what David Hargreaves calls 'the culture of teaching'.[15] Under the combined weight of these influences drama in some schools is rapidly becoming part of the problem some thought it might help to solve.

Education As Conservation

Schools are complex institutions. Like all institutions they are inherently conservative and resist innovation. Institutions exist to formalize and stabilize evolved and imposed patterns of social relations and organization. The institutional functions of schools in this respect are clear enough:

> ... The school is required to perpetuate and transmit ... the culture handed down to it by the intellectual creators of the past.... Further, it is obliged to establish and define systematically the sphere of orthodox and the sphere of heretical culture.[16]

Schools as institutions derive a number of structural and functional characteristics from the fact of having to fulfil these functions, in particular their allegiance to traditional subjects. Any attempt to introduce curriculum change in the school must contend, therefore, with the established routines and traditions which are implicit in the logic of the institution itself. Changing the curriculum is much more, therefore, than a question of logistics.

Professional Identities

These general institutional restraints are strengthened by the professionalization of education by which specific roles are strongly identified with particular functions of the institution. Secondary teachers are employed to teach subjects rather than children. Their professional identities are strongly rooted in the institutional and strongly classified forms of educational knowledge.[17] Attempts to change or to mix subject categories may be seen as a threat to these identities.

New methods of teaching may be accommodated relatively easily in secondary schools, provided the boundaries of existing subjects and professional identities are not breached. New or extra 'subjects' may be accepted under the same conditions. Attempts to change subject classifications may be resisted for this raises questions of demarcation – of property relations – and thus of the distribution of educational power. The strength of resistance is a function of the strengths and traditions of the existing power structures in the school. These are considerable obstacles to innovatory work such as drama, and tackling them needs enormous care.

It would be misleading, however, to picture drama specialists as a universally enlightened group in conflict with a sclerotic system of hardened educational categories. This is not because there is no sclerosis but because drama teachers in their own drive towards further specialization are, to some extent, becoming part of it.

The World of the Specialist

Drama has obvious applications across the curriculum. Many drama teachers have long recognized that they are not dealing with a subject in the conventional sense. For the reasons noted, however, gaining specialist status is a distinct professional advantage for teachers in secondary schools and establishing and running a separate, independent department is a bigger one. The development of drama has now become associated, therefore, with the whole panoply of the subject specialist, including examinations. The trend of this was plotted in 1977 by a commentator on drama in Scotland. In the search for status, he asked, are we now to:

> ... heap on drama the familiar trappings of academic respectability: a separate section of the library for drama, a Central Committee for Drama, 'O' Grade Drama, Higher Grade Drama, Certificate of Sixth Year Studies Drama, Alternative 'O' Grade Drama, The Scottish Association of (Qualified) Drama Teachers, The British Association of Drama Teachers? Drama by that time will have arrived and drama specialists will have established their monopoly.[18]

This might be good for the career prospects of drama teachers, he adds – and a good many of these measures have since come to pass – but is it good for the pupils' education? Are drama teachers, he concludes:

> ... in their search for professional identity, in danger of exacerbating an already unsatisfactory situation? Opportunities for drama activities emerge organically from the work of many teachers of other subjects. Are they to bide their time till the drama specialist is free? Or do they refuse to exploit these opportunities altogether for fear of creating a demarcation dispute?[19]

One of the problems of subject specialization is a kind of tunnel vision through which curriculum problems appear as peculiar problems of drama, of music, of history, rather than as general and common problems of the whole school. Attempts to change the curriculum thus become chauvinistic, for example, more time for drama at the expense of music. This tends to compound the problems of innovation by increasing the competition for resources. One of the features of this specialization is a strong sense of territory, and often of isolation, which ultimately divides one department and one institution from another.

First, there is a horizontal division – teachers in different departments in the same school having very little contact with each other. This minimizes opportunities to identify and address common problems. Second, there is a vertical isolation between the three main sectors of formal education – primary, secondary and tertiary. Third, there is the isolation of teachers from other practitioners in their own art form. Fourth, there is a general lack of contact between teachers working in different regions. The need to exchange experiences and strategies becomes even more important for teachers when they are under external pressures. As it is, few of them ever see other teachers at work or come into contact with projects and schemes operating elsewhere. The result of all this is a sense of working alone which can be profoundly demoralizing.

The Examination Trap

These various problems of developing drama in schools are not to be underestimated. The trouble is that they often are. The principal strategy in many schools for improving the status of drama has been to introduce an examination. I have indicated the probable redundancy of this so far as future school leavers are concerned. There are other reasons to think twice about this which are to do with the general process of curriculum development. For the most part examination courses compound the problems of changing the curriculum by promoting:

1 subject specialization;
2 conservative tendencies – through the emphasis on set syllabuses.

They constrain the arts in particular by promoting:

3 the use of predetermined objectives as the principal basis for assessment;
4 an emphasis on product rather than process;
5 academic values.

Many forms of examination are also antipathetic to the practice of the arts in school in two further respects:

1 they are competitive;
2 they involve a high level of failure.

Much formal assessment in schools, and most examinations, are norm-referenced. They seek to establish not *absolute* but *relative* achievement, by locating children at points along a pre-specified ability range. Children are commonly given grades from A to E with C as the 'average'. The graph of results is expected to etch a bell-shaped curve with the majority clustered around the middle range and a minority of high and low scores at either end.

Bloom has pointed to the self-fulfilling prophecy in the giving of such grades. Teachers begin courses with the expectation that about a third of the pupils will adequately learn what they have to teach – about a third will fail or just get by. A further third are expected to learn a good deal. This set of expectations:

> ... supported by school policies and practices in grading becomes transmitted to students through the grading procedures and ... creates a self-fulfilling prophecy such that the final sorting of students ... becomes approximately equivalent to the original expectations.[20]

For Bloom, this is the most destructive and wasteful aspect of the current system in that it *reduces* motivation for learning and '... systematically destroys the ego and self-concept of a sizeable group of students who are legally required to attend school.'[21] Discussing some of the restrictive tendencies of conventional methods of public assessment and examination, the distinguished American evaluator, Ernest House, puts the criticism more pungently:

> ... I believe that such schemes are simplistic, unworkable, contrary to empirical findings and ultimately immoral. They are likely to lead to suspicion, acrimony, inflexibility and cheating and finally control ... which I think is their real purpose.[22]

None of this amounts to an argument that aspects of drama neither can be nor should be examined in some form. It does question whether examinations should be used to legitimize this work. For the broader problem is not that drama and the other arts are not fully examined – it is that, for the reasons which we have discussed, the developments and interests with which the arts, *qua* arts, are associated are neither fully understood nor valued in schools – examined or not. The real task is to promote this understanding. It seems unlikely that the kinds of provision and status which teachers seek will be forthcoming otherwise.

Changing the Curriculum

Given these various constraints, what kind of strategy is required for the development of drama in the curriculum? A number of points emerge from this discussion. First, the problems which drama teachers see themselves facing are not unique or peculiar to drama. They are common problems of curriculum innovation and arise from a range of cultural, institutional and professional pressures. Second, drama and other arts activities do challenge existing academic and instrumental assumptions about the purposes of education. This should be taken into account. Third, these existing problems can be compounded by teachers themselves adopting territorial attitudes to their own specialism and by their seeking to legitimize the arts in terms which do not apply. The arts represent a broader view of education and of personal capabilities than the purely academic. This should be recognized in attempts to assess and evaluate work and achievement in these areas. Although examinations may provide a short-term solution to the problem of status, they provide no useful strategy for change and development in the long term. These considerations suggest a number of steps for drama teachers to take in developing such a strategy.

1   To identify specifically and in detail in individual schools the kinds of change which are sought in the curriculum.
2   To seek to understand the ideology of the school in question and of other staff so as to identify the particular obstacles which obtain.
3   To recognize other legitimate curriculum interests and to see planning as a collective task involving staff and other interested groups including parents and employers.
4   To recognize the need for the interaction of interests and the exchange of information and ideas to achieve this.

The general need is to resist the tendency to see the curriculum as an inanimate thing. Schools are not things at all. They exist as patterns of relationships and human actions: like drama itself, the curriculum as a whole is best seen as a process.

The Curriculum As Process

The concept of process implies a reciprocal relationship of elements – that each part is in some respects in every other. Thompson, in his analysis of social history argues that the various elements of the social culture cannot be understood if they are looked at as separate and isolated 'things'.[23] This is precisely the danger in the institutionalization of education when knowledge and experience are reified into 'subjects' and the actual and potential relationships between these are overlooked or ignored. The school timetable may be written down: the curriculum takes place as a process of action. It can therefore be adapted and modified to meet changing circumstances. This suggests five basic needs in devising a strategy for change.

The Need for a Policy

Few schools have thought out a curriculum policy from first principles.[24] There are no possible grounds, argues the Schools Council, for assuming that the sum total of objectives of subjects in the curriculum is equal to the total objectives of the whole curriculum. Indeed, where curricula are so enormously fragmented by subjects it is difficult to see how this could be so. What is needed is: '. . . a framework of principles within which individual teachers, teams or departments can consider how best they might each contribute to the whole curriculum.'[25] More often, the curriculum is an accretion of unquestioned tradition, superimposed with piecemeal attempts to accommodate innovation. Two factors challenge the wisdom of this:

1   the general rate of cultural change;
2   the specific variations in the local circumstances of individual schools.

There are two challenges here:

1   to balance the need for curriculum stability with the need to respond to change;
2   to balance the need for an understanding of general cultural themes with that of the specific cultural communities in which children actually live their lives.

The normative pressures of national assessment procedures can easily override these variations in local need and provision.

Two of the problems with existing subject divisions as a basis for curriculum planning are:

1   there are too many of them;
2   the logistic problems they entail enforce an institutional rigidity which resists change.

In *The Arts in Schools* we argued that whatever their differences, all the arts – music, dance, drama, visual arts, literature – have certain elements and educational functions in common.[26] Equally, those ways of knowing which comprise science may be argued to extend across its present division into subjects: chemistry, physics and the rest. The principle to which this points is to look beyond existing subject barriers to the forms of logic and procedure which identify the various and related ways of knowing.

Lawton refers here to 'disciplines' and argues that, to some extent, it is less important that the number and names of these disciplines are agreed than that the value of the principle is recognized.[27] Certainly it lies beyond the scope of this discussion to embark on a general classification of this kind. We can assert, however, that in so far as the arts have common elements, of function and procedure, it is not a separate policy for drama which is needed in schools but a general policy for the arts which relates them to the curriculum as a whole and in which drama has a part.

The Need for Specifics

No two schools are the same. Although, necessarily, we have been concerned with general questions of restraint and innovation, these will appear differently in different settings. Schools differ in almost every respect – size, catchment, staff/pupil ratios, facilities and so on. It is only through analyzing the specifics of their own situation that teachers can begin to devise practicable strategies for change. In some schools the attitudes of the headteacher and of other members of staff will be the key. Moreover, just as the curriculum policy must respond to different cultural settings, so drama will have varying functions within it. Just as individual factors question the value of prescribing methods of teaching drama, so these curricular factors question the wisdom of prescribing this or that form of provision. Nevertheless, detailed planning is precisely what is required. When the headteacher asks, 'What is the value of drama in *this* school?', it is crucial that the question is answered in the same specific terms.

The Need for Specialists

An adequate curriculum policy must recognize the need for drama to be given time to itself. In common with all arts processes, drama is difficult to use productively and requires considerable skill in the teacher. The arguments against defensive specialization are not arguments against the need for special training for drama teaching, nor for time to be given to the work in its own right. Enabling children to understand experience in different ways is at the heart of education. Drama, in common with all ways of knowing, can be used across the curriculum and is not a teaching monopoly. Nevertheless, the different skills of knowing need to be given their due if they are to be used effectively. All teachers help to develop children's use of language, for example. This does not discount the special role of the English teacher. Equally, specialist teachers in the arts are needed to enable children to use these processes as fully as possible. It does not follow that their use should be restricted elsewhere. It is isolationism and territorialism which need to be overcome in schools – while maintaining the skilful teaching of the various disciplines.

The Need for Information

All systems are held together by information. Each of these points is derived from that principle. The difficulties of innovation in schools are compounded by the extent to which the flow of information, within the school and between it and outside agencies is interrupted, blocked or inadequate.

The defensive trends of specialization exacerbate this. The development of a more comprehensive and informative process of evaluation and assessment would increase the flow of information in forms which report on the complexity of the experiences in question. In doing so this could begin to promote the interaction of interests at the levels of both planning and implementation, in which the evolutionary nature of the curriculum must be rooted.

Given the current rate of social change, policies and principles should not only be coordinated, they must also be open to revision in the face of new experience and changing circumstances. Evaluation of the curriculum process and assessment of pupils' attainment are essential to this. In place of the normative and summative assessment procedures which now dominate the curriculum, drama teachers should be aligned with those who are developing and promoting more informative, descriptive and naturalistic styles of evaluation.[28]

The Need for Training

Schools have become increasingly intricate as organizations, incorporating split sites, ability bands, streams, options, vertical and horizontal groupings and the rest. Teachers who want to change the curriculum may well feel outfaced by the logistics, especially since professional training, being subject-based, gives little grounding in curriculum theory and planning. Many teachers lack the skills and the confidence to tackle the curriculum problems which they face. Planning the curriculum is the assigned task of yet another specialist. In addition, the job of curriculum research and innovation has become largely the province of other experts outside the schools – the universities. This extension of specialization has the effect of 'deskilling' teachers in an area with which they are critically concerned.[29]

Nevertheless, as Lawton puts it, there can be no curriculum development without teacher development.[30] No amount of prescription from outside schools will compensate for a lack of direct action within them by teachers themselves. If teachers are genuinely concerned with innovation, they need the will and the skill to analyze problems in their own schools and to devise and promote the relevant strategies for change. This means a direct emphasis in initial and in-service training, not only on teaching methods in drama but on these complementary areas of professional responsibility – curriculum management and evaluation.

Ends and Means

Education is in crisis. Economic, industrial and technological changes are questioning some of the most deep-seated assumptions about what schools are actually for. The public priority is to intensify the pressures of academic qualifications. This is no solution and the realization is beginning to spread. More than ever before young people need a broad-based general education to equip them adequately to meet the increasing perplexities and demands of life during, after and beyond school.

The arts – all the arts – have an inestimable role to play here, not as appendages to a regressive curriculum but at the centre of curriculum reforms which have now become urgent. Status is important because it affects resources and the atmosphere in which the work is done. It is also important because it reflects public values and priorities. It may be expedient in the short term to demonstrate the relevance of drama to existing priorities. In the longer term the strategy must provide for changing what these priorities are. In our concern with status, we should not mistake the means for the end.

Notes

1   The most recent national survey of secondary provision was that done by the staff and working parties of the Schools Council Project (10–16) and published: McGREGOR, L., TATE, M. and ROBINSON, K. (1977) *Learning through Drama*, Heinemann Educational Books. The project also drew on a statistical report on drama provision which I had prepared for the School Examinations Department, University of London: ROBINSON, K., *Find a Space* (mimeo). For a full account of practice and provision of drama in primary schools see STABLER, T. (1979) *Drama in Primary Schools*, Macmillan.

2   For a fuller discussion of the development of drama in education see, for example, ROBINSON, K. (Ed.) (1980) *Exploring Theatre and Education*, Heinemann Educational Books; also ALLEN, J. (1979) *Drama in Schools: Its Theory and Practice*, Heinemann Educational Books.

3   This continues to be a contentious issue in drama education. For a detailed consideration of the relationships between drama and theatre see ROBINSON, K. (*op. cit.*) Chapter 6, 'Drama, Theatre and Social Reality'.

4   COX, C.B. and DYSON, A.E. (1969) *Fight for Education: A Black Paper*, Critical Quarterly Society. Other 'Black Papers' appeared under the same editorship in 1970, 1975 and 1977.

5   It was interesting to note, as Barry MacDonald has argued, that where Risinghill was seen as an aberration, William Tyndale was seen as an early warning signal. (MACDONALD, B. (undated) *Who's Afraid of Evaluation?*, Centre for Applied Research in Education, University of East Anglia, mimeo.)

6   For the facts and implications of falling rolls see BRIAULT, E. and SMITH, F. (1980) *Falling Rolls in Secondary Schools*, Part 1 and 2, NFER Publishing Company.

7   It was announced in the House of Commons on 20 March 1975 that teacher training capacity outside the universities would have to be reduced to about 60,000 places in response to falling rolls. As a result, about thirty colleges were expected to give up teacher training altogether. (See DES, *Reports on Education: No. 82*, March 1975.)

8   Association of Chambers of Commerce (1979), *Education and Employment*, p. 2.

9   For detailed discussions of each of these points see Calouste Gulbenkian Foundation (1982) *The Arts in Schools: Principles, Practice and Provision*.

10   For a detailed profile of the facts, causes and implications of youth unemployment see *Youth Unemployment: A Background Paper*, Youthaid, 1977 and 1980.

11   Kenneth Baker MP in *The Guardian*, 17 May 1977, quoted in Youthaid, *op. cit.* (1977) p. 6.

12   The inflationary tendencies of the qualification market are incisively analyzed in DORE, R. (1976) *The Diploma Disease*, Unwin Education Books.

13   For a critique of these assumptions see SIMON, B. (1978) *Intelligence, Psychology, Education: A Marxist Critique*, Lawrence and Wishart.

14   HEMMINGS, J. (1978) 'The betrayal of the adolescent', in ROSS, M. (Ed.) *Arts Education: Towards 2000*, Conference Report, University of Exeter School of Education, p. 20.

15   HARGREAVES, D. (1982) *The Challenge for the Comprehensive School: Culture, Curriculum and Community*, Routledge and Kegan Paul.

16   BOURDIEU, P. (1971) 'Intellectual field and creative project', in YOUNG, M.F.D. (Ed.) *Knowledge and Control*, Collier-Macmillan, p. 178.

17   See BERNSTEIN, B. (1971) 'On the classification and framing of educational knowledge', in YOUNG, M.F.D., *op. cit.*

18   KIRK, G. (1977) *Drama and the Curriculum*, Education Department, Jordanhill

College, Scotland, mimeo, p. 6.
19 *Ibid.*, p. 7
20 BLOOM, B. (1971) 'Mastery, learning and its implication for curriculum development', in EISNER, E.W., *Confronting Curriculum Reform*, Little, Brown, p. 17.
21 *Ibid.*
22 HOUSE, E.R. (1973) *School Evaluation: The Politics and the Process*, McCutchan Publishing Co, p. 3.
23 THOMPSON, E.P. (1968) *The Making of the English Working Class*, Pelican.
24 DEPARTMENT OF EDUCATION AND SCIENCE (1981) *The School Curriculum*, London, HMSO.
25 SCHOOLS COUNCIL (1975) *Report of the Schools Council Working Party on the Whole Curriculum* (1971–4), Schools Council Working Paper 53, Evans/Methuen Educational, p. 24.
26 Calouste Gulbenkian Foundation, *op. cit.*
27 LAWTON, D. (1975), *Class, Culture and Curriculum*, Routledge and Kegan Paul.
28 These points and their practical implications are elaborated in *The Arts in Schools*, Chapter 6, 'Assessment Evaluation and Accountability'.
29 SIMONS, H. (1978) *Process Evaluation in Practice in Schools*, University of London, Institute of Education, mimeo.
30 *Op. cit.*

2 Context or Essence: The Place of Drama in the Curriculum

Cecily O'Neill

The author continues debating the theme that the arts should be perceived as an essential part of the school curriculum. However, whereas Robinson emphasized drama's 'contextualist' function, arguing that drama should be valued for its contribution to personal and social education, O'Neill suggests that, while this function is important, at least as a survival strategy, it must not be allowed to subvert the prime 'essentialist' function of drama. Here the act of drama is valued as a unique mode of learning to know about human behaviour and its consequences. It is the quality of the enactment, then, that must be considered in planning, teaching, and evaluating drama. This chapter, together with Robinson's, deals with issues at the heart of the debate within drama concerning its intrinsic value as an educational activity and its contribution to learning generally. In this sense the two form a necessary preface to the issues raised in the following sections.

The arts have seldom been regarded as an essential part of the school curriculum, even in periods of expansion in education, and nowadays they are likely to seem mere luxury subjects, educational frills which are far from central to the training of children for real life. Teachers of the arts in schools are increasingly faced with this attitude to their subjects from administrators, headteachers, parents, colleagues and even pupils. Although they may believe passionately in the value of their work, it is not always easy to convince others of its importance, possibly because many teachers lack a sound theoretical base for their work in the arts, but also because the very substance of the arts seems inimical to what is accepted as the function of the school. In many instances, the hidden curriculum of drama is far removed from the norms of the school in which it is taught, as Chris Day points out.[1] Using Bernstein's analysis of the transmission of learning in schools as three message systems – curriculum, pedagogy and evaluation – he contrasts these in drama with those in other areas. In drama 'the curriculum is problematic rather than given, pedagogy is viewed as negotiable rather than imposed, and evaluation is viewed as individual rather than comparative'. The implication of these differences for the arts generally, which share to a large extent the same 'hidden curriculum', is that teachers must be able to identify for themselves and others what part their subject *does* play in the education of children, and what part it plays in the context of the school.

In the past many teachers of the arts, and especially of drama, recognizing that their subject operates in a different way from those taught by their colleagues, have sought justifications for their work in these very differences. Drama produces unconventional interactions between pupils and teacher, therefore drama must be about relationships and social learning. Drama provides a release from the strait-jacket of academic learning, therefore drama can be justified as 'fun' or therapy. Both these claims may be true, but neither is likely to recommend itself highly to a headteacher trying to squeeze the subject into an already overcrowded timetable. Under present circumstances, it is no longer appropriate for drama teachers to try to operate an incompatible system within the school. This is likely to further isolate them from their colleagues, strengthen a siege mentality, and do nothing but disservice to the subject. Until teachers of the arts in general, and drama teachers in particular, are able and willing to share their thinking with their colleagues and superiors, the impression that their subjects exist at the fringe of school activities, rather than at the centre, will continue to be reinforced.

Many drama teachers today are engaged in an attempt to construct a clear theoretical framework to support them in their work, and are searching for aims and objectives to provide an adequate basis for action. Ways must also be found to define drama in broad educational terms. Elliot W. Eisner, an American educator who has been very much involved in curriculum planning and development, makes a far-reaching investigation of the philosophy and history of the arts in education in his book, *Educating Artistic Vision*.[2] Although he is primarily discussing the visual arts, what he has to say has great relevance for drama teachers. He identifies two major kinds of justification for the teaching of the arts in schools, which I propose to relate specifically to the teaching of drama in the remainder of this chapter.

The first type of justification for the teaching of the arts Eisner calls 'contextualist'. This approach emphasizes the instrumental consequences of art, and utilizes the particular needs of the students or society as the basis for objectives in the work. The orientations which Eisner discerns in this approach will be familiar to all drama teachers, and may include arguments which they themselves use in support of their subject. He lists these orientations as follows:

1. the arts as leisure pursuits;
2. the arts as tools in the child's physiological development;
3. the arts as therapy – encouraging the release of emotion and physical tension;
4. the arts as instruments in the development of creative abilities;

5   the arts as ways of developing understanding of academic subject-matter.

I have altered the order of Eisner's orientations to fit in with what I see as a kind of historical development in the teaching of drama, but all of these approaches can be found in the past and present teaching of the subject.

The idea of the teaching of the arts and drama as a leisure pursuit has been emphasized time after time in various reports on education. In such reports, art is seen to be concerned with the transmission and exploitation of the best of the cultural heritage, which is expected to exert a powerfully civilizing influence. The importance of the cultivation of finer feelings is stressed. This orientation is strongly reflected in many a theatre arts CSE syllabus, where the cultivation of an interest in theatre as a leisure activity is often stated as an aim of the course, and is supported by education authorities who subsidize theatre experience for schoolchildren. Teachers interested in developing their pupils' taste and appreciation of culture may be accused of trying to indoctrinate their pupils with middle-class values, but it would appear that the majority of pupils continue to find theatre less significant in their lives than football or rock music. Support for this approach is demonstrated by the Schools' Council Drama Project's book, *Learning through Drama*.[3]

> At the end of five or six years of drama, pupils ought to be able to appreciate other people's drama, to be aware and critical of the drama they encounter outside their school lives. This includes television, radio and films. It is also hoped they will be informed about the theatre as a basis for future enjoyment.

The notion of art as an aid to physiological development, through the child's growing coordination, is best illustrated in drama terms by the BBC's programme, 'Music and Movement'. Although generally regarded as rather out-of-date, it is a view which still has considerable currency among infant teachers and those wishing to help gauche or physically inhibited teenagers. It is an approach which can be seen today in the work of dance and movement teachers.

The next of Eisner's orientations of the contextualist justification for the teaching of the arts is the therapeutic. This is an extremely familiar justification for drama, which has had both age and respectability bestowed on it by Aristotle's notion of catharsis. The release of pent-up emotions and energy is seen as conducive to mental health and valuable for pupils as a contrast to the academic disciplines in which they are usually engaged. Both Peter Slade and Brian Way put forward the view that 'illegal' behaviour in real life can be avoided by the release of emotion through drama. Robert Witkin claims that teachers are torn between encouraging this release of emotion and trying to control it. He defines this kind of emotion, which he does not regard as being meaningful in art, as 'subject-reactive' – where the emotion is merely discharged, and contrasts it with 'subject-reflexive' emotion, which he sees as leading to expressive action and providing the foundation for the intelligence of feeling. Some teachers see value for their pupils in re-enacting their real-life problems in therapeutic role-play. But again, there is often ambivalence from the teacher who recognizes that such work may assist pupils in understanding or coming to terms with their problems, but who also knows that he himself is not trained to deal with any deeper conflicts which may arise from the work. As Witkin says: 'The drama teacher is involved in a continuing contradiction between his need to engage the emotional responses of the pupil and his discomforting awareness of the dangers of doing this.' Where the drama teacher sees the justification for his work lying in the area of therapy, he is particularly likely to be prey to these fears. Drama as compensation for the underachievers also fits into this orientation. Children who have little chance of succeeding at any academic subject can be given a sense of achievement in the arts. Although this fact may be apparent, too great an emphasis in this direction can lead to an undervaluing of the arts by pupils and teachers alike. Another important element in the work of drama teachers, which fits in with this approach, is the significant social learning which may occur and whose effects on the pupils can be far-reaching.

The development of creative abilities is Eisner's next orientation. In drama teaching during the 1950s and 1960s, the main emphasis was on the necessity of unlocking the creativity of the child. It was assumed that the child develops from the inside out, and that the teacher must refrain from interfering with the child's own vision. This approach has a lengthy parentage in educational philosophy, from Plato through Rousseau, and is one which many of the most influential writers on drama have espoused. Teachers whose initial training in the subject may have been less than adequate could find comfort in this approach. Their task became the relatively simple one of facilitating the natural self-expression of the child. More recently, this orientation has developed towards an emphasis on creative thinking, in which work in the arts is used to engage pupils in problem-solving activities. The basis for this approach lies in the fact that the aesthetic experience faces the student with a situation in which the normal expectations which guide his characteristic modes of action are interfered with. It is a kind of discrepancy-resolution that has been described as a genus of which problem-solving is one species. The teacher of the arts who views his work in this light is concerned with developing the divergent aspects of his pupils' thinking. Mel Marshak recently reinforced this view of the arts:[5]

> The arts, through their imagery, afford the possibility for independent thinking, as alternatives to the exactitude of standardisation, of uniformity, of predictability and of single-valued thinking enjoyed by analytical philosophy, scientific calculations and their technical applications.

The drama teacher is able to confront his pupils with alternatives, challenge their thinking, and help them to place ideas and relationships in a new perspective.

This approach merges with Eisner's last contextualist orientation – the arts as tools in the teaching of cognitive skills. In recent years, drama teachers who have become profoundly dissatisfied with the paucity of aim and content in their lessons have begun to see a way forward in the use of drama as a means of understanding academic subject areas. They look to the example of such teachers as Dorothy Heathcote and Gavin Bolton, whose work is patently full of learning for their pupils. Teachers find it possible to identify this learning, and see its value, so that the idea of drama as a method – a tool in the teaching of cognitive skills – is gaining acceptance. It has become obvious that specific kinds of learning, particularly in language and social studies, can be promoted through the use of drama. Fines and Verrier's excellent book, *The Drama of History*, has shown how effective the drama method can be in the service of an academic discipline.[6] Some drama teachers, seeing in this kind of work a solid reason for the existence of their subject in the curriculum, are asking to be included in humanities departments, or as part of integrated studies, rather than in arts departments, or as additions to the English department. In primary schools, the idea of drama as a weapon in the armoury of the classroom teacher which can be used to teach almost any cognitive skill has led, I believe, to an increased interest in the subject, and has received support recently from the publication of the Bullock report.

Although all or any of these kinds of learning identified in Eisner's five contextualist orientations may take place as a result of teaching drama, and may be appropriate as aims for certain teachers in particular circumstances, each can be achieved by other subjects in the curriculum. To justify the arts in education satisfactorily we must turn to what Eisner calls the 'essentialist' justification. This emphasizes what is unique and indigenous to art. For Eisner, the prime value of the arts in education lies in 'the unique contributions it makes to the individual's experience with and understanding of the world'. Each of the arts will deal with one aspect of human consciousness that no other field touches on. This view of the arts is less readily grasped than the idea of the arts in the service of the individual and the community. It demands from the teacher a real understanding of the special nature of his subject, and a sound theoretical grasp of its basic principles. Drama can find itself in difficulties here, since its special nature is most readily recognizable as theatre, an aspect of the work which many teachers of educational drama might not wish to emphasize.

Until teachers of drama can think and express themselves in essentialist terms, they are doing less than justice to their subject. The most determined and successful attempts to move the arts out of their peripheral role in education are taking place where teachers explore the intrinsic educational value that the process of art can have – the quality of thinking and feeling it can bring to the children's understanding. Jerome Bruner identifies art as a mode of knowing, which he sees as profoundly complementing the 'knowing' of science, and as having the power to free us from the forms of instrumental knowing which occupy the centre of our awareness.[7] He refuses to accept that education is merely the process of transmitting a society's culture, but demands the kind of education which will provide alternative views of the world and strengthen our will to explore them. The experience of art ideally does just this, in each of its manifestations. It can give the child deeper, more gripping and subtle ways of knowing the world and himself. Suzanne Langer develops this idea of two major modes of knowing, which she defines as discursive and non-discursive.[8] For her, art is in the latter category, and is concerned with developing forms which are expressive of human feeling. She believes that art is a cognitive activity based on feeling, and that to claim that the artist does not think as intently and penetratingly as a scientific enquirer is absurd.

Louis Arnaud Reid makes the point that art cannot be accepted fully as part of liberal education without what he calls 'cognitive perspective'.[9] This sounds perilously close to Eisner's last contextualist orientation, but Arnaud Reid is not satisfied to focus merely on the instrumental qualities of the experience.

> There is a cognitive perspective which is attainable not so much by going beyond or outside the art itself, as by going deep down inside it. It is an expansion of outlook by cultivation of aesthetic depth, an increase of understanding through the feeling of the involved mind-and-body.

Arnaud Reid is aware that the potential cognitive content of the study of the arts is enormous. But he insists that this cognitive content can only be a part of education in the arts if it is constantly related in feeling and thought to the intrinsic aesthetic experience. There have been many attempts by aestheticians and philosophers to identify the unique and essential learning which takes place within the aesthetic experience. But aesthetic learning is not a single type of learning. Every different art form will be likely to elicit a particular kind of experience. If it were possible to define and analyze that unique experience precisely, there would cease to be a need for the art form which produced it. The non-discursive mode would give way to the discursive.

In drama, as in each of the other arts, the kind of learning which takes place will depend on the unique meaning embodied in the work. Because of the special nature of drama, this meaning is likely to be concerned with human behaviour and its consequences. It is the task of the teacher who justifies his work in essentialist terms to help his pupils to experience and explore that behaviour, its implications and consequences, from within the creative process that is drama, and to develop an understanding of the ambiguities and complexities of meaning in the work. Art is a form of experience which vivifies life. Such experience is relatively rare and intrinsically valuable. To subvert it to other ends is to violate the very characteristics which art, as experience, possesses. Ann Shaw emphasizes this point with specific reference to drama:[10]

> Drama's potential is best realised when we emphasise the process and the particular understandings with which drama is involved and able

to illuminate; when we purposefully involve children in the enactment of their imaginings of the development and outcomes of significant and universal experience. To the extent that we do this, we may propose drama as a central part of education. To the extent that we promote drama as a panacea for personal development and the problems of schools, we are profligate. Drama may well be an effective teaching methodology, but to relegate it to the role of hired hand is an appalling waste.

Both essentialist and contextualist views will have profound consequences for the teaching of the arts, as Eisner recognizes. Each will determine the kind of curriculum which is planned, the kind of teacher who is employed and the teacher education which is provided. If headteachers and curriculum planners were sufficiently knowledgeable about the different aspects of drama, they could be extremely precise in providing for particular needs. For example, if drama as therapy were required, a teacher with a background in psychology and psychodrama could be employed. If drama were regarded as important for social learning, a teacher with a knowledge of group dynamics and sociology would be required. If physiological development were the main aim, a teacher trained in movement skills would be appropriate, and so on. As art departments advertize for a potter, or a graphic designer, so a school needing a drama teacher might expect to appoint someone with the skills of a Veronica Sherborne, a Sue Jennings or a Dorothy Heathcote. No one need quarrel with the notion that a drama teacher should have particular skills at his command, so long as he knows why and to what end he is using his skills, what kinds of learning they are likely to promote, and how far these arise because of the unique quality of the art form in which he is working. It may be useful for drama teachers to get the following structure clear, and to decide which parts of their teaching accomplish the different kinds of learning:

Learning which arises because of the social and interactional nature of drama: drama for leisure, as therapy, social learning, as a remedial activity.	Cognitive and imaginative skills: drama which gives rise to creativity, imagination, problem-solving, discovery, language learning, the study of other subjects.	Learning which is unique to the art form: drama as a way of knowing. Learning which arises as a result of the unique nature of the dramatic experience.

To some extent, it may be necessary for the drama teacher to use both contextualist and essentialist approaches when he has to justify the inclusion of his subject in the curriculum. If the drama teacher is to operate effectively within the political structure of his school, he may have to support his work with contextualist justifications while being, in reality, a crypto-essentialist. Yet this need not mean a loss of integrity. Even such a firmly instrumental and contextual document as *A Language for Life* recognizes the essentialist nature of literature: 'It is not the function of literature to provide a kind of social comprehension test; nor to serve as a glib and instant illustration, its true significance left unexplored.'[11]

Malcolm Ross has stated categorically that the relevance of the arts in education is to the life of feeling.[12] Nothing less, he says will serve. Yet inevitably the themes and goals of the arts in education are context bound. Steps forward are usually followed by steps backward, in the acceptance of the arts as central to education. Eisner recognizes that the content, goals and methods of art in education change over time, and the aims to which the field is directed are related to the social, economic and ideological situations in which they function. In times of recession, practical utility will be the main criterion by which the contents of the curriculum will be judged. The Great Debate has shown that we are now operating in such a time. Institutions in a changing social order must change to survive. Teachers of the arts must use the arts as tools when necessary without sacrificing what the arts can uniquely contribute to learning. But these other purposes should be conceived of as short-term goals which are necessary for the eventual achievement of those aims which only the arts can provide.

The importance of the arts in education lies in the fact that learning in the arts does not, finally, remain a merely individual experience. It 'remakes the maker' but it can also be a remaking of the experience of the community.'

Notes

1 DAY, C.W. (1977) 'Drama: A means of educating', in *The Times Education Supplement*, November 1977. 4th Nov. (P. 27)

2 EISNER, E.W. (1972) *Educating Artistic Vision*, London, Macmillan.

3 MCGREGOR, L. *et al.* (1977) *Learning through Drama*, Heinemann Educational Books, p. 145.

4 WITKIN, R.W. (1974) *The Intelligence of Feeling*, Heinemann Educational Books.

5 MARSHAK, M. (1976) 'Symbol, myth and art', in *New Destinations*, Greater London Arts Association Publications.

6 FINES, J. and VERRIER, R. (1974) *The Drama of History*, New University Press.

7 BRUNER, J.S. (1962) *On Knowing – Essays for the Left Hand*, Harvard University Press.

8 LANGER, S.K. (1953) *Feeling and Form*, Routledge and Kegan Paul.

9 REID, L.A. (1965) *Meaning in the Arts* Allen and Unwin, p. 297.

10 SHAW, A. (1975) 'Co-respondents: The child and drama', in MCCASLIN, N. (Ed.) *Children and Drama*, New York, David Mackay.

11 BULLOCK (1975) *A Language for Life* London, HMSO, p. 149.

12 ROSS, M. (1975) *Arts and the Adolescent*, Schools Council Working Paper 54, Evans/Methuen Educational.

2
Concepts of Drama in Education

3   Drama as Game

Brian Watkins

This chapter presents an apparently radical view of drama per se and its function in the curriculum of the school. It is, Watkins argues, explicitly concerned with celebrating and challenging social values, and so promoting social change which, the author believes, is necessary to the health of the community. Watkins suggests that authority in the drama lesson must be vested in the individual pupil, that drama should be both provocative and child-centred. He claims that drama represents 'a truly democratic model' of learning which is consensual. The chapter thus raises issues of teacher and student role. Watkins criticizes teacher-directed drama work, extols the virtues of 'contract' drama, and finally offers a set of criteria to assist teachers in their decision-making as the drama progresses. So far, then we have identified the third major issue for drama teachers. Robinson's chapter was presented as a critical overview of the status of drama in relation to the broad social context; O'Neill argued for drama itself as a unique mode of learning; and Watkins claims that the prime function of drama is to promote social change. He brings the reader to the door of the classroom in asserting that the relationships between teacher and pupils and attitudes to knowledge and control must inevitably be different from those which exist in the normal curriculum of a school.

For more than a decade there has been among educationists with a concern for drama a search for structure. More recently a severe decline in staffing, affecting provision for the arts, and an emphasis on accountability have made that search more intense. At the same time there has been pressure to commit programmes to paper in a way that will make explicit not only the content but also the educational objectives. The behavioural modification that these anticipate, especially in the group context that drama requires, has revealed more clearly the links that the subject has with sociology. Such topics as role, group dynamics, interactional analysis and aspects of social order and control have seemed to be especially relevant.

Nevertheless, although such titles as Goffman's *The Presentation of Self in Everyday Life*[1] have found their way onto many a course booklist, we should beware of substituting the study of sociology for that of drama. We should always be clear that in drama we observe the social process but through a model; as Aristotle described it, 'an imitation of an action'.[2] It is perhaps the work of the symbolic interactionists, therefore, that is most apt for the purposes of the drama teacher because they regard men in social encounters as actors playing a succession of roles. This view is articulated in the following definition of the game framework: 'The game framework is a model of behaviour of man under consciously problematic situations of a similar nature.'[3] The drama might be similarly defined as an imitation of people's interaction. It deals with relationships under stress; a problem that requires resolution or alleviation, and the need for decisions that will affect others for better or worse.

There is, however, a fundamental difference between the two and it lies not so much in the content but in the purpose of the investigations. The 'symbolic interactionists are interested in searching for and analysing the areas of negotiation and innovation that exist within interactions. They are interested in the interpretation and negotiation of shared symbols and meanings within interaction, but not in where these symbols and basic everyday rules and procedures come from.'[4] The drama, on the other hand, is a mirror of moral values, a mirror that reflects the great concerns of men, 'a concern for God, for society, and for the individual....'[5] Therefore, a study of the drama must include not only the social-psychological but also a philosophical appraisal of the bases of social behaviour.

The argument is that drama does not merely admit to the use of game theory but is actually game itself. This view in former times would not have seemed exceptional when men did not make the distinction between drama and other games that they make now. This modern view is maybe only an extension of that fragmentation of social experience that separates religion from politics, politics from education and the arts from common forms of leisure. For whatever reason though, we seldom associate such terms as 'a play', 'players', 'the playhouse' with the more familiar world of play and game. Yet the continued existence of these terms is proof of its earlier synonymity with popular concepts of game. In medieval times it was its existence as game that made the representations of God and Christ in popular drama acceptable and not the heinous crime of blasphemy. A less tolerant view of game in the seventeenth century brought the Puritan attack dismissing drama along with other pastimes as mere frivolity and a waste of time. Certainly no distinction was made then between drama games and others but all were regarded for good or evil as an integral part of the life of the community at play.

Exactly what part game plays in the life of the community needs closer study because the function it once performed seems now to be less apparent. Nowadays we tend to regard games as being merely an escape from the real traffic of our lives; 'time out'. We do not see in the structure of the game a reflection of the complex social process in which we are involved. Nor do we appreciate as we once did its ritualistic function often preserving unconsciously echoes of the profoundest chords of man's being: 'Primitive, or let us say, archaic ritual is . . . sacred play, indispensable for the well-being of the community, fecund of cosmic insight and social development but always play in the sense . . . [of] . . . an action accomplishing itself outside and above the necessities and seriousness of everyday life?.' We may agree that the content of the play does indeed appear 'not serious' and outside the necessities of everyday life, yet its conduct reflects a profound aspect of social behaviour. That is, that its rule regulation, upon which its continuance depends, affirms in man a tendency towards order.

The drama game not only shares these orderly characteristics with all other games but like many others draws its substance from an observation of human affairs. We reflect upon social values when they are presented to us as analogy in drama, that is, as a series of model encounters involving human behaviour in stress situations. Thus, as in all art, the game of drama 'serves as a lifebelt to rescue us from an ocean of meaninglessness.'[7]

The importance of the social experiences that are reflected in the drama will be discussed further, especially in relation to the classroom. More immediately, we should establish a common understanding of what we mean when we use the term 'play the game'.

In his book, *Homo Ludens*, the Dutch anthropologist, Huizinga, described play as 'a free activity standing quite consciously outside ordinary life, . . . not serious but at the same time absorbing the player intensely and utterly. It proceeds within its own proper boundaries of time and space according to fixed rules and in an orderly manner.'[8] Caillois, too, isolates the same properties as, 'free, separate, uncertain and unproductive, yet regulated and make-believe'.[9] This activity, play, as it becomes more socialized and institutionalized also becomes more structured and repeatable through its rule regulation. We now recognize the activity as that phenomenon we term game, and though we may see both as separate from real-life affairs yet their substance is based upon an observation of reality, though distorted. Indeed, it would be true to say that the players create a symbolic world within our normal world which by its order and harmony lends a coherence to the original.

That the activity absorbs the player utterly indicates the power of the game, that it is at the same time a 'free activity' shows its intrinsic motivation. These two aspects are both the strength and the weakness of drama as a way of learning for when they are present the process is like no other in the curriculum; when they are absent the drama game is impossible to achieve. Perhaps it is possible to carry through a task in, say, maths that one dislikes, but not so in drama. To play a game requires a basic desire to do so and anything less will render it unenjoyable and probably unplayable. Thus it may not be enough to have prepared materials such as work cards to anticipate success. Above all one must be satisfied that those essential game conditions exist to enable the task to be established.

The progress and the enjoyment of the game rely also upon its structure, its own proper boundaries of time and space, and upon its being conducted in an orderly manner. Here again one may spy a problem in drama teaching where too much structure destroys spontaneity and yet too little rule regulation can result in chaos. As we shall see later it is imperative that the drama teacher is able to conduct work that is essentially empiric, for the experience in drama, as in any other game, is concretely dynamic.

Lastly in this context, we might consider how the drama game relies upon the suspension of disbelief, the operation of make-believe. It is essential that a corporate fantasy be agreed to in order that the game can go forward and that social implications become apparent. Again the immense difficulty of achieving and maintaining this condition with a group of more than 30 boys and girls must be appreciated. And it is not merely an agreement to observe the rules as obtains in many games, but a respect for content as well as its conduct.

If we agree that the drama is game, then what sort of game is it? How can we define the process of drama in such a way that it reveals its essential game characteristics? Perhaps we might define it thus – drama is a game in which the players, in role, present an analogy of social behaviour. They employ verbal and non-verbal skills in a series of encounters that cumulatively reveal the form of the analogy. The players do not aim at a convincing imitation of reality but at the illusion of impending outcomes from immediate actions. The operation of this sense of destiny is the particular province of the drama game.

Within the above description there are many social implications which apply both to the school as community and to the larger world beyond. On the one hand, there is the real-life experience of role, of 'sanctioned orderliness arising from obligations fulfilled and expectations realised',[10] and of the whole complexity of the language of speech and gesture which is related to social class. There is also the drama game that models these experiences and which maintains its own social structure and democracy among players. In both there are certain accepted views that are either being confirmed or challenged and which underline those social norms and values that we both consciously and unconsciously adopt from our childhood. The social mechanisms that condition us to conformity and which serve as social regulator make a fascinating study in themselves, but rather than pursue this in isolation, it may be more relevant to look at how they appear in the classroom and the way in which drama may also be seen as such a regulator.

Perhaps because we have all experienced living in classrooms we often only perceive the instructional and not the social aspects of the curriculum. Jackson identifies the latter as appearing in three major ways: 'as members of crowds, as potential recipients of praise or reproof, and as pawns of institutional authorities.'[11] Thus 'students are confronted with aspects of reality that at least during their childhood years are relatively confined to the hours spent in classroom'.[13] And whatever else may be learned during those long hours, it seems likely, Jackson continues, that 'adaptive strategies having relevance for other contexts and other life periods are developed.'[13]

'Crowds, praise and power' make up the environment in which learning takes place and are themselves a major part of what is learned. They represent areas of social control to which we learn to respond and comply, and in the process we lose at least temporarily our individuality and the significance of individual experience. This is especially true of being part of a crowd where 'delay, denial, interruption and social distraction' prevent not only one's own desires being fulfilled but also an effective contribution to the fulfilment of those of others. These frustrations produce not a productive anger but an all-pervasive lethargy, the celebrated apathy about which organizers wring their hands. We learn to live in schools with unutterable boredom brought about by time unsatisfactorily handled and through the death of desire.

Neither the praise nor the anger of the teacher ultimately can do very much to change the attitudes that living as a crowd induces. Children, especially at secondary school level, give up trying because praise comes to be seen not as a reward for genuine effort but as a veiled exhortation always to do better. Evaluation by the teacher or by peers in classrooms so often represents a process external to the child's influence. Rarely is he consulted about his own estimation of his progress nor indeed what for him represents progress. A child-centred approach is a rarity and the 'norm' is more likely to reflect training that stresses the need for the teacher to be always in control of everything that happens in the classroom. Surely there can be few situations in which a crowd of people are expected to comply so consistently with the orders of one individual.

Like the apathy we so often deplore in our society, the roots of an un-questioning acceptance of authority in adult life may very well begin in the classroom. Rules become restrictions because they do not represent a genuine contract but a situation in which there are oppressors and oppressed. Yet such is the ease and the security of the adaptive strategies that the occurrence of the unusual or the challenge of the innovative to the individual initiative is met with resentment and anger. Approaches in the classroom that depart from the traditional will often spell disaster, as we shall see when we consider how the experience of drama threatens dead, institutionalized attitudes by stirring the essential individuality of the class members.

Before the claims for the effects of drama in the classroom appear to become incredibly excessive, let us return to the game association to underpin the assertions. In particular, let us examine those same characteristics – crowds, praise and power – in relation to the drama game.

Central to the examination is the question of authority and rule-regulation in particular. 'Obedience to rules is a freely given act of the will among equals.... In obedience to rules we reserve the right to question and criticize, but since the will of equals is the basis for the authority of rules, differences must be resolved through arbitration.'[14] If we apply this statement to the conduct of any game we know that the progress of the game, indeed its very existence, depends on the desire to play for the satisfaction gained therefrom. Heavy authoritarian control of games, as again we remember from schooldays, can destroy for ever our desire to participate. And it is even more applicable to the drama game where the content is so dependent upon a corporate act of willing suspension of disbelief. Authority is vested in each member of the class through a self-restraint exercised in order to achieve the desired goal. Such power-sharing does not eliminate the need for the teacher, but his role is clearly that of facilitator and not policeman.

Equally it may be the function of the teacher to be arbiter but not the sole judge of the work of the children. The criteria for the evaluation of what is achieved by the class, either collectively or individually, must arise from the nature of the task. Once the class are clear about what they want to do then they will be equally clear about whether they have succeeded in their aim. Especially in the arts where the affective is paramount there comes a satisfaction from creative expression that is unmistakable. In terms of skills of performance, as Brecht says, 'If it works, it works.' The same may be said of the content or the form of the piece, for both may have their own inbuilt logic. Therefore, for the teacher to criticize using alien criteria for assessment is to be merely irrelevant. He must instead be able to come to terms with what is being created, to enter the child's world and obey its logic, as indeed in the theatre we submit ourselves to the circumstances and characters with which we are presented. And by so penetrating the fantasy the teacher is able to provoke the child's thought, but always contextually. As Joan Tough has said, 'the teacher is projecting into what is meaningful for the child, knowing his background and using that, reporting upon what has happened to him outside, making his own past experience important to her as a teacher.'[15] What is wrong is when the teacher praises or blames children either because he assumes his job is to hand down judgments or because he believes that his own experience is definitive.

Finally in this part of the argument, it would be ridiculous to assert that drama in the classroom is not subject to the same frustrations of 'delay, denial, interruption and social distraction.' Indeed, because the basis of the work is consensual, all these factors may be even more apparent. There is however a difference in that there is a positive fervour to overcome the obstructions in order to reach one's goal. A parallel may be seen in play and game of any sort where a number of people are involved. Their desire to play enables them to accept interruptions, to settle differences along the way and to recognize that the pace of the game must accommodate the slowest player. It is truly a shared experience and to a certain degree the solving of the problems of distractions is part of the strength of the overall success of the group. Clearly there is a limit to the extent to which the momentum of the play can be interrupted for it can kill the desire to play altogether. Here is a good lesson for the teacher who feels the need constantly to stop the progress of what is happening in order to gain what he considers to be clarification. Like football players shivering on the field waiting for the recommencement of play, drama players too may feel their inspiration dissipating while details of plot or character are being exhaustively analyzed by the teacher.

The watchword that applies throughout is 'sharing'; shared motivation, shared experience, shared responsibility and shared success. Living in crowds, which happens both in and out of school, does not pose a threat to individuality if the life of a community is one of shared experience. Problem-solving and decision-making need to involve the talents of us all; tolerance and respect for others grow from an assurance that they are extended to oneself; rewards and privileges, if they have a place at all, should emerge from a genuine communal acclaim.

These are all social experiences that we would claim are possible where the mode of government is democratic. We extol the values that they represent and often act as though the society in which we live practised them. Yet this is patently not the case and so it seems that the education of the young prepares them to accept the lie with equanimity. They are not taught to question the obvious and obscene discrepancy between life as it is claimed to be and as it actually is for many millions of people. It would be easy to pillory the press, politicians, the media and other social institutions for these double standards, but we are all guilty, for we are all so compliant. But as we said earlier, it may be that part of that unquestioning acquiescence begins in the classroom.

Education should assist the appreciation and conservation of socially healthy and beneficial norms and values but it should do this by encouraging question and debate. We should know what we believe in and why, for without that conviction our worthwhile social institutions will be destroyed. Yet it remains that in our classrooms we conduct activities that do not encourage children to question, to debate, to evaluate, to live together as socially healthy and responsible people, to help to fashion the world of which they are its most optimistic part. Our hope for a better future must be the result of our confidence in the young for they must achieve what we have failed to do. And unless we offer them the means through education, we have only ourselves to blame.

Ideally then, drama serves as a truly democratic model, for it is above all else consensual. It both celebrates social values and challenges them, thereby assisting the process of social change so necessary to the health of a community. This has been its social function since its origins, a function that has been increasingly neglected as industrialism has destroyed community life and community consciousness. But the roots remain and the drama represents one of the ways in which they can be nourished. This is the genuine educative use of the drama and yet it is not yet widespread in our schools, perhaps because the school system as we know it is not conducive to the democratic relationships that are essential for the conduct of the work.

Nowhere is this clearer than in many of the drama manuals where the lesson plans are teacher-centred, authoritarian models posing as open-ended lessons. One such manual says explicitly that it contains what should be done but not how to do it, while others offer a host of ideas for the teacher unable to conceive his own and too insecure to invite others from the class. Above all, the models do not attempt to change a school environment of authoritarianism, but accommodate it by advocating activities that deny the pupil freedom of choice, freedom of speech and even freedom of movement. And increasingly we have moved nearer to a drama image that is indistinguishable from other lessons where the emphasis is on conformity to externally set standards through prescribed curriculum.

Arts and the Adolescent[16] and Witkin's *The Intelligence of Feeling*[17] have stressed the necessity for an area of genuine creativity in the creative arts. Too often, though, teachers not only provide the stimulus but also, by a variety of means, determine the response of the class. The DES report, *Education Survey 2: Drama*,[18] back in 1968 despairingly looked for the children's contribution in much of the work they saw. Nor should we comfort ourselves by saying that things have changed, for recent films showing drama teachers at work reveal the same imposition, though the accompanying notes suggest that the teacher's view of what he is doing is the exact opposite. Unconsciously teachers mould the work to fit the prevailing school situation which is one in which the teacher has the ideas and the pupils have none.

Certainly a notable exception to this pessimistic view of drama teaching is that work that has been developed in the north-east of England. Dorothy Heathcote and Gavin Bolton have explored the area of provocation in drama teaching. They are the spike in the side of a class urging them on to make their own choice of play and then to follow through the implications of their choice in role-playing. Further, they have concentrated upon the analysis of the teacher/class interaction in the drama lesson. They identify clearly what the role of the drama is in the learning situation and in what ways the teacher can assist, allowing the play to remain child-centred. Their approach rarely calls into question the admissibility of drama in the school context largely because their approach is essentially contract learning. The contract is established through a series of questions, the answers to which commit a class to a course of action. Throughout there are reminders of their original intention which can be changed but only as a conscious decision backed by reasonable argument. In this way the class is caused to reflect upon the cause and effect of human actions, how they confirm or deny social values and how they affect others for better or worse.

Working in this way requires that the teacher should be aware of not only what ways the question can further the progress of the work by provoking thought and feeling, but also when is the most effective time to do so. This is the intuitive area of teaching that requires the teacher to penetrate the concious level of the thinking of the class and to feel for the developmental possibilities of what is yet half-formed. Above all, the teacher must be clear about the direction in which the work is heading and where is now stands. Without such insight the play becomes too diffuse; the blind lead the blind. So it is crucial that the teacher has access to some means of analysis, some map that is sufficiently familiar in its appearance that he can learn where he and the class have got lost.

Such a guide can be found in the consideration of drama as game, for experience of games is something with which we are all very familiar. And though skills and strategies are learned, it requires an intuitive grasp of what is happening to enable players to apply them effectively in the dynamic of play. At any time, however, in the progress of the game it is possible to stop and take stock, whether it be to sort out a problem, review a piece of play that has taken place or plan the strategy of the moves ahead. All of this is possible in the drama game which can help the teacher and the class to enjoy playmaking through effective planning and operation.

The progress of the drama lesson may be thought of as occurring broadly in six stages: *enquiry, decision, definition, committal, reflection* and *appraisal* (see Figure 1). Whether a class completes all stages will depend upon a number of factors: time, the clear definition of the goals and how to achieve them, social cohesion, etc. Certainly they do not represent a definitive lesson plan, completion of which signifies success. One stage will overlap another and at any time a class may choose to return to an earlier stage to redefine their goals or objectives. Perhaps a closer examination of each stage will help us to recognize its characteristics, especially if we use game to identify its intention.

Figure 1. Stages of a Drama Lesson

Enquiry

Exploring an idea   Is a game possible?
verbally, visually,
aurally

Decision

Arriving at an understanding   What is the game?
of the group's intention

Definition

The intention explored   How do we play the
in action   game?

.... TO PERCEIVE RELATIONSHIPS .... ACTING .... TO EXPRESS THE RELATIONSHIPS ....

Committal

Declared relationships   Playing the
in action   game

Reflection

Redefining the problem   Looking back
                                on the game

Appraisal

The teacher evaluates the experience. Did the game assist the learning process?

The *enquiry* represents that initial encounter with a stimulus that will arrest the attention, interest and potential involvement of the class. Whether it be music, a picture, a piece of movement or a set of questions, its appeal must be obvious and immediate. Very often it is teacher initiated but can arise from a preoccupation of the class, but whatever its origin it must embody the child's interest and not the adult's. Of course the subject may be of mutual interest but sometimes the things that teachers agonize over and see as being potentially rewarding bore the class to distraction.

This stage is that which poses the question, 'Is a drama game possible?, do the essential conditions exist or can they be created so that the game contract can be made?' This is a highly neglected area of consideration, for there is still a prevailing view that children are highly motivated to work in drama whereas the real school situation does not always bear this out. Assuming that there is this fund of goodwill, a teacher will often plunge a class into a subject for dramatic exploration and the work founders. The class may not be socially healthy, there may be too many disruptive elements that destroy the essential consensual base on which the make-believe fabric can be constructed. Again, the children may be too excited, too tired, too preoccupied with other things. A class smarting with the injustice of a detention peremptorily given at the close of the previous lesson will not respond eagerly to the drama teacher's attempts to win their cooperation. Dinner ladies laying dinner tables during the lesson, the caretaker trundling chairs across the stage, all of these sorts of distractions destroy concentration and a serious involvement with the work. Indeed, if one were to apply a comparison with the sports field the ridiculousness becomes only too obvious. What game of cricket or football could continue with groundsmen marking the pitch during the game or survive the sudden removal of the goal posts?

Many lessons do not progress beyond the *enquiry* stage and are none the worse for that. The teacher may spend the time attempting to discover what aspect, if any, of the topic under discussion interests the class. This is in itself a lesson and may involve exercises, games, questions, writing, and many other activities, all directed towards eliminating an overabstract approach, where the clear, concrete understanding is essential. Nor is this time ill spent for without the cooperation of the class – the desire to play the game – progress is impossible.

At this stage particularly, the problem of innovatory approaches can become apparent. Marten Shipman[19] sums up the situation thus:

> The more a lesson departs from the traditional, the greater is the risk of disorder through lack of definition. This is why senior forms do not jump eagerly at new methods and content, for these threaten to break up secure routines, customary ways of doing things, established groupings, while simultaneously introducing the prospect of new demands for improved performance and new chances of humiliation.

We must be careful that the proposal to play the drama game does not appear as an irresponsible invitation to anarchic riot.

The *decision* stage of the lesson is marked by agreement to undertake a task, to explore some facet of human relationships, some aspect of human life. This agreement cannot be merely faint support but must amount to a genuine understanding by all of the group's intention; they are all aware of what game they have chosen to play. This need not necessarily appear as an explicit agreement but might be implicit in the questions the class might ask of the teacher, or of each other, their comments and suggestions. Above all, the teacher's task is to assist to establish the clarity of their intention and to support their construction, even by playing devil's advocate, or by requiring to be reassured on certain points about the plot that is the setting they have chosen for the exchange of human relationships.

This agreed intention will be the conscious rationalization of an unconscious preoccupation of the class. The teacher must beware of taking it at face value, so that when the class say they want to make a play about ghosts, it does not result in mere hooting and shrieking. 'Who has ever seen a ghost?' he may ask, 'What are ghosts?' The belief that they are spirits unable to find rest might lead one back to the conditions surrounding their death. Such a scenario once produced a play about a kitchen below stairs, where envious servants murdered one of their fellows because he was a favourite of the master and figured, so they thought, in his changed will. The overall picture that emerged was a play about money, or the lack of it, and this from poor children in a Midland city. The decision stage is truly the consideration of the question, 'What game?'

Once the decision has been made about what game, there is a need to further define the nature of the game and how it is played. In the drama lesson the *definition* stage determines what is the problem that affects the people that the class have invented. To be able to do this they have to penetrate the abstract of the fiction, to 'live through' their experience by being them. By acting out the lives of these people and their situation we perceive how they relate to each other. That relationship becomes tested in the next stage when they confront each other in the stress of the moment. The moves or strategies of the game have been determined, in the *committal* they are put into action.

This experience is very much akin to workshop or rehearsal when the actor gains perception of the pattern of relationships implicit in the text. As a way of learning it is dynamic, for the player uses his own experience to find the truth of the human situations he explores. In this way too he discovers significance in his recalled experience; he finds his lifebelt in 'an ocean of meaninglessness'.

It is in the committal to the game, though, that the players put themselves, as in all games, at risk. They live from moment to moment but always within the agreed structure, realizing the characters' problem, clarifying the issues and probing the motives. Their group agreement is demonstrated in action, their insights into human conduct expressed in the significant present of the problem played out.

It may well be that at this stage further clarification is required and that the players return to the earlier stage. There is, perhaps, a pause for conversation or a certain incident is enacted to examine another way of looking at these fictitious people. Such recycling is a familiar feature of the play of young children, easily recognized by their disputes over rules or strategies employed. Their play too may be accompained by a constant flow of regulatory language, a commentary that defines not merely the plot but the motives of the characters.

The *reflection* assesses the effectiveness of the decisions taken and the possible consequences of the behaviour of the people in the dramatic invention and, by implication, its relevance to real life. It is a stage that, together with the *appraisal*, can lead the class to further enquiry or to a new interpretation of the original *enquiry*. The players can look back on the game with a discerning eye, critical of strategies or ineffective rules, knowledgeable and skilled in the operation of the dramatic form of expression.

All the stages of the lesson are important for the reasons that are implied in the description of their functions. None is more important, however, than the *decision* for this is the point at which there must be a transfer of power from the teacher to the class. If there is to be a genuine creative element then it must start with the children's choice of play. If the conditions for the playing of a drama game obtain, then the desire to do so may reside in the choice of what game in particular. As we have said earlier, that desire is crucial not only for the progress but also for the very existence of the game. Above all, it must be a child-centred choice with its own logic, its own perceptions and based upon a child's experience. Unless the teacher respects this need then it would be as though he were to write the child's essays or paint his pictures. None would deny the necessity for the teacher's support for these exercises but not his domination.

Because the class establishes its own aims then the degree to which they achieve them they, themselves, can estimate. The teacher may have to remind the class of their intention, to help them resist the distraction of easier, more superficial routes to their goal. This can easily occur if there is too great an emphasis on the incidents rather than the relationships between participants. But ultimately the responsibility lies with the players who will recognize when the game loses its appeal because it becomes too easy.

Lastly the *decision* represents an achievement in corporate living. Embodied in the act is tolerance, generosity and the assurance of respect for self and for others. Potentially in the projected enterprise there are roles for everyone, for leaders and for followers, both equally and mutually dependent.

So we see that not only does the content of the drama game reveal for examination values that are the basis of social order, but also its progress reflects the same foundation. Like all games, drama has its roots deep in the earliest manifestations of our civilization. Now as we devise ever more efficient ways of destruction, it may be wise to reflect upon the powers of play and game to preserve social order by example. Perhaps nowhere is this better expressed than by Huizinga when he says:

> real civilization cannot exist in the absence of a certain play-element,
> for civilization presupposes limitation and mastery of the self, the

ability not to confuse its own tendencies with the ultimate and highest goal, but to understand that it is enclosed within certain bounds freely accepted. Civilization will, in a sense, always be played according to certain rules, and true civilization will always demand fair play. Fair play is nothing less than good faith expressed in play terms. Hence the cheat or the spoil-sport shatters civilization itself. To be a sound culture-creating force this play-element must be pure. It must not consist in the darkening or debasing of standards set up by reason, faith, or humanity. It must not be a false seeming, a masking of political purposes behind the illusion of genuine play-forms. True play knows no propaganda; its aim is in itself, and its familiar spirit is happy inspiration.[20]

Notes

1 GOFFMAN, E. (1969) *The Presentation of Self in Everyday Life*, Allen Lane.
2 ARISTOTLE (1940) *Poetics*, Everyman.
3 LYMANN, S.M. and SCOTT, M.D. (1970) *The Sociology of the Absurd*, Appleton Century Crofts.
4 SALAMAN, G. (1972) *Symbolic Interaction*, The Sociological Perspective Units 5–8, Open University Press.
5 WICKHAM, G. (1962) *Drama in a World of Science*, Routledge and Kegan Paul.
6 DUNCAN, H.D. (1962) *Communication and Social Order*, New York, Bedminister Press.
7 BENTLEY, E. (1969) *The Life of Drama*, Methuen.
8 HUIZINGA, J. (1970) *Homo Ludens*, Temple Smith.
9 CALLOIS, R. (1962) *Man, Play and Games*, Thames and Hudson.
10 GOFFMAN, E. (1973) *Encounters*, Allen Lane.
11 JACKSON, P. W. (1968) *Life in Classrooms*, Holt Rinehart and Winston.
12 *Ibid.*
13 *Ibid.*
14 DUNCAN, *op. cit.*
15 TOUGH, J. (1974) *Early Years at School*, BBC TV Programme.
16 ROSS, M. (1975) *Arts and the Adolescent*, Schools Council Working Paper 54, Evans/Methuen Educational.
17 WITKIN, R.W. (1974) *The Intelligence of Feeling*, Heinemann Educational.
18 DES (1968) *Education Survey 2: Drama*, HMSO.
19 SHIPMAN, M. (1968) *The Sociology of the School*, Longmans.
20 HUIZINGA, *op. cit.*

4 The Activity of Dramatic Playing

Gavin Bolton

Whereas the authors so far have taken a broad critical view of the nature, purposes and structure of drama, Bolton deliberately focusses his chapter on one aspect of the activity itself – dramatic playing. He analyzes the activity by identifying what it has in common with and how it differs from play. He judges that it is more than simply an extension of play as earlier writers have sometimes suggested. Certainly it contains spontaneity, symbolism and passive-active elements. In addition, both play and dramatic play are rule-governed. However, Bolton argues that in dramatic play the quality of meaning depends on appropriateness, integrity and collectivity of response. In this sense dramatic playing is nearer to games than to symbolic play. He suggests also that in dramatic play it is not enough for the participant to enjoy a sense of satisfaction. Rather, it is important to move beyond the intuitive, discovery learning towards objectifying experience, and this suggests a generalizing, conceptualizing requirement of the participant. The type of teacher intervention is crucial here, for it is his responsibility, the author claims, to identify potential learning areas and ensure as far as possible a balance in drama between the child's play and the teacher's play. In terms of the activity of dramatic playing, the teacher's role is to provide further refinement of feeling values. It may be argued that this is a complicated way of saying that whereas play is natural, dramatic play is structured by the teacher, and so, inevitably, each is likely to have different intentions, processes and outcomes. However, like the writers of all the chapters, Bolton is essentially concerned with clarifying the meaning of drama in relation to teaching and learning. The chapter, therefore, is both important in itself, and contributes in the progressive focussing of issues in educational drama.

In this chapter I propose to conduct a theoretical analysis of a certain kind of dramatic activity in schools. It is an attempt to analyze the *activity per se*. The function of the teacher will be discussed insofar as the teacher controls the activity in terms of its potential for learning. Regrettably, because the subject is so vast and complex, neither methods of teaching for implications for teacher training can be explicitly included in the discussion.

Gavin Bolton

Three Kinds of Dramatic Activity

The Schools Council Secondary Drama Project team usefully coined the phrase 'acting-out' as an umbrella term to cover seemingly countless varieties of dramatic behaviour to be found in schools.[1] A popular way of categorizing acting-out is to use the criterion of *outer form*: movement; mime; dance-drama; role-play; improvisation; scripted-work; performance, etc., but I find it more useful to classify the activity according to its *orientation*.

There are two basic polarities in dramatic activity: (1) moving in a direction of 'being' or 'experiencing' and (2) moving in a direction of giving someone else an experience, that is, performing. The former tends to be characterized by a spontaneous, existential quality that is perhaps found at its most intense in children's playing; the latter tends to be characterized by a 'demonstrating', 'calculating the effect' quality that is found, *par excellence*, in professional theatre. But just as there is an incipient degree of 'demonstrating' at the heart of a child's play, so vestiges of 'spontaneity' can linger in the most rigid theatre performance. These two orientations can be seen, therefore, as a continuum rather than as divisions.

Towards   ⟵———⟶   Towards
experiencing   performing

Whether the children in school are using mime or movement or improvisation, the drama work will have one or other of these basic orientations, unless it is directed towards the third form of orientation – *exercise*. Here the purpose is primarily neither experiencing nor giving experience: it is practising. Usually a skill that is felt to be appropriate to drama (at any point on the above continuum) is isolated for training, for example, sensitivity, concentration, group awareness, voice skills, movement skills, acting techniques, etc. may be practised.

This classification implies a relationship between intention and quality of experience:

1 orientation towards experiencing – a quality of spontaneity;
2 orientation towards performing – a quality of demonstrating;
3 orientation towards exercise – a quality of practising.

It may be that in isolating *quality* I have successfully determined the most fundamental criterion affecting different educational drama practices, for a basic difference in quality implies a basic difference in learning potential in each kind of activity. A justifiable inference might be that the first orientation leads to skills of 'discovery' learning, the second to 'communication' skills and the third towards an acquisition of technical skills. But quality is not the only significant aspect of the three orientations. The outcome in terms of learning derives from equally significant factors such as teacher function, meaning and structure.

The whole of the school drama scene is so complex that I propose to confine this examination to the first of these orientations[2] – *towards experiencing*. I shall call this kind of school drama 'dramatic playing'. Our findings may, at least by implication, throw some light on the significance of the other two. Reference has already been made in the second paragraph to children's play. Indeed a tradition of English writing on educational drama, started by Caldwell Cook[3] and Peter Slade,[4] has made the linking of the two a *sine qua non*. But for me it is not a matter of following faithfully in the paths of pioneers. I consider an understanding of the relationship between play and drama to be critical to a theoretical basis for drama in education. Certain characteristics essentially found in play are also central to the activity of dramatic playing. I shall discuss them using the following dimensions:

1   quality of experience, (already touchèd upon above);
2   awareness;
3   meaning.

1   Quality of Experience in Play and Dramatic Playing

What is this quality of spontaneity that characterizes the experience? It is a sense of the immediate, of being in the here and now. It is both an active and passive mode, both controlling and being controlled, both making it happen and submitting to it happening. For example, the host gives a smile of welcome to set the tone of a greeting and at the same time responds to the hand proffered for shaking; the swimmer agitates the water for propulsion and at the same time submits to the water so that his body floats. In other words, the quality of spontaneity is what we experience a great deal of our waking time: living in and responding to the present. My suggestion in the second paragraph, therefore, that this spontaneous quality is perhaps found 'at its most intense' in children's play, hardly seems to make sense when spontaneity clearly belongs pre-eminently to 'living' rather than to a specially contrived activity known as 'playing'.

Piaget distinguished three categories of play:

> games: where there are socially determined rules, for example, playing tennis;
> practice play: where some action is repeated for its own sake – practising a tennis stroke;
> symbolic play: where an absent or fictitious context is represented, for example, 'pretending' to play tennis.[5]

Practice play, by its repetitive nature, implies non-spontaneity, but its difference from symbolic play and games lies deeper than that. It has to do with the degree to which it is a self-contained activity. In fact, although it can be seen as contrived, it is not as separate from the normal 'web of purposes' as the other two. Thus practising a tennis stroke does not have the *special* quality of spontaneity of a tennis game: 'this is it now' might describe the feeling that colours the game, whereas 'getting ready for it' is more likely to describe the predominating feeling behind the exercise. I stress this of course because of the parallel difference we find in school between 'dramatic playing' and 'exercise drama'. An explanation, which may also hold true of some dramatic playing is that play activity both constrains and liberates. The constraints are in the form of rules which require a disciplined commitment; the subsequent release into freedom is an experience unhampered, as Dearden puts it, by the 'prudence and obligation' that belong to ordinary life. 'Play stands apart from the web of purposes which make up the serious, and in this sense is self contained.'[6] Thus, in a sense, play allows a spontaneity that is, if you like, in a purer form than in everyday living because it is liberated from the moral and legal consequences that normally temper freedom of response. To summarize the paradox: it is a self-contained non-serious activity the very separateness of which permits a serious commitment to its specially contrived rules. It is this submission to the rules that liberates the participant into the freedom of spontaneous behaviour. This quality is not a characteristic of all kinds of play, however, any more than it is shared to any significant degree by the other two orientations of drama.

The reader may be puzzled by my reference to games when clearly it is symbolic play that is closest to drama. This essay may well, to some extent, challenge that view, for I am more and more impressed by the logical connections between games and drama. Vygotsky makes the interesting point:

> Just as we were able to show at the beginning that every imaginary situation contains rules in a concealed form, we have also succeeded in demonstrating the reverse – that every game with rules contains an imaginary situation in a concealed form.[7]

We may not wish to go all the way with Vygotsky in finding a concealed imaginary situation within every game – I find it very difficult to discern make-believe in, for example, cricket apart from the agreement to identify with two opposing sides – but we can agree to an important similarity between games and symbolic play in terms of self-containment, and the special quality of spontaneity, that is, a 'living-through' that is freed from the normal pressing needs of living.

One of the obvious differences between symbolic play and games is that whereas in the latter the rules are social, collectively agreed before the activity starts, in the former they are open to negotiation. In symbolic play the rules affect a greater number of levels of spontaneous behaviour from the purely physical to the deeply imaginative. On the other hand, spontaneity has a greater chance of breaking down in symbolic play if the rules are too vague to be trusted. That the negotiation often requires such fragile handling clearly has implications for the teacher working in dramatic playing. It is no wonder that so may drama teachers fall back on drama games which give the children an active spontaneous experience without the risk of inadequate negotiation of rules. Often children who commit themselves freely to 'living-through' in games will not trust the drama context to the same extent.

2   Self-Awareness in Play and Dramatic Playing

I suggested earlier that spontaneity in play implies both a passive and an active aspect – both 'making it happen and having it happen', as it were. But the question arises to what extent is a participant *conscious* of controlling and being controlled. Can he in fact *knowingly* say, 'I am making it happen; it is happening to me?' Spontaneous action in real life seems to vary in the degree to which a participant is conscious of his behaviour, that is, the extent to which one is, say, talking as opposed to being *aware* that one is talking. Usually the circumstances have to be rather special for one to become a spectator of oneself in this way – an interview situation is an example. Indeed, in such an example we may say that an interviewee's 'self-consciousness' is not allowing him to 'be himself'. This ability not to be oneself is crucial in the process of self-evaluation (cf. Chapter 6). Self-awareness implies a heightened awareness of a moment of living that remains unspoiled by the act of observation. We can probably all recall some moments and have forgotten many others when we have, as it were, 'caught sight of ourselves'.

I shall now argue that the nature of symbolic play, and subsequently dramatic playing, is such that opportunity for this kind of self-awareness is increased. It seems to me that because the child is his own agent contriving his own 'self-contained' situation, he can claim with some force: 'I am making it happen, so that it can happen to me.' Thus he has a vested interest in the activity which no doubt invites a special attentiveness to what is happening within it. But there is more to it than that. Again it is the paradoxical nature of play and drama in allowing the participant to be both in and yet not in the symbolic situation that critically affects potential for awareness. The activity is a metaphor relating two contexts, the actual world of the child as controller of events and the fictitious world in which events have control.[8] The relationship is a dialectical one of controlling and being controlled. The experience *is* the dialectic. It is this act of both contriving and submitting to a *metaphorical* context that gives symbolic play and drama, and indeed all art forms, a richness and intensity that sharpens awareness. Vygotsky makes the point that 'the child weeps in play as a patient, but revels as a player.'[9] It is this juxtaposition of two effects, of the fictitious world and the actual world, that invites heightened attention rather than the total absorption as in weeping in real life.

But heightened attention to what? We cannot discuss the possibility of awareness without attempting to specify what is being perceived. *Self-awareness* supplies an answer, but we perhaps could be more precise. I prefer to talk about the MEANING of the experience for it is the dialectic between the *self* and the *fictitious context* that gives the experience meaning. Thus any perception is of 'the-self-in-the-fiction'. The participant is not aware of some general self, but of a particular self in a unique relationship. That relationship is the meaning of the experience. But let us give this problem the detailed examination it deserves.

3 Meaning in Symbolic Play and Dramatic Playing

Vygotsky has pointed out that play is a step in the direction of abstract thinking, where the meaning created is something other than the actions and objects present in the child's immediate field of perception.[10] Let us picture two 3-year-old children playing at riding a horse. One, astride a stick, is dashing in mad circles around the garden. The other, perched on a high kitchen stool, is jogging up and down on it. In these examples, the meaning is to do with horses; the objects and actions are a stick and a stool and running and jogging. Vygotsky writes, 'In play, action is subordinate to meaning, but in real life, of course action dominates over meaning.'[11] It seems clear then that one of the purposes of plays is seeking of meaning. It will be useful here to analyze further the factors that might contribute to the meaning created by the two children in the illustration.

Although both children might well describe what they are doing as 'playing horses', in fact their experiences are significantly different from each other. The aspect abstracted by the first child (running around in circles) is one of speed and/or direction; the second child (on the kitchen stool) has abstracted height and/or being jogged. The meaning created might then be tabled like this:

	Child A	*Child B*
Context	Horse	Horse
Abstraction	Speed/direction	Height/jogging
The action and object employed	Running astride stick	Jogging on kitchen stool

But this is only half the picture. Something has given the two children the energy to set up these actions. There is an affective, motivating factor which brings another dimension to the meaning. The abstraction on the second line of the above diagram we will call the 'objective' aspect of the meaning in order to distinguish it from this second source of meaning, which we will term 'subjective'. Let us confine ourselves, for the time being, to child A. What are some of the possible range of feelings that might have prompted the 'running astride a stick' action?

Child A's motives

I like the sensation of riding a horse
I like to ride a horse at speed

I would like to be a fast horse
I'm a cowboy on TV
I would like to ride away
I am scared of horses.

. . . .

I like rushing around
I like showing off
Teacher says I am a fast runner
I'm like my dad
I know it's really bedtime

Any one of these motives or combination of them may give the impetus to the playing. A more definite meaning is often implied in the motives as I have described them, for example, 'I like rushing around' may imply a feeling of 'it is *exhilarating* to rush around', 'it is *joyful* to rush around' or the more ambivalent 'I'm a bit *nervous* about it but I think I like doing it.' On the other hand, 'I'm like my dad' may imply more than that he has a horse-riding father; it may, more specifically, imply a feeling of 'dad is *powerful*, 'dad is *fun*', 'dad is *important*' or 'dad is *frightening*.' Note that I have described these implications as 'feelings of'. In other words, they are *'felt values'* given to whatever the context is. It is these felt values that contribute to the child's subjective meaning in playing and are a feature of the search for meaning central to the activity of drama.

Child *A's* subjective meaning may stem from a combination of the following felt values:

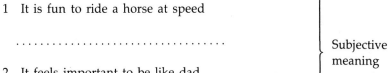

1   It is fun to ride a horse at speed

. . . .   Subjective
                                                                                  meaning
2   It feels important to be like dad
3   It feels risky but exciting to carry on, although it's
    bedtime.

Notice the dotted line in each of the two lists. I have classified the motives and values into two kinds. Above the line are those motive where the selection of 'horse' as the topic is highly relevant, whereas below the line alternative actions and objectives might have served the purpose just as well. We have a degree of interdependence in some cases between the subjective and objective meanings. For instance: 'I like rushing around' does not *necessarily* require that he be 'riding a horse', compared with, 'I'm a TV cow-boy.' On the other hand, 'I know it's really bedtime' is simply using horse-riding as a pretext. This becomes important later in discussing dramatic activity. Let us see what child *A's* diagram will look with a few subjective meanings added:

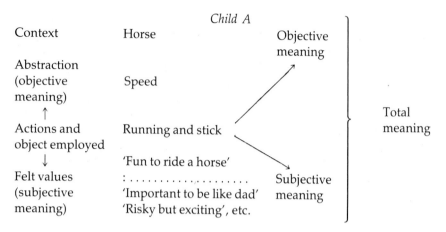

Notice how the action and the object may both serve as a vehicle, as Vygotsky suggests, but also may control the meaning both in its subjective and objective aspects. Suppose that child *A* who 'wants to ride a horse at speed' is confined (because it's raining outside, poor chap!) to child *B*'s kitchen stool, that particular object is certainly going to restrict his capacity for 'speed' experience. Similarly, his drive to be like dad may be somewhat thwarted if the new physical conditions (the kitchen) do not have 'dad' associations for him.

We seem to have established so far that symbolic play is concerned with creating meaning that is a variable mixture between subjective and objective. The meaning is both controlled by and freed from the action and objects.

But I still haven't answered the question posed at the end of the previous section. Although I have attempted to outline a model to explain the way meaning evolves in symbolic play, I still have to relate this to the claim that the child is experiencing a 'heightened awareness'. In what way is the child aware of the meaning that is created? Certainly the meaning accessible to our hypothetical child will have but a slender connection with the examples given above. They are merely theoretical, hypothetical samples which are not describing a play activity but the author's *notion* of a play activity. And the notion of a play activity is expressed in a written, discursive form that has nothing to do with play. Thus although a reasonable interpretation of a particular playing activity might be that she is taking a long time undressing her doll because she wants to delay going off to bed herself,' the meaning for the child herself *lies within the action and the images in her head*. Greater awareness implies, to use Bruner's terminology,[12] an enactive and iconic knowing not amenable to verbal or other symbolic explicitness. To put it crudely, she understands what her fingers tell her. If there is some kind of change, it is a differentiated understanding at an intuitive level, which may or may not result in her recognizing her own true motives. The 'discovery' learning may be no more than a reinforcement of what she already knew about the order in which clothes come off!

This brings us a bit nearer to a discussion of some of the ways in which dramatic playing moves away from symbolic play. So far, by selecting the dimension of quality, awareness and meaning we have been able to treat the two activities as if they were the same, but whereas one might be impressed with the potential within a self-initiated playing activity for a particular pre-school child's growth in intuitive understanding, it surely cannot be that dramatic playing in school is simply a perpetuation of child play. Many play theorists, Vygotsky included, argue that, developmentally, the older school-child does not require this action-based activity. So let us examine what dimensions we have to consider when we look at educational drama as an activity apart from play, still confining the discussion to the orientation I have called dramatic playing.

Dramatic Playing

(a) *Appropriateness, Integrity and Collectivity*

We have seen in our hypothetical illustrations of symbolic play that the relationship between subjective and objective meanings may vary according to the degree to which it is important to the child to imitate the external world. Thus a child proving to himself what a good car driver he is would be likely to give more attention to physical detail than if he were an 'escaping robber' who happens to have seized a car for his getaway. This variable emphasis on accuracy of representation is found in drama too. In the early days of drama teaching we used to think that accurate simulation was a top priority; we failed to recognize that it depends on the *meaning* of the experience. Thus one might find a class enacting a story about body snatchers whose divided fears between the imminence of the law and the supernatural are such that they fail to take the right body, simply using *token* gestures to represent digging with spades, as compared with another class who were in role as expert gardeners teaching the new apprentices. Both forms of action could be considered appropriate.

On the other hand, suppose one of the boys who elected to role-play a policeman arriving on the scene did so with a 'mock' seriousness or an openly flippant attitude, then, insofar as this runs counter to the meaning of the experience as it is understood by the rest of the class, you could say that his behaviour was inappropriate. Thus in drama it is the *collective* meaning of the context that dictates appropriateness. Similarly, if the second class had pre-decided that the 'apprentices' were totally committed to learning the trade and one of them clearly shows from his behaviour that he could not care less, his contribution could be described as inappropriate, for in terms of the drama he is breaking the agreed rules.

Could the two boys' behaviour also be described as lacking in integrity? On the surface yes, but supposing they do not know what their behaviour is communicating – like 'Smiler' in Wesker's 'Chips with everything', whose compulsive smile was always misinterpreted by his superiors as disrespect; or supposing they are intellectually incapable of grasping the rules; or emotionally frustrated at failing to find the rules credible; or, in the case of the apprentice gardener, wishing to break the agreed rules in order to move the drama on? One of the difficulties for a teacher of drama is deciding the extent the above types of inappropriate behaviour should be tolerated and contained by the drama, because the recalcitrant individual is, by his own light, behaving with integrity.

Such tolerance may be therapeutically beneficial, but in terms of the drama and education the work for the group may become undermined. And here, in speaking of the activity as 'work', we have moved away from playing. In playing, connotations of wish fulfilment and personal satisfaction rather than appropriateness may prevail. But in the reference to 'the work' there is a hint that some created group entity exists. This links with Dearden's comments about the non-seriousness of play. It is significant that when he talks of the arts, he feels compelled to qualify his position:

> Before leaving the question of what play is, however, something ought to be said about an important class of activities which on the face of it do satisfy the criteria suggested, yet which we should not call 'play'. These activities are the various arts and sciences when they are pursued quite apart from any obvious applications which they may have to the serious business of living. On the face of it, therefore, they could well be non-serious, but a closer look shows this not to be so. Though they often do give satisfaction to those who pursue them, the reason for pursuing them as worthwhile in themselves is rather that they seek to establish or to create something of objective value, whether this is some mathematical proof, scientific law or object of aesthetic merit. They are to be assessed not primarily by the satisfactions which they give, but by impersonal criteria of truth and of merit. Furthermore, though not themselves dictated either by prudence or by obligation, and hence not in that sense serious, they do have a very intimate connection with the serious in that they explore aspects of the conception of ourselves and of our situation which is the background against which our objective evaluations of seriousness are made. They are concerned with the various sorts of 'reality' which are presupposed in asserting the validity of all such judgments. The similarity of these activities to play, therefore, is not more than apparent.[13]

We may not feel that drama of the dramatic playing kind is in the same class as a work of art. Nevertheless, there is an important shift from playing to dramatic playing that qualifies the latter for consideration in terms of 'the impersonal criteria of truth and merit'. Significance in drama in schools should not be confined to personal satisfactions but the meaning of what is created should have some kind of universal application.

The recognition of universality in an experience suggests a generalizing, conceptualizing requirement of the participant that goes beyond the intuitive, discovery learning of play (beyond, but not independent, let me emphasize). It also implies teacher intervention. We are now moving into an educational process where teacher expertise is crucial if the activity is to be seen as more than 'just playing'. I shall now proceed to discuss the teacher's function insofar as it affects the structure of the experience.

(b) *Structure*[14]

It is perhaps in terms of structure that dramatic playing differs fundamentally from symbolic play. Geoff Gillham has usefully coined the phrases 'the play for the teacher' and 'the play for the children' as a way of describing the double negotiation that goes on between the children's goals and the teacher's educational objectives.[15] In other words, the meaning which the teacher wants to draw out from a context is not necessarily the meaning immediately available to the children. Thus a teacher's responsibility, if drama is to be used as a medium for learning, is to structure the experience so that learning can take place. But he must find a balance between 'his play' and 'theirs'. An example occurred for me when a group of adolescents chose to make a play about a druging. I immediately structured into that dramatic context an exploration of how entering this kind of legally and morally doubtful commitment can conflict with the way one might normally wish to be open in one's relationship with close friends and family: the adolescents experienced their own domestic 'cover-up' as a lead into but, more importantly, as a microcosm of the larger-scale 'cover-up' they had chosen to be involved in. They were still able to pursue 'the play for them', the drug-ring activity, but it was now coloured by the more universal reference to do with deception, etc. On the other hand, if a teacher gets the balance wrong, very little can be learned. When I worked with a class of first-year secondary children who chose 'killing scientists', I so loaded the intellectual requirement of 'my play' with the problem of assessing which invention has done most harm to mankind that there was a danger that the only one having the dramatic experience was the teacher!

Unless the teacher can 'fold in' his meanings with the children's meanings, nothing worthwhile will happen. The chief means at his disposal are structural. We established earlier that a quality distinguishing symbolic play and dramatic playing is the spontaneity that is released by the mutual negotiation of rules. I will now argue another paradox: that because the teacher takes a large measure of responsibility for structure, dramatic playing undergoes a tightening of form that brings the activity *structurally nearer to games than to symbolic playing.*

The Dutch anthropologist, J. Huizinga, makes the following interesting point about games. He says they demand 'order' and their elements, which also belong to aesthetics, are 'tension, poise, balance, contrast, variation, solution, resolution etc.'[16] But these are the very elements of theatrical form.

Thus it can be argued that as dramatic playing moves in structure nearer to a game, so it is also nearer to theatrical form. Indeed, insofar as it is the business of the playwright to create tension and contrast – and I would add *focus*, for it is the focus that defines the rule – so it is the business of the teacher to negotiate these elements with the children.

In summary, the teacher's function in drama is to 'fold in' a level of meaning above, beyond, wider than or deeper than the level readily accessible to the class. One of the most effective ways of doing this is to tighten the inner structure while retaining the spontaneous existential quality or mode of the 'play for them', thus achieving a quality of living through within a theatre form.

Learning in Dramatic Playing

This last section, while discussing potential learning from dramatic activity, will also summarize what has gone before, for the preceding analysis has guided me to certain conclusions about the importance of dramatic play in children's learning.

It seemed that symbolic play, a self-initiated activity, is a kind of 'standing outside' what one has already experienced in order to 'discover' what it means. Three kinds of understanding seem possible: an intuitive grasp of facts, a development of skills and a recall of feeling about something. In our earlier illustration of the boy riding a stick, he could be, for example, (a) reminding himself of what he knows about horses, (b) practising running fast in a circle, or (c) testing his attitude to his father. The *meaning* of the experience is a compound of the child's attitude/physical running/horse context any aspect of which may be emphasized at any one moment, but each is coloured by the others. The meaning then is unique to a particular feeling/action/mental imagery experience. This it seems to me is a reasonable description of the intuitive thinking process of symbolic play. Theorists like Piaget see this as an egocentric form of thinking, distorting reality. Others, like Smilanski, perceive it as a process of imitating reality.[17] We have noticed earlier that there appears to be a variable dependence on accurate representation of the objective world.

If we move away from play towards dramatic playing, an educational arena which a teacher must enter, how does this affect the natural thinking process of symbolic play? A great deal of play reinforces what a child already knows. A drama teacher may help a child to new knowledge by offering a new context or by giving practice in new skills, but I suggest that the most significant change in understanding through drama must be at the subjective level of feeling. By 'feeling' I do not imply untethered emotion but as mentioned earlier, a 'feeling-value', that is, a feeling tied to judgment. Piaget states it quite dramatically: 'We do not love without seeking to understand, and we do not even hate without a subtle sense of judgment.'[18] It is in this area of feeling-value, or attitude, that a drama teacher's responsibility lies when he is negotiating meaning. Whatever the topic, that is, the context for the drama, the teacher is concerned with refining in some way the feeling-judgment the children bring to it. The refining may take the form of a clarification, a broadening, a breaking of stereotyped thinking, a challenging of prejudice, a questioning of assumptions, making the implicit explicit, seeing something in a new light. Thus it may be that as a direct result of a drama experience, some children in a class might for the first time realize that being an historian is like being a detective or that a scientist's persistence in examining what is natural is a way of ignoring what is supernatural, or that motherhood is a mixture of joy and pain or that freedom has limitations or that policemen are real people with houses and families or that heroes not are without blemishes, and so on.

Differentiated understanding then implies that whatever feeling appraisal a child brings to a dramatic metaphor (unless what he brings is lacking in integrity, in which case drama cannot even start for him) his judgment becomes modified in some way by the dramatic experience. But does differentiated understanding imply explicit generalizations such as those listed in the previous paragraph? For if it does, it means an intellectual shift, as Bruner puts it, from the left hand to the right hand.[19] Is this the learning objective in drama to reach cognitive explicitness, to see the particular action of the drama experience as an instance of a broader category, something labelled and classified? Does the pupil literally say to himself: 'Ah! I now know not to include heroes in a category of perfection?' The answer, it seems to me, is both 'yes' and 'no' – more 'no' than 'yes'! To objectify experience is what we do in most subjects of the curriculum. It is an important way of handling knowledge. It seems, therefore, that it is of educational value to identify what one has learnt through drama in these objective terms that can, at least partially, make one's experience available to others and for one's own intellectual recall.

It is this 'partially' that challenges that conclusion, for we have to consider to what extent the limitations of abstracting only what can be made verbally explicit have in reality removed the experience. The meaning embodied in the drama experience is a personal meaning. A child may conclude that being an historian is like being a detective, but it is *himself in that conclusion* that is the meaning. The statements about historians, scientists, motherhood, policemen and heroes are only objective out of context. Implied in their meaning is the feeling of the child who makes the discovery. It is uniquely his knowledge. The intuitive process that we discussed in symbolic play essentially retains its power in drama. I believe it may be useful for children of all ages to engage in an intellectual explanation of an experience, but it is those meanings that are not amenable to a discursive form of communication that give differentiated understanding through the dramatic art form its essential identity. Although a participant or an observer may, as I have done above, intellectually pinpoint a particular attitude or feeling appraisal, such a labelling has to be seen as a recognition of a door to be opened to things that cannot be labelled. But unless the teacher, at least recognizes which door he is trying to open, unless he goes through some labelling process, he may simply allow drama to do what play does most of the time: reinforce what the child already knows – the meanings beyond the door do not become available.

Which brings me to the aspect of the activity that could be described as the principle feature of dramatic playing: the symbolization process.[20] I emphasize *process* to distinguish from the way Piaget and the Schools Council Secondary Drama Project use the word symbolic. They both use symbol or symbolic to refer to an action that represents something else. This perfectly valid use, however, is not particularly helpful for describing those significant moments in drama when there is an enriching of meaning – when, to use the same metaphor, the children 'go through the door'. It is a fascinating feature of educational drama work that, although it may be necessary as I have suggested for the teacher to identify the door with an intellectual label, once identified, it is the non-intellectual theatrical symbol with its potential for crystallizing as opposed to conceptualizing meaning that will take the children through. Perhaps this is one of the marks of the good drama teacher, that he can both identify the door and then work the magic – thus employing two entirely different thinking processes.

Dramatic playing, in its most pedestrian moments, will involve actions and objects that have for the participants just a single, collective, uni-dimensional, functional meaning; in its most heightened moments the actions and objects will accrue for the participants many-layered, personal as well as collective, non-functional as well as functional meanings. Put crudely, the children will have gone through the door. It is not my place here to discuss how this might be done, but to draw attention to its significance for learning. In the discussion on structure I tried to establish that it is the teacher's responsibility to change the form of symbolic play in injecting a tightness of structure, employing such basic theatrical devices as focus, tension and contrast. I will now add to this list the making of available symbols. A teacher can only *make available.* He cannot guarantee that a particular symbolic action or object is going to resonate meanings for the participants. He can do no more than be sensitive to the potential.

Mary Warnock, in summarizing Kent's view of imagination, claims that: 'What we appreciate or create in the highest art, is a symbol of something that is forever beyond it.'[21] This is the other *partial* answer to the overall picture of learning through dramatic playing.

Conclusion

The reader may have wondered why I chose to confine my discussion to just one aspect of drama in schools – I have neglected drama towards performance and drama training in skills. I hope I have now made it clear that in terms of learning potential, dramatic playing has the greatest educational value. Its strengths lie in the unique relationship it offers in combining theatrical structure (not outer shape, of course) and a quality of spontaneous living that belong to both symbolic play and to games.

Notes

1 McGregor, L., Tate, M. and Robinson, K.L. (1977) *Learning through Drama*, Heinemann Educational Books.
2 The reader may refer to Bolton G.M. (1978) 'The Concept of "Showing" in Children's Dramatic Activity', in *Young Drama*, 6, 3, pp. 97–101, for further discussion on the relationship between dramatic playing and performance.
3 Cook, Caldwell H. (1917) *The Play Way*, Heinemann.
4 Slade, P. (1954) *Child Drama*, University of London Press.
5 Piaget, J. (1972) *Play, Dreams and Imitation in Childhood*, Routledge and Kegan Paul.
6 Dearden, R.F. 'The Concept of Play', in Peters, R.S. (Ed.) *The Concept of Education*, Routledge and Kegan Paul.
7 Vygotsky, L.S. (1976) 'Play and its role in the mental development of the child' in Bruner, J.S. *et al.* (Eds), *Play: Its Roles in Development and Evolution*, Penguin Educational, p. 543.
8 The metaphorical nature of drama and its implications for teaching are discussed in 'Drama as metaphor', in *Young Drama*, 4, 2, 1976, pp. 43–7.
9 Vygotsky, *op. cit.*, p. 549.
10 *Ibid.*
11 *Ibid.*, p. 551.
12 Bruner, J.S. (1974) *Beyond the Information Given*, Allen and Unwin.
13 Dearden, *op. cit.*, p. 85.
14 For a detailed examination of structure in dramatic playing, see Bolton, G.M. (1979) *Towards a Theory of Drama in Education*, Longmans.
15 Gillham, G. (1974) 'Report on Condercum School Project', unpublished.
16 Huizinga J. (1970) *Homo Ludens*, Temple Smith, p. 29.
17 Smilanski, S. (1968) *The Effects of Sociodramatic Play on Disadvantaged Pre-School Children*, John Wiley.
18 Piaget, *op. cit.*, p. 207.
19 Bruner, J.S. (1962) *On Knowing: Essays for the Left Hand*, Harvard University Press.
20 For further discussion of symbolization, see Bolton, G.M. (1978) 'The process of symbolization in improvised drama', in *Young Drama*, 6, 3.
21 Warnock, M. (1976) *Imagination*, Faber and Faber, p. 63.

3
Planning and Evaluating Drama in Education

5 Curriculum Planning and the Arts

Desmond Hogan

The author believes in the needs of contemporary society for more personal and decision-making opportunities. His particular concern is with institutionally-based curriculum development, and the contribution that drama teachers may make by virtue of their specialized knowledge and skills in social interactive learning processes so necessary in implementing this.

He presents a critique of the widely used and accepted models of curriculum planning which are characterized by 'an essential reliance on "cold", objective analysis of objective needs and strategies' and argues that it is divorced from the reality of the learning process which he regards as essentially exploratory, responsive and social. He suggests that the planning of teaching should be based not so much on an often diversive discussion of 'aims', but on the use of the more pragmatic device of viewing classroom action in terms of specific teacher intention in relation to observed practice. This kind of planning, so much an implicit part of the drama teacher's work, would contain within it a consideration of both instructional and expressive objectives.

In focussing on the traditional divide between curriculum planners and those who teach the curriculum, Hogan's chapter emphasizes the contribution that drama teachers may make both in school through their knowledge of group dyamics and negotiating strategies; and on behalf of schools as they debate with local and central government issues of the common core curriculum and assessment and performance and attempt to resist pressures for a firmer central control of the curriculum.

In discussing a subject as potentially vast and complex as the title 'curriculum planning in the arts' suggests, it seems necessary to focus on what is really only one facet of the planning problem but one in which drama teachers have a unique contribution to make.

I am increasingly unhappy with titles which may imply that curriculum planning is a process whose nature is constrained more by its subject-matter content (for example, the arts) than by the 'cultural' assumptions of the planners. I feel increasingly strongly that, in curriculum planning, we are concerned with the whole problem of how people learn. Learning, if we leave aside maturational issues (and acknowledge honestly that, as a whole, it is a phenomenon about which we know shockingly little), is a process which must have similar characteristics whether the central actor is a child facing new material in a lesson, an adolescent facing his first job, or a teacher in mid-career facing a new curriculum proposal. When we have widened the definition to cover all people faced with the problem of how to respond to, and how to make use of, new knowledge or new situations, then we surely begin to enter territory with vaguely familiar landmarks for drama teachers.

The learning process seems to involve probing and exploring the new information or situation; to involve tentative responses in interaction with other people involved to test whether our interpretation is similar to theirs; consequently, to involve a process of negotiation in which broad agreements on meanings and acceptable responses are hammered out; and, as a result of all this, to be a form of 'successful coping' which, operationally, reduces what was at first unknown and potentially threatening to something broadly 'familiar' and predictable. Thus, platitudinally, learning is a process of social interaction; and social interaction is characterized – at periods other than those of acute confrontation and crisis – by a rising spiral of shared experiences, shared emotions, shared meanings, which, in turn, facilitate the process of environmental control, if one uses the term 'environment' to embrace the social, cultural and psychological, as well as the physical, context of thought and action. The implication of such a view is that hitherto accepted models of curriculum planning, characterized as they were and are by an essential reliance on 'cold', objective analysis of objective needs and strategies, bear as much resemblance to reality as the basically identical and equally mythical image of the natural scientist alone in his laboratory pursuing objective truth. However, it is a model which is so deeply embedded in contemporary culture that it is dangerous to underestimate its strength. It is the model behind the expenditure of £100 million on the planning of a new Ford car, or several thousand million pounds on a Concorde, and it has as its goal the production of a user-proof commodity. It is also the model behind certain crucial aspects of the work of the Nuffield Foundation and the Schools Council in which sums in excess of £10 million have been spent in an attempt to produce curricular plans which will guarantee improved learning outcomes in spite of deficiencies in large sectors of the teaching profession.

I want to focus on just a few aspects or issues in the planning process. Firstly, I am conscious that there are, in our present social situation, two conflicting forces at work which have relevance to this discussion: on the one hand, there is a growing alienation experienced by almost all of us – by the industrial worker through the separation of his daily work from the ultimate product, and by the teacher faced by a separation between the planning and design process involved in a new curriculum package and his or her daily work in the classroom. In a sense, there is a dehumanizing division of labour between those who plan and those who implement, and this has expression, at least in some of the extreme versions of detailed course planning, in a sort of contempt for the user. The 'good' package is one which is user- (that is, pupil *and* teacher) proof – one which guarantees results regardless of the idiot consumer. Of course, this is a classic self-fulfilling prophecy: treat someone this way and boredom and backlash follow. I suppose one of the most extreme (short of full, programmed learning courses) versions of this was the Holt Social Studies Curriculum kit[1] which came out in the 1960s: here you had, in a neat plastic attaché case, pupil books, teachers' guides (replete with hundreds of detailed aims and objectives), Banda masters for duplicating notes, OHP transparencies to obviate blackboard work, slide or film strip sets for 'enrichment', together with records for media variety, and assessment tests and mark schemes to ensure 'correct' evaluation. I leave you to imagine the impact on users in the British cultural context of such an approach: great, if your consuming interest is golf or gardening rather than teaching. And, given more teachers turning to golf, you have an inexhaustible demand for more teacher-proof packages.

On the other hand, and emerging from the same complex of social conflict which generated the first response, is the demand for *participation* – hardly yet recognized in teaching at a level of involvement above *consultation*. This demand is not only associated with a politically divergent view of what a healthy society needs to be, but also with the idea that one cannot, usefully, separate wholly the design and implementation phases of an innovation. For one thing, the study of organic systems has forced industrial and economic planners to think in terms of 'feedback': unless the field experience of use is 'fedback' into the ongoing design/redesign process, disaster is ultimately inevitable. In education we call this process, in the jargon, 'formative evaluation'.[2] Its recognition as a central link in curriculum planning calls into question the whole previous model – as well as the model of a hierarchically organized (as opposed to an organic) society with which it is basically linked. This is an area where no easy solutions can yet be seen but I would suggest that one useful approach already exists in education and has its roots as far back as the early 1950s in the birth period of the Welfare State: it was Aneurin Bevan who questioned the detailed planning approach which derived from the Soviet GOSPLAN machinery and suggested that it was impractical for the modern, complex, advanced technological economy. He preferred, instead, a process of planning involving control of the 'commanding heights' of the economy – below which individual initiative and local circumstances must be allowed to apply creative initiatives. I would suggest that the British economy is no more complex than the learning process and that the 'commanding heights' concept involves a very difficult but potentially fruitful approach to our work.

Only a little thought will lead to the conclusion that this model, if it is to work, will involve a far greater attention to the *people* involved: rather than a process of abstract analysis (of 'needs', of objectives, etc.), 'planning' will involve attempting to influence social process – 'social' in the sense of the dynamics at work within groups of users. Once one has reformulated the problem in this way a whole new area of research findings can be brought to bear. For example, it seems clear that the flow of new information into and through a 'social system' (that is an ongoing group engaged in a common task), is affected by, for example, the 'location' of those receiving the information: new ideas are often first picked up by 'loners' who are relatively isolated and who, perhaps as a result, are primarily members of other groups. In practice, in the staffroom, they may be the chronic 'course attenders' who may not, as a result, be very popular but who, if properly 'managed' may be vital channels for new ideas. I say 'properly managed' because, by definition, as they are peripheral to the group their ideas and information are not quickly or easily passed on in 'normal' circumstances: their ideas only slowly percolate until, quite suddenly, they can become 'respectable' and important. Here, again, research suggests that someone may be playing a vital role in the group – that of 'opinion-leader', who can judge both the needs of the group and the potential of innovating ideas and bring them together. Without being too cynical, it seems to me that a good head is one who uses the peripherals like an old-style general used his cavalry: their function was to find out where the enemy was and in what strength. Basically the only way to do this was to get shot at – so they were expendable. The head encourages new ideas and experiments by and from peripherals (young enthusiasts with nothing to lose and everything to gain?): if they are failures then the failures are those of the authors; if they are successes they automatically enhance the authority of the leader who 'encouraged' them. That is an example of the management of a group learning process and can be seen as 'natural' because the survival of the leadership is often closely linked to the survival of the group.

We must recognize how basic are social interaction processes like these. Most of us, for example, don't carefully analyze a possible new textbook: rather we rely on 'old Joe's' opinion – and if many of us turn to him, he is an 'opinion leader'. Similarly GPs with new drugs or girls with new fashions. However, we must also recognize the strengths of the *R.D. and D.* model and somehow synthesize the two – for example, by restricting central planning to decisions on broad knowledge structures in a curriculum (for example, the traditional decision to treat physics under heat, light, sound), on the basic concepts to be acquired, and on a range of *exemplificatory* resource materials. Adaptation, implementation and development would be left to local initiative. This would be the application of restricting central planning decisions in complex systems to the 'commanding heights'.

Contemporary ways of looking at behaviour in organizations are derived from the same social and philosophical assumptions as are modern ideas on drama. For example, it is argued that the communication of ideas just does not happen unless there is a degree of 'openness' in the climate of the audience group; that 'openness' depends upon a sense of security, a sense of trust, as well as on an awareness of the *need* for new information if current problems are to be successfully solved. There is a fine line between these countervailing faces of need, often associated with a growing sense of insecurity, and security itself as the foundation for the risk-taking inherent in change. And the dynamics of a sense of group security based upon trust – a characteristic of all good 'lessons' surely? – is, to me, complex and obscure: for example, I found that it took me almost three times as long to establish that sort of situation with children in London's East End as it had during my spell as a headmaster in West Africa. My colleagues in the humanities teams in a London comprehensive spent a great deal of time thinking about the constraints upon the growth of a sense of security: for example, and at a basic physical level, we worried about the agoraphobic pressures of open-plan learning spaces on 12 girls – and found that teachers suffered at least as much as the kids when they felt they were openly watched by colleagues; we provided locker-bases for the children under the influence of ideas like those of Ardrey on the significance of a sense of territory, and compromised many of our early, radical ideas in favour of form – basis and desk clusters. It shouldn't take too long to realize that, if you adhere to a model of learning which involves meaning-exploration and negotiation, you really ought to look at your classroom furniture and seating plans – but it took me ten years to take that seriously. However, the physical aspects of security are no more than the foundations of the structure: security, in the sense of a form structure of shared *understandings*, is far more complex and fragile. Communication is fundamentally dependent upon a large – but not too large – degree of homophily within the group. People can grow old when they share too many assumptions and values: the young radical at university can become middle-aged in ten years if he joins a stock-broking firm, moves to Esher, travels up to town on the same train each day, reads the same paper, goes to the same golf clubs and cocktail parties, and buys the same furniture from Heals or Habitat as neighbours in similar jobs! There is never the discomfort of an idea forced on you from outside your value system and you cease to be alert and flexible in critical areas of the mind. But the development of a working team cannot occur, on the other hand, without a degree of homophily: I remind you of the phases which, it is said, every stable group must go through: forming, storming, norming, performing.[3] No successful 'performing' will take place until the group has agreed the norms to govern its behaviour, and they cannot be generated until everyone has put their beliefs and values on the table for criticism and debate; the membership of the group has to form and reform before this can happen – and I have a clear picture in my mind of a drama group in action when I say this. But how often do we organize our classes so that it happens? How often do staff meetings continually attempt to 'perform' while politely avoiding 'unpleasantness' involved in 'storming'? Is it not true, in your experience, that where this is allowed to happen, it is not participation in decision-making which is the reality, or teacher-pupil cooperation in a common learning experience, but a naked imposition of power? And is much of this not due to our own incapacity to handle conflict, (that is, to handle the unexpected, the antipathetic, the new?) due, in turn, to our groups not having thoroughly 'normed', or generated the shared meanings on the basis of which they could develop competence in solving problems? The head who seeks to build an empire for himself by adopting five major curricular innovations is almost certainly exposing his group (the staff and pupils) to an area or zone of uncertainty far greater than they can handle creatively. Since cope they must with his use of power, they will respond by sabotage at worst, or, at best, making the novel familiar: by cannibalizing the projects until they can use them for their old purposes and in familiar ways.

This response of teachers raises another fascinating aspect of organizational behaviour and development. I have no doubt that one can usefully think of a 'psychological contract' as existing between members of any group, and that the head in my previous example had breached that 'contract'. It is this 'contract' which is not only the basic security of the members but the springboard from which innovation and risk-taking can be attempted. The contract is quite 'hard': members have the right to expect predictability in the behaviour of colleagues (think how disturbed we all feel if the known persona of the head is replaced by a wild 'swinger' in the latter stages of the Xmas party!) and the responsibility to be consistent in their own. But predictability and consistency alone spell fossilization and death. There must be experiment, even a healthy degree of subversion. In the past far too much institutional experience has been dependent upon staff replacements and appointments: now that this is a thing of the past we must somehow generate change *internally*, actually put a premium on some subversion, on 'awkwardness' and 'difficult' behaviour amongst colleagues. I see some aspects of this in the 'normal' way subgroups form: for example, if I feel discontented and frustrated I grumble to people who might be sympathetic, that is, share my discontents. If this proves the case we adjourn to the 'pub' and explore our feelings. Later maybe we agree on some common course of action – like trying a new teaching method or pattern of relationships. We don't ask permission: we go ahead and do it. If the 'Old Man' is wise and judges that it can't do any great harm, he turns a blind eye. Immediately this happens the 'subversion' has won important informal status and will continue and probably spread. Ultimately, when it is widely accepted, the wise head will formally adopt it (probably giving the impression that he thought of it first!). Thus a healthy open system 'learns'.

But the least of my argument is that this sort of dynamic can and must be managed if we are to take charge of change and not just suffer it. The situations most likely to facilitate it can be designed like a good party can be delayed. The interactions require skills which we, as innovators, must acquire. They involve attitudes which value these developments and we all need help to acquire these – for example, how to cope creatively with conflict. Management of these interactions may, for example, require the projection of conflict issues out of the real into an imaginary situation where the audience can come to terms with them 'safely'. – Of course, I'm talking about dramatic catharsis and need not further labour the point of how much drama teachers have to contribute to this aspect of managing curriculum change. Many of us have experienced the creative catharsis of well-produced school cabarets which, by externalizing heated issues in the forms of 'skills', do a superb job of reducing tension and reopening communication.

I would like now to turn to another issue and approach which, eventually, will, I hope, illuminate the same argument. This is the question of how to initiate the planning process.

I was cynically amused to read (in *Learning through Drama*, 1977[4]) of the 'typical' drama teacher walking into the classroom wondering 'What on earth can I do with them today?' I would suggest that that is how the great majority of lessons are 'planned' regardless of subject. And while all the authorities would hold up their hands in horror, and all the training institutions redouble their demands for lesson plans, nevertheless, in my view, this behaviour of teachers as a profession must be recognized as relevant to their perceptions of their job and of pupil needs. In terms of the job they see themselves as craftsmen (if not artists!) rather than technicians; they instinctively reflect the industrial model where the pupils are raw materials to be processed into saleable products. And, in so doing, they reflect the prescriptive planning model which demands a prior formulation of aims and objectives, followed by the selection of strategies most likely to achieve them, followed by an assessment of how far these objectives have been achieved. They believe that serendipity plays a large part in their lives; that most outcomes are not only unpredicted and unpredictable, but most of them – good as well as bad – are unintended! And they work on the assumption that, in general, it's best to try and start each lesson at the point where the *mids* are. Now I do not support an approach that can be, all too often, sloppiness piled on laziness, but I do recognize the strength of the implied critique of the linear model of lesson planning which is still taught in colleges and universities. Above all, I want to stress the implications of starting where the learner is – whether the learner is a pupil or a teacher.

Firstly, I question whether, in this era of loss of value consensus, it is ever worthwhile – outside the confines of a small, ideologically committed group – to *start* the process of planning by an attempt to agree on aims. In my experience that is a recipe for civil war which will only die down when key people leave or retire. I think we need to accept that we will seem, at the outset, to disagree about what sort of society the children are being educated for; on whether Skinner is the best guide for classroom practice; or which are the key concepts involved in understanding the problem of pollution, etc. But I particularly suspect the linear approach because it divorces the planning from the teaching, and because, in practice, it tends to reinforce our assumptions rather than open them to question. I suggest, in its place, a very pragmatic approach which seems of use in most situations, with the exception, perhaps, of where we are starting a new school. This would begin with the belief that what is needed is a useful discussion based on questioning existing practice by working colleagues. Thus a team would discuss with each other their *intentions* in teaching a particular lesson or course; the lessons would then be observed and the observer would attempt to analyze whether, in *action*, the explicit *intention* of the teacher were guiding his action; and/or what other intentions appeared to be involved (including those of the pupils, of the authors of the textbooks in use, etc.). The observation would then switch to analysis of the *actual* outcomes of the learning: what was 'intended' set against what we realized. Without going further into detail, the purpose would be to make as much of current practice as possible problematic: not to argue that 'you *ought* to be doing *X*', but 'you seemed to be doing *X*', and to examine how far this was seen as successful. Thus a genuine *supportive* strategy, aimed at helping the colleague to do what he wanted would generate the trust necessary to go on later, perhaps, to the question as to whether he should be doing it at all. This is to start where the learner is. It is an attempt to clarify exactly where the present world does and does not work and to generate a working consensus on that, before proceeding to design the new Jerusalem.

Secondly, when it comes to making suggestions for necessary changes I want to suggest that all who work in the arts are generally far too quick to deny the validity of attempting to formulate intentions very clearly because, perhaps, 'clarity' in the past has been associated with prescriptive, behavioural objectives. The work of Eisner suggests that we might progress in the arts if we could examine each other's intentions and teaching in order to clarify what concepts and tools we all, implicitly or explicitly, assume are prerequisites for what Maslow calls 'self-actualization'. We recognize them in oracy, and literacy and numeracy at a low level, but I believe colleague-observation and discussion of our lessons would highlight an increasing body of them which we share in recognizing as essential. Now these objectives Eisner would call *instructional*[5] and claim as capable of planning and evaluating in fairly traditional ways. However, they represent only a part of what teaching intends: the other objectives are termed *expressive* and involve the internalization and transformation of learning by the individual learner – the cultural regeneration and transformation process if you like. In a practical primary science example, the former would involve a visit to the village pond for the purpose of collecting a given list of materials; while the latter would involve an exploration of the pond. The former could be assessed using a straightforward scoring technique; the latter would be far more complex and open-ended. I suggest that this sort of approach would not only generate a creative discussion in the arts departments, but would also involve them speaking the same language as that of other curriculum departments – thus helping to break down the 'cultural isolation' that characterizes them in schools attempting to plan change . . . and, indirectly perhaps, ensuring a rather higher place in the queue for resources than is often the case at present?

One example of the sort of thing I have in mind you will find in Maurice Barrett's *Thinking about Art Education*[6] where, amongst other things, he tries to stimulate discussion on intentions and means by producing a typology of different 'schools' of art education with their associated styles of teaching and criteria for evaluation. It is not the correctness or otherwise of his typology which is of interest but the value of this sort of approach as a heuristic tool which generates openness amongst teachers by questioning how well-articulated are their intentions with their methods; whether the information they are getting on learning outcomes is accurate or adequate and what they are doing with it, etc. The purpose is to generate a diagnostic process on the part of the teacher. I have stressed security and trust as essential for change: now I am stressing the other factor in the equation – the self-diagnosis of need, which is the driving force behind change. Here again, the teacher trained in self-awareness in terms of the impact he or she is making on an audience is surely vital to the spread of that awareness amongst colleagues in other disciplines. The act of diagnosis will always be extremely threatening and most of us need help to cope with and defuse it.

Lastly, I want to stress that I don't believe that a drama department in a school or college can *afford* to focus solely on improving its own work. The planning models I have recommended can only be applied within a favourable institutional climate. The drama teacher can lead, or demonstrate, or help others, but the whole institution must change if change anywhere within it is to be radical. At Sussex we are now defining the curriculum as the 'collectively acknowledged body of norms and decisions within which teaching is planned and learning takes place'[7] and thus are stressing the collectivity of the planning process. It is out of the institutional norms that resource allocation criteria emerge, that subject status is determined. It is out of a healthy articulation of classroom practice and staffroom discussion that norms are generated and regenerated. I want to stress staffroom discussion because this is an arena where surely the drama specialist can, above all, contribute by his or her analysis of the dynamics at work. So many discussions generate heat not light because of assumptions not shared, styles of debate which just don't mix, language which generates defensiveness rather than openness, etc. I find increasing concern amongst teachers at the poor dynamics of the average staff meeting. Surely drama teachers have many insights to apply here?

And I believe that there *is* a change to institutionally-based curriculum development, at the very worst period of crisis most of us have known when we either innovate by pulling ourselves up by own bootstraps in the foreseeable future or we don't innovate at all. We'll have to put up with old Jim Bloggs the arch resister of experiment, because he won't and can't move away from the school. Consequently, we'll need every ounce of expertise we can find in the art of talking and living and working together.

Notes

1 FENTON, E. (Gen. ed.) (1967) *Holt Social Curriculum Studies*, Holt, Rinehart and Winston.
2 SCRIVEN, M. (1966) 'The methodology of evaluation', in STAKE R.E. (Ed.), *Perspectives of Curriculum Evaluation*, AERA Monograph Series on Curriculum

Evaluation, Chicago, Rand McNally and Co.

3   BION, W.R. (1948) 'Experiences in groups', in *Human Relations*, Vols. 1–3.

4   MCGREGOR, L. *et al.* (1977), *Learning through Drama*, Heinemann Educational Books.

5   EISNER, E.W. (1969) *Instructional and Expressive Objectives: Their Formulation and Use in Curriculum*, AERA Monograph Series on Curriculum Evaluation, 3, Chicago, Rand McNally and Co.

6   BARRETT, M. (1974) *Thinking about Art Education*, London Borough of Redbridge, Education Office.

7   This first occurs in MICHAEL ERAUT's contribution to ERAUT, M.E., SMITH, G. and GOAD, L. (1975) 'The analysis of curriculum materials', Sussex University Education Area Occasional Paper No. 2.

6 Teaching Styles in Drama: Theory in Practice

Christopher Day

This chapter, which echoes Desmond Hogan's view of the negotiated curriculum, is concerned with helping teachers increase their professional effectiveness. It focusses on problems of theory and practice as two interactive parts of a 'theory of action' which governs each teacher's practice.

The chapter is in two parts. The first considers the practical problems facing teachers who wish to improve their practice in an education system which encourages learning by students but positively discourages learning by teachers. The author argues that in spite of the many constraints placed upon them, if teachers wish to enhance their effectiveness in the classroom, they need to learn to identify and take responsibility for inconsistencies between their intentions and practice.

In the second part a number of discovery-based teaching models are presented then examined within the context of various orientations of dramatic activity. By this means, the author makes explicit a number of principles underlying drama thinking and practice, and challenges teachers to evaluate their work by reflecting on themselves both as educationists and as practitioners.

Throughout, the author contends that in any consideration of teaching we must not only discuss 'the what' but also – perhaps more importantly – 'the how' of teaching. He thus raises two of the most significant issues in education: the problem of clarifying teaching values and translating these into classroom practice.

This chapter is in two discrete but related parts:

1. It discusses the practical problems that exist for teachers who wish to become more effective in the classroom. In this, there is an implicit judgment on the kind of education system which, on the one hand, encourages learning by students by providing environments, time and resources, and on the other, discourages learning by teachers – as if the two were not connected.

2. It focusses on the teaching of drama, and seeks to make explicit the relationship between the essential nature of the drama activity and the

use of this activity by the teacher to promote learning. The purpose is to assist teachers in the process of what I believe to be a natural activity of reflecting on their teaching.

Professional Learning: Purposes, Needs and Constraints

Every teacher who takes his work seriously ... holds in mind a vision of his teaching style that he believes is most effective. Not every teacher is able to describe his vision upon request, but it remains nonetheless ever-present in his mind. It is the teaching style that he actually exemplifies in his classes during those moments when external reality and inner-vision meet. It is an image of teacher-at-his-best.... (Axelrod, 1973)

It is assumed that teachers do take their work seriously, do have in mind a vision of effectiveness towards which they strive, and use reflection as a means of assessing the effects of previous actions in order to take decisions about future actions. It is argued, however, that because of the day-to-day demands of teaching, and for perceptual and contextual reasons, the ability of teachers to reflect systematically on their work is often seriously impaired.

It is worth investigating at this point what 'professional learning' involves and what are the obstacles which stand in its path. There are three main principles of learning (and I am assuming that learning involves changes in understanding):

1 Effective learning occurs in response to the identification and confrontation of problems by the learner.
2 Decisions about teaching should stem from reflection on the effects of previous actions.
3 Effective confrontation of problems requires the maximizing of valid information (about teaching).

The 'maximizing of valid information' implies that teachers need to identify and investigate consistencies and inconsistencies within and between their teaching ideologies (intentions) and their teaching acts in the classroom in order to become more effective; for the teacher's planning of a lesson and his/her behaviour in the classroom reflects his or her *theories* of planning and behaviour. I should like, therefore, to debunk immediately the long-standing myth held by many educationists whether they be administrators, consultants, teachers – or even university professors! – that theory and practice are separate entities. On the contrary, they are two essential parts of everybody's 'theory of action'. These two parts have been termed 'espoused theories' (teaching intentions or aspirations) and 'theories-in-use' (behaviours in the classroom, or teaching acts) (Argyris and Schon, 1976). In order to become more effective in our work, then, we need to confront our espoused theories in the context of our theories-in-use. If we do not, knowledge about our teaching will remain at the level of espoused theory only.

The obstacles that lie in the path of any comprehensive and systematic examination of discrepancies between intentions and practice are three-fold.

1 The time and energy constraints of day-to-day teaching do not allow teachers the practical reflection necessary to identify events in the classroom, find causal relationships (assessing the consequences of direct actions) or reflect on these consequences.

2 Not only are teachers' actions limited by the context in which they work, but their perceptions are also limited, both by the 'norms' of the specific social context and by wider norms of their profession.

3 Much knowledge about practice is implicit rather than explicit (Day, 1981).

All schools as systems, and classrooms as subsystems, operate on the basis of assumed and negotiated 'norms' of behaviour. These are often characterized as making up the 'ethos' of the school; and in order to join in the life of the school, both teachers and students quickly learn to adopt the expected behaviour.

> Teachers operate within a framework of expectations, which is initially shaped by their previous life-experience, their professional training and their professional socialisation in schools; and subsequently modified by their changing school experience and external influences both from within the education system and from outside it. They are acutely aware of some of these expectations, particularly those empha-sised in transactions with people outside the school (eg. employers), but less aware of others. Some professional norms are so internalized that they only become apparent when somebody questions them or some unusual incident draws attention to them.... (Eraut, Barton and Canning, 1978)

For a teacher to survive in a school it will be necessary for him to accept into his system of behaviour what are often unstated norms and expectations of the community and his colleagues in school. Jackson (1968) identified the system of norms and values which influence both teachers and students in schools and which are created by cultural inheritance and professional socialization as the 'hidden curriculum'.

This 'hidden curriculum' is not disinterested, for in each school it represents a particular view of what a teacher is and what an ideal pupil should be, what knowledge is important, how this knowledge should be transmitted by the teacher and how learning should be assessed. Any process of learning for the teacher will involve making these tacit assumptions explicit. Insofar as assump-tions about (a) school and (b) classroom practice remain unquestioned and unproblematic, these are likely to act as limitations on a teacher's capacity to evaluate his work and hence increase his professional effectiveness. The problems of increasing knowledge about practice have been highlighted by

Keddie (1971) in her distinction between teacher as educationist and teacher as practitioner:

> ... While, therefore, some educational aims may be formulated by teachers as *educationists*, it will not be surprising if 'doctrine' is contradicted by 'commitments' which arise in the situation in which they must act as *teachers*. . . .

There may be ,therefore, a difference between what people say and what they do. In the staffroom setting, for example, talk about teaching is governed by tacit assumptions about the nature of talk about teaching; whereas in the classroom setting, teaching actions are governed by tacit assumptions about the nature of teaching actions. What we do is based on our tacit and thus unstated knowledge of the nature of practice in any given setting.

When we are planning or carrying out practice, decisions often involve making explicit what we already 'know' tacitly – about, for example, what is 'good' and 'bad', what is 'right' and 'wrong', and what will or will not work. Practice specifies the kind of behaviour which, under normal conditions, will lead to predictable results. It is, therefore, also the means for maintaining certain kinds of constancy and control.

The world in which we live contains much more information than we can handle, and our decisions about practice are ways in which we can make our world constant. Thus practices are in a sense rules of action which allow us both to maintain a stable view of, for example, the classroom or the school, and to give priority to certain kinds of information while ignoring other kinds. They are theories of control. A new teacher very quickly develops assumptions about practices which allow him to cope with the complexities of teaching and being a member of staff. However, since it is rare for these to be made explicit or tested, the possibilities for evaluating those assumptions which underpin his teaching are minimal. Our explicit actions as educationists and practitioners are therefore often based on tacit knowledge of what to do (Polyani, 1967).

It would seem, therefore, that teachers are not, under normal conditions, able to be autonomous or self-critical since they are limited in what they can see and do by both perceptual and contextual constraints. If they are to extend their knowledge about practice and thus gain the possibility of increasing their professional effectiveness they will need intellectual and affective support.

It has been argued thus far that in the normal course of events there are often contradictions between a teacher's intentions and practice; that the practice of teaching is the expression of teaching theory; that much of the curriculum remains at the implicit level because of contextual, perceptual and professional constraints; and that in order to become more effective teachers need to be allowed more opportunities for practical reflection which involves confrontation of both congruities and incongruities within and between intentions and practice.

The second part of this paper attempts to provide, indirectly, one such opportunity to those teachers involved in the use of drama as a means of promoting students' learning. It begins by

(a) defining the essential nature of the drama activity process by
(b) attempting to tease out or make explicit the underlying theories of learning and principles of practice implied by this definition, and concludes by
(c) presenting various models of teaching which are both consistent and inconsistent with the nature of the drama activity and the theories and principles upon which it is based.

Drama is 'acting out', a use of the enactive mode of learning. The process of acting out means that the participants in the drama must place or project themselves into 'as if' situations. Almost always, more than one person is involved in the enactments or dramas. The plays that are created are the vehicles for the student's learning. Central to the process of the acting out is *investigation* (Day, 1977). This process is as important as the communication of what has been investigated. Indeed, one may say that the quality of the communication is directly related to and dependent upon the quality of the process.

Inevitably, the question of what is drama and what is theatre is raised. There are many definitions of the distinction between the two, including one of my own (Day, 1975). However, such a distinction is, I believe, spurious. Theatre is a part of drama. Whether child drama arises out of children's play or whether drama in schools arises out of a need to pass on our cultural inheritance of theatre, the two are inextricably parts of one whole – learning through enactment, as a member of an audience, as a participating member of the cast, in public and non-public drama work. So drama in schools, and the teaching of drama, must be discussed in terms of 'orientations' of work in which teachers are engaged at different times and for different purposes. These may be characterized as being:

1   *towards exercise* – which involves qualities of practising (skills of mime, voice and speech, movement, techniques of expression, etc.);
2   *towards performing* – which involves qualities of demonstrating and public performance/communication (techniques of stagecraft, etc.);
3   *towards experiencing or living through* – which involves qualities of spontaneity and empathy (improvization, role-play, etc.) (Bolton, 1979).

These three orientations deal with both dramatic experience and dramatic form.

We have defined the nature of drama as involving two essential components, participation (learning through use of enactment) and social interaction. Thus whatever the orientation, the teacher's task must be to:

(a)   engage students in participation in enactment as a means of learning (to establish and build/extend belief in 'as if' situations);

(b)   to assist students in developing skills of social interaction at a 'real' (life) and 'symbolic' (drama) level which are necessary to (a).

So, intrinsic to the drama teaching situation is participation in enactments with other people. Because there is participation (of the moment/at life rate) it is not possible for the teacher to instruct, nor is it possible to view students as passive receivers of knowledge. They must be regarded as active participants in the shaping/making of knowledge. Because students are engaged in social interaction the teacher must exercise active social influence. His ideology must be *discovery-based learning* and his intervention strategies must take account of the *nature of learning* and social influence.

The Drama Teacher's Ideologies

There can be little doubt that a teacher's belief about teaching affects the self-concepts of pupils in the class (Barker Lunn, 1970; Ferri, 1971) and the kind of learning which is being promoted. Because he/she is 'having to organize and control the activities of a large number of people, the teacher is continually having to present a particular kind of self which serves to maintain an appropriate relationship between himself and his pupils, and which indicates to them those areas of conduct which he wishes to control' (Esland, 1977; Goffman, 1959). A teacher's style may be said to represent the teacher's idea of what the classroom should be like: 'It is as if he had a model in his mind, and operated consistently to make the classroom conform to his model' (Thelen, 1954).

I would suggest that although it is true to say that drama teachers are engaged in promoting discovery-based learning it is vital to distinguish within this paradigm between learning by discovery and learning to discover, since each will affect differently the way teachers conceptualize and carry out their teaching.

Learning to Discover/Inquiry-Based Learning

Discovery-based learning has been defined as that in which the teacher introduces his pupils into situations 'so selected or devised that they embody in implicit or hidden form principles or knowledge which he wishes them to learn' (Stenhouse, 1968). Within the paradigm of discovery-based teaching a distinction may be made between learning by discovery and learning to discover (Schulman and Keisler, 1966), and this may well be useful in identifying more accurately the differences which exist in the practice of drama teaching.

In *learning by discovery* the teacher has certain content objectives in mind, for example, knowledge and principles to be learned, but he uses indirect (non-instructional) influences in the learning process. For example, he may use 'guessing games' or guided discovery processes or employ project work which often simply involves 'a transference from uncritical dependence on the teacher's views to uncritical dependence on the views in books' (Elliott, 1973). In *learning to discover*, the teacher is concerned with helping pupils learn procedures for critically evaluating knowledge and principles, leaving what is to be learned as a result of this process an open matter. Elliott (1973) distinguishes these two kinds of discovery-based teaching by calling them discovery-based – where objectives are specified by the teacher in terms of knowledge content – and inquiry-based – where the emphasis is on the process (how to inquire) rather than the products of past inquiries.

It is likely that in discovery-based learning the teacher is essentially employing 'closed' methods of teaching which involve 'suppression of the pupils' freedom to disagree with the teacher', whereas in inquiry-based teaching he will be employing 'open' methods, which 'give pupils the right to disagree with people's beliefs, including the beliefs of the teacher and those of the majority of people in our society (established knowledge).' These understandings may be expanded, elaborated and made idiosyncratic. Where the problem set has no predetermined resolution – as with issues raised in most drama work which is usually concerned with conjecture, interpretation, considered opinion – there can be no 'right' or 'wrong' answer, and thus, logically, no distinction can be made between 'valid' or 'invalid' thinking by pupils.

Drama teachers are concerned not only with asking questions to which there are ready-made, 'correct' answers, but also with the investigation of issues through the use of enactive, iconic and symbolic techniques. The inquiry, where it involves acting out, is the drama. Through acting out experience may be represented more adequately than either the written or spoken word alone, since in drama the child, uniquely, has the opportunity to involve himself both in the creation and interpretation of meaning and as the medium of expression for symbolizing that meaning, through 'acting out'. Kamii (1974) summarized the pedagogical principles of inquiry-based learning when writing about Piaget's view of learning: 'The task of the teacher is to figure out what the learner already knows and how he reasons in order to ask the right questions at the right time so that the learner can build his own knowledge.' In Dewey's (1939) view, an inquiry which is successful is an inquiry which resolves perplexing situations. Whenever children are given 'the opportunity to do about exploring a situation' they are engaged in discovering and developing their own thought structures and finding new ways of organizing experience. The more they are able to engage in these activities, the more likely it is that they will be able to generalize methods of problem-solving and lines of inquiry. Indeed, for Dewey the rules of successful inquiry are the rules of logic. These rules of inquiry are derived by analyzing what is done as perplexing situations are resolved, for when the rules are formed they become the norms by which to assess future inquiries. Between the 'perplexing' and 'resolved' he places 'reflective thought'. Isn't this just what a drama class does between, say, the initial improvization and any succeeding stage of work? Dewey suggests that individuals will learn best when, as in drama, they are placed in 'at risk' situations. Smith and Meux (1970), in discussing motivational factors in learning, summarize what they call the 'psychologized version of Dewey's theory of logic':

> ... the individual is moved to act when he is in an unsettled situation – one for which he has no ready-made response. In such a situation, the individual is moved to try various ways of acting to overcome the barrier to his reaching a goal. By working himself out of such circumstances he learns.

Essentially, then, the learning model with which drama teachers would expect to be closely associated would be a discovery-based model in which students would be expected to attempt to learn through *problem-solving*. In problem-solving, learning is associated with change in the individual's system. (See Figure 1)

Figure 1   Rational Problem-Solving Model

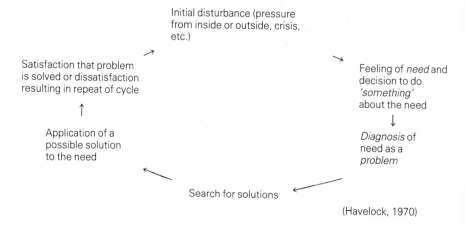

(Havelock, 1970)

In Piaget's terms, learning occurs when new knowledge is assimilated (into existing interpretative categories) and accommodated (whereby we modify our existing categories in order that we may explain events more adequately). This change takes place when the new knowledge has become transformed or recoded. It is not acquired simply by adding new parts to existing parts. The drama teacher discovers what the learner has learnt by helping him apply this new knowledge to *other* situations – by making it operative.

We are concerned then with both our own and the *pupil's* knowledge, and helping him build on it. As Barnes (1976) says, 'knowledge ... can be explained as the operations or interpretative schemes upon the data presented

to our eyes and other senses.' If we define 'learning' as 'changes in understanding', these changes are more likely to be of a permanent nature if they are
internalized by the pupil.

RefBook

Intervention Strategies in Drama Teaching

Social Influence of the Teacher

Clearly the drama teacher whose ideology is discovery-based cannot have
teaching strategies for child development. He can only have strategies for
promoting or fostering child development. Since this is regarded as natural he
will be concerned with providing the right environment and with removing
constraints rather than with creating master plans. Eraut (1977) suggests that
the child will often learn best when an appropriate variety of concrete
experiences are acted out, reflected upon, talked about and assimilated or
accommodated:

> According to Piaget, the child organises his experience through
> 'schema', and according to Kelly, people organize their experience
> through 'personal constructs'.... Child development has to build on
> those schema and constructs which already exist. They cannot easily
> be promoted in any other way.... Finally, the child is best motivated
> when following his own interests ... pursuing them can lead to the
> development of a wide range of knowledge and skills. (Eraut, 1977)

The type of social influence practised by the teacher will 'tell' the student about
the kind of learning in which he is expected to engage.

Three processes of social influence have been defined (Kelman, 1961):
compliance, identification and internalization.

COMPLIANCE

> When an individual accepts influence from another person because he
> hopes to achieve a favourable reaction from the other.

IDENTIFICATION

> When an individual adopts behaviours derived from another person
> ... because this behaviour is associated with a satisfying self-defining
> relationship to this person or group.

INTERNALIZATION

> When an individual accepts influence because the induced behaviour
> is congruent with his value system, thus it is intrinsically rewarding.
> The individual adopts it because he finds it useful for the solution of a
> problem, or because it is congenial to his own orientation, or because it
> is demanded by his own values.

It has been hypothesized that this latter process – based as it is on principles of relevance (to the student), changes in understanding (to the student's own value system) and thus problem-solving – is that which is most likely to result in permanent change.

Teaching Styles

What has been promoted so far is a particular version of teaching which has been variously described by writers as open rather than closed (Esland, 1977), integrative rather than dominative (Anderson and Brewer, 1946), person-centred rather than production-centred (Paisey, 1975), liberation rather than domestication (Friere, 1972), curriculum as practice rather than curriculum as fact (Young, 1976), progressive rather than traditional (Bennett, 1976), and interpretation rather than transmission (Barnes, 1976).

Barnes characterizes a 'transmission' type of teacher as one who, he hypothesizes:

1 Believes knowledge to exist in the form of public disciplines which include content and criteria of performance,
2 Values the learners' performances insofar as they conform to the criteria of the discipline,
3 Perceives the teacher's task to be the evaluation and correction of the learner's performance, according to the criteria of which he is the guardian,
4 Perceives the learner as an uniformed acolyte for whom access to knowledge will be difficult since he must qualify himself through tests of appropriate performance.

He contrasts this with an 'interpretation' type of teacher who:

1 Believes knowledge to exist in the knower's ability to organize thought and action,
2 Values the learner's commitment to interpreting reality, so that criteria arise as much from the learner as from the teacher;
3 Perceives the teacher's task to be the setting up of a dialogue in which the learner can reshape his knowledge through interaction with others,
4 Perceives the learner as already possessing systematic and relevant knowledge, and the means of reshaping that knowledge.

Certainly, the drama teacher cannot operate exclusively in the classroom as the 'expert' or fount of knowledge.

It follows that flexibility of action by the teacher becomes the *criterion* of rational action, if he is to respect the complex nature of independent inquiry. He cannot predict accurately what the end product is going to be. He cannot predict in advance what is to be learnt if he believes that problems arise from current activities and that future activities are shaped by the identification, resolution and reflection of these problems. In short, he cannot pursue particular ends, come what may (Day, 1977).

The appropriateness of interventionist strategies (in the past called 'leadership behaviour') of teachers in classrooms is of course relative to the nature of the group and the task in hand. We will assume for the purposes of this discussion that teachers use personal leadership and not institutional leadership styles so that they rely on the use of their own personal qualities and abilities to adapt to different situations and different pupils' needs rather than use status, power and sanctions (Hoyle, 1969). It is assumed also that the teacher:

1 has no significant problems in terms of ability to maintain social order, that, like many other teachers, he is in a position of authority both by right (*de jure*) and in fact (*de facto*) in that he exercises authority without being authoritarian. Authority in this sense is a means of bringing about social conformity. It is only when the teacher as an individual loses his authority that he will have recourse to the use of power by, for example, operating sanctions (Peters, 1973);

2 is able to form mutually satisfactory working relationships with his pupils. In short, there exists a mutually acceptable definition of teacher-pupil interpersonal relationships in which the teacher is seen, for example, to be firm but fair, friendly, understanding and good at explaining things (Meighan, 1977; Nash, 1976; Hargreaves, 1972).

Various attempts have been made to characterize leadership styles adopted by teachers, but perhaps the most appropriate for considering the use of teaching styles in relation to teaching ideologies in drama is that by Joseph Axelrod (1973) who, through empirical research, distinguished two broad prototypes of teacher – craftsmen and artists. Craftsmen usually plan work where 'inquiry on the part of the student is not required or encouraged for the successful completion of the learning tasks set', whereas artists plan work where 'inquiry on the part of the student *is* required if he is to complete successfully the tasks set by the teacher.' With the former prototype *objectives* would be 'instructional', or 'behavioural', stressing 'either cognitive knowledge acquired primarily by memorisation, or mastery of skills acquired primarily by repetition and practice.' The lesson would be planned and evaluated in terms of outcomes which are homogeneous in character insofar as the students are regarded as being at similar stages of development. With the latter – the teacher as artist – objectives would be 'expressive' (evocative rather than prescriptive). They would 'identify situations in which students are to work a problem with which they are to cope'. However, they would not specify *what* from that situation or problem the students are to learn. Students are regarded as being at different stages of development (Eisner, 1969). The major means employed would be inquiry or discovery. When the teacher is engaged in promoting learning by discovery, his objectives would tend to be instructional, and when he is engaged in providing opportunities for students to learn to discover, his objectives would tend to be expressive.

Within the evocative teacher-as-artist model, Axelrod identified the following teaching prototypes:

1 Subject-matter-oriented (principles and facts prototype);
2 Instructor-centred;
3 Student-centred: (a) student as mind; (b) student as person.

The assumption is that since there are three component parts to the teaching-learning process, that is, teacher, learner and subject-matter, emphasis on one requires adjustment in the other two. He identified characteristics associated with each of these prototypes.

CHARACTERISTICS OF SUBJECT-MATTER-ORIENTED TEACHER

1 Learner and teacher must adjust to the subject matter.
2 The teaching is organized around the teacher's desire to help students master principles, concepts, analytic tools, theories, applications and relevant facts.
3 The emphasis is on cognitive knowledge.
4 There is systematic coverage of a given segment of knowledge in each course.

CHARACTERISTICS OF INSTRUCTOR-CENTRED TEACHER

1 Learner and subject matter should be accommodated to their teacher.
2 He is the possessor of knowledge and a model for learners.
3 If he were to push himself into a shape that is not his own, his humanity and individuality would be lost.
4 Lessons are organized around the teacher's desire to help the pupil learn to approach problems as he himself would approach them.
5 The emphasis is on cognitive knowledge transmission, but through the force of the teacher's own personality and unique points of view which give shape to that knowledge.

The student-centred teacher sees the pupils and himself as constituents of a larger and more powerful organism – the total teaching-learning group.

CHARACTERISTICS OF THE STUDENT-AS-MIND TEACHER

1 He emphasizes the personal development of the pupil, but limits the scope to the pupil's mind.
2 He organizes lessons around his desire to help his students acquire a set of skills and abilities that are intellectual in nature.
3 He teaches pupils to adopt reason and language as their major tools, and to use problem-solving as the major means of investigating subject-matter.

1   The emphasis is on the personal development of the pupil – his entire personality, not just his mind.
2   Lessons are organized around the teacher's desire to help pupils as individuals along all dimensions where growth appears necessary or desirable – particularly the non-intellectual dimensions.
3   The teacher uses the pupil's peer group as a means of accomplishing such development.

Whatever the leadership style, drama teachers will be concerned with fostering a child's confidence in his own ability to learn by processes of inquiry, to foster the value of cooperative learning through the almost exclusive use of projects which necessitate socially interactive groupings of children, to foster the value of the child's own directly experienced life by basing at least a part of the subject-matter on the child's imagination and experience and, significantly, to encourage children to learn about the nature of certain 'key' social under-standings dictated by the particular teacher. In the last respect, the drama teacher does not differ from any other teacher in that it is he who decides on the content of what is learnt, except that since drama is not yet a traditional public 'discipline' (as are history, geography, English, maths, etc.) there is as yet no publicly acknowledged curriculum or syllabus. I suspect, however, that a close look at drama work in schools would reveal a high degree of consensus on the subject matter used by teachers, for example, structures involving conflict, ritual, social mores, 'life' role rehearsal etc. Indeed, these may well reflect Heathcote's 'universalistics' (Wagner, 1979). Much drama may be categorized as 'moral education' and, contrary to many drama teachers' claims, it *is* involved with values of 'right' and 'wrong', 'good' and 'bad'.

Let us look systematically, therefore, at the way drama teachers might be expected to conceptualize knowledge, learning, pupils, and their classrooms.

Knowledge

Unlike many so-called subject 'disciplines', drama (unless it be theatre arts) has no publicly recognized body of knowledge that is expected to be transmitted. Indeed, this is seen by drama teachers to be a strength rather than a weakness, for it enables them to demonstrate a high regard for pupils' knowledge, capacities and personal experiences by often using them as the content of lessons (or to use knowledge from other disciplines where appropriate). They see knowledge as personal, relative and justified in terms of a particular culture or particular purposes and occasions, rather than as objective or universally valid. Consequently, they would not view knowledge as hierarchical, where some knowledge is viewed as being inherently more difficult, that is, not able to be learnt until other knowledge has been mastered.

Learning

We would expect the drama teacher to see learning as (a) collective rather than individual, (b) cooperative rather than competitive, (c) intrinsically rather than extrinsically motivated, (d) being achieved through doing (direct experience) rather than hearing or talking about (indirect experience). Learning would involve the production of new knowledge rather than the reproduction of old. Its path would, therefore, be perceived as biologically given (through the 'game' structure) rather than culturally imposed (through passive assimilation of facts). There would thus be no distinction between 'work' (seen as productive) and 'play' (seen as unproductive).

Pupils

We would expect the drama teacher to regard learning as inevitably occurring in the course of everyday life. He would, therefore, hold an optimistic rather than pessimistic view of pupils. He would believe in pupils' willingness to learn and work rather than believe that they have an inherent dislike of learning which causes them to have to be coerced into learning in which they wish to be directed and avoid responsibility. He would evaluate pupils' action in terms of particularistic rather than universalistic criteria. That is, their actions would be explained or identified in terms of their individual responsibilities and backgrounds rather than in terms of deterministic standards or rules of behaviour and work which would be applied to all pupils regardless of individual backgrounds. Pupils would not be seen as adults or apprentice adults expected to conform to adult 'norms', but as 'licensed', that is, having sets of rights, obligations, capacities which are seen as appropriate to childhood.

Classroom Organization

We would expect to see an informal classroom where pupils are working in groups or as a class and where the teacher is not engaged in constant supervision and intervention or the hub of the activity, for example, acting as question-master as in formal organizational structures.

Classroom Control

Though like other teachers drama teachers would be concerned with order, the rules for both behavioural and cognitive domains would relate to the process rather than product. Thus they are less definitive in their interpretation of order than those involved in discipline-based teaching; a wider range of pupil behaviour is allowed. However, even this 'progressive' social order relies on the socialization of pupils into the rules which constitute it. As with order, the kind of control one would expect to see in drama work is different in kind from control as it is defined in discipline-based teaching. In the latter it is the teacher who controls, whereas in drama work one would expect to see relatively less control over content, pacing and process being exercised by the teacher and relatively more being exercised by the pupils. This is often incorrectly interpreted by discipline-based teachers as disorder. Social order is negotiated, with teachers exercising a lower level of control over pupil activity and learning, and pupils contributing more. Control as exercised by the drama teacher would thus be based on personal appeals, for example, contract making, rather than on imperatives or positional (status) modes.

Classroom Action

All this implies that the predominant teaching strategies would be those of participation rather than supervision. We would expect teachers of drama to be primarily concerned with a method-based approach rather than a knowledge of the curriculum approach. Thus they would be concerned with the thinking underlying the production of any product (the process of learning) rather than a product-based approach in which pupils' actions are evaluated in terms of their conformity or deviance from certain specifications laid down by the teacher, with the process by which the product is reached being unproblematic or unimportant.

Evaluation

We would expect informal reports which measure pupil performance now in relation to performance at some previous time rather than the use of normative class tests in which pupils' performances are measured against those of other pupils (Hammersley, 1977).

The pupil engaged in learning through drama, then, may be expected to be involved with others in a group for a large part of the time in cooperative and not competitive activities which are relevant to his interests and concerns and to some degree of his own choosing and at his own pacing. He may expect to have far more responsibility for self-control and self-discipline than in other lessons; he may expect to negotiate social order and the activity with his peers and the teacher; and he may expect his present performance to be evaluated in relation to his past performance.

Conclusion

I have presented a set of values which I would expect the drama teacher to hold. These values are expressed to the pupils in his teaching where he is, in effect, socializing the pupils into the acceptance of certain modes of thinking about learning.

> Values are involved in education not so much as goals or end products, but as principles implicit in different manners of proceeding and producing ... in my view, many disputes about the aims of education are disputes about principles of procedure rather than 'aims' in the sense of objectives to be arrived at by taking appropriate means. The so-called 'aim' in part picks out the different valuations which are build into the different procedures like training, conditioning, the use of authority.... (Peters, 1968)

My contention here is that if teachers are to evaluate their teaching, they must consider not only objectives and ideals expressed in the organizational strategies adopted but also as values expressed by procedural strategies. For example, a teacher who is engaged in teaching the class as a unit is not necessarily instructional anymore than one engaged in small group work is necessarily expressive in his procedures; for an apparently weak organizational framing may still have an overlay of strongly framed task and talk by the teacher. In any consideration of teaching we must, therefore, discuss not only the content of a teacher's teaching – his style – but also the meaning of the teacher's teaching – the use of his style (Elliott, 1975).

Finally, the complexity of the teaching and learning which may occur in improvised, negotiated whole class drama work as well as small group drama work is revealed most clearly in the roles played by the teacher and pupils. Certainly, there will be no clear role expectations if each pupil is to be able to contribute according to his/her own identity:

> ... in strong frame settings, because roles are expected, the talk relates to the expectations of action. Participants know what is going on from others in the school and classroom. The tradition in strong frame schools of having only a limited number of roles, eg. 'jester', 'sleeper', 'swot', 'stupid' etc. to play allows the teacher to take for granted aspects of social control which the teacher in weaker frame settings must negotiate....
>
> In weaker frame settings, situations have to be restructured continuously; talk and actions as contributions to this restructuring are expected from all participants. There is no stereotype of teacher or pupil talk or action. Each encounter, if successful (to the teacher) is an exploration of ideas in which the pupil is allowed power to interrupt and interpret the resources and tasks provided by the teacher and pupils. (Walker, 1972)

Typically, drama work does occur in situations which have to be restructured continuously. Each lesson encounter is an exploration of ideas. The extent of the exploration will, however, be determined by the degree of negotiation of task between teacher and pupil, whether it be its planning or its process. It follows that the teacher should at all times attempt to ensure that his practice in the classroom is consistent with his teaching intentions, and that modification of one will require modification of the other. It has been the intention of this article to raise issues of intentions and practice in order to assist the reader in this process.

References

ANDERSON, H.H. and BREWER, H.M. (1945/46), *Studies of Teachers' Classroom Personalities*, Applied Psychology Monographs, Stanford University Press.

ARGYRIS, C. and SCHON, D.A. (1976), *Theory in Practice: Increasing Professional Effectiveness*, Jossey-Bass.

AXELROD, J. (1973), *The University Teacher as Artist*, Jossey-Bass.

BARKER-LUNN, J. (1970), *Streaming in the Primary School*, Slough, NFER.

BARNES, D. (1976), *From Communication to Curriculum*, Penguin.

BENNETT, N. (1976), *Teaching Styles and Pupil Progress*, London, Open Books.

BOLTON, G. (1979), *Toward a Theory of Drama in Education*, Longmans.

DAY, C.W. (1975), *Drama for Middle and Upper Schools*, Batsford, England.

DAY, C.W. (1977), 'Drama: A Means of Educating', *The Times Education Supplement*, 4 November 1977.

DAY C.W. (1981), 'Classroom based in-service teacher education: The development and evaluation of a client-centred model', Education Area Occasional Paper 9, University of Sussex.

DEWEY, J. (1939), *Theory of Valuation*, University of Chicago Press.

EISNER, E.W. (1969), 'Instructional and expressive educational objectives: Their formulation and use in curriculum,' AERA Monograph Series on Curriculum Evaluation, No. 3, in GOLBY, M., GREENWALD, J. and WEST, R. (Eds) (1975), *Curriculum Design*, Croom Helm.

ELLIOTT, J. (1973), 'Is instruction outmoded?', in *Cambridge Journal of Education*, 3, 3.

ELLIOTT, J. (1975), 'The values of the neutral teacher', in BRIDGES D. and SCRIMSHAW P. (Eds) (1975), *Value and Authority in Schools*, Hodder and Stoughton.

ERAUT, M.E. (1977), 'Strategies for promoting teacher development', in *British Journal of In-Service Education*, 4, 1 and 2.

ERAUT, M.E., BARTON, J. and CANNING, A. (1978), 'Some teacher perspectives on accountability', SSRC Working Paper, University of Sussex.

ESLAND, G. (1977), 'Schooling and pedagogy', *Schooling and Society*, Unit 6, Block 1, Schooling and Capitalism, E. 202, Open University Press.

FERRI, E. (1971), *Streaming: Two Years Later*, Slough, NFER.

FRIERE, P. (1972), *Pedagogy of the Oppressed*, Harmondsworth, Penguin.

GOFFMAN, I. (1959), *The Presentation of Self in Everyday Life*, Penguin.

HAMMERSLEY, M. (1977), 'Teachers perspectives', *School and Society*, Units 9 and 10, Block 2, The Process of Schooling, E. 202 Open University Press.

HARGREAVES, D.H. (1972), *Interpersonal Relations and Education*, Routledge and Kegan Paul.

HAVELOCK, R.G. (1970), *A Guide to Innovation in Education*, Ann Arbor, University of Michigan.

HOYLE, E. (1969), *The Role of the Teacher*, Routledge and Kegan Paul.

JACKSON, P.W. (1968), *Life in Classrooms*, Holt, Rinehart and Winston.

KAMII, C. (1974), *Pedagogical Principles Derived from Piaget's Theory: Relevance for Educational Practice*, Reader 1, Open University.

KEDDIE, N. (1971), 'Classroom knowledge', in YOUNG, M.F.D. (Ed.) (1971), *Know-*

ledge and Control, Collier-Macmillan.

KELMAN, H. (1961), 'Three processes of social influence', in *Public Opinion Quarterly*, 25, Princeton.

MEIGHAN, R. (1977), 'The pupil as client: The learner's experience of schooling', in *Educational Review*, 29, 2.

NASH, R. (1976), 'Pupils' expectations of their teachers', in STUBBS, M. and DELAMONT, S. (Eds) (1976) *Explorations in the Classroom*, John Wiley and Sons.

PAISEY, H.A.G. (1975), *The Behavioural Strategy of Teachers*, Slough, NFER.

PETERS, R.S. (1968), 'Must an educator have an aim?', in PETERS, R.S. (Ed.) (1968), *Concepts of Teaching*, MacMillan and Nelson, Rand McNally and Co.

PETERS, R.S. (1973), *Authority: Responsibility and Education*, George Allen and Unwin.

POLYANI, M. (1967), *The Tacit Dimension*, Garden City, NY, Doubleday.

SCHULMAN, L.S. and KEISLER, E.R. (Eds) (1966), *Learning by Discovery: A Critical Appraisal*, Chicago, Rand McNally and Co., Ch. 15.

SMITH, B.O. and MEUX, M.O. (1970), *A Study of the Logic of Teaching*, University of Illinois Press.

STENHOUSE, L. (1968), 'The Humanities Curriculum Project', in *Journal of Curriculum Studies*, 1.

THELEN, H.A. (1954), *Dynamics of Groups at Work*, University of Chicago Press.

WAGNER, B.J. (1979), *Dorothy Heathcote: Drama as a Learning Medium*, London, Hutchinson.

WALKER, R. (1972), *Towards a Sociography of Classrooms*, SSRC.

YOUNG, M.F.D., 'Cultural change: Limits and possibilities', in DALE, R., ESLAND, G. and MACDONALD, M. (Eds) (1976), *Schooling and Capitalism: A Sociological Reader*, London, Routledge and Kegan Paul/The Open University Press (Course Reader), Reading 20, pp. 185–91.

7　An Operational Approach to Evaluation

Haydn Davies

This chapter offers a way of looking at aims and objectives which, Davies claims, 'might prove helpful to teachers in the planning and appraisal of their work'. Unlike other authors, he adopts the predictive instructional objectives model and attempts to apply it to four areas of drama – learning to use the process; understanding themes through acting out; participation in presentation; interpretation and appreciation of dramatic statements by other people (McGregor, Tate and Robinson, 1977).

There are many problems with using this particular approach, as the writer himself observes. The most crucial of these is the identification by the teacher of any 'affective' learning which may result in both the process and as a product of drama work. Many of his examples are, therefore, concerned with measuring acquired social behaviour, the ability of participants to recognize the 'rules of the game' and cognitive understandings. They do not provide means of measuring 'sensitivity', 'concentration', 'attitude change' or emotional congruence of each participant's behaviour with the given objective. Indeed, they do not measure progress in drama. Nevertheless, the chapter provides an important contribution to the use of objectives in drama and may most usefully be viewed as a means of approaching the structuring of what Eisner describes as 'instructional objectives' – 'a predictive model of curriculum development i.e. one in which objectives are formulated and activities selected which are predicted to be useful in enabling children to attain the specific behaviour embodied in the objective. . . .' By placing it in this context we may distinguish it from those chapters about drama work which concerns itself principally with expressive objectives. Interestingly, it also contributes to the debate on education and social engineering.

The natural and logical planning of the drama work in the school should begin with the teacher's aims and objectives for drama as a whole, in the context of the school. Methods of assessment should grow out of this.[1]

In this chapter I seek to present a somewhat unusual point of view concerning the formulation of aims and objectives in drama in education. The accusation has often been made that the aims of drama are woolly and ill-defined. Here I offer a way of looking at aims and objectives which might prove helpful to teachers in the planning and appraisal of their work.

I make the following points.

a That learning is change in behaviour.

b That teachers set out to change the way people behave and that learning objectives are statements of these intended changes.

c That all 'subjects' can be described in terms of particular kinds of behaviour.

d That behaviours relevant to drama lie in the areas of:

   i the process, that is, ways of working, the skills used by participants as they seek to find meaning through drama;

   ii the kinds of thing a person can learn because they have used the process of drama – in other words, learning through drama;

   iii participation in theatrical presentation;

   iv interpretation and appreciation of dramatic statements by other people such as playwrights.

(I have been influenced in my choice of categories by the writers of *Learning through Drama*, though I interpret each area in my own way.)

e That aims and learning objectives for drama are to be found in these four areas, and that it is useful to state these intentions in terms of pupil behaviour, for it clarifies thinking and allows for clear communication leading to curriculum development.

I outline a way of structuring learning objectives using Mager's instructional objectives model,[2] give examples from each of the four areas, and invite teachers to look at their own work from this point of view.

Education is a process, and process inevitably means change. The teacher intervenes to facilitate change; he enters the environment of the learner with this express purpose. The learner can think, can feel, can move, and it is in these three areas, cognitive, affective, psychomotor, that change can occur. Teachers, whether they like it or not, are facilitators of change, and learners, whether they like it or not, for the purposes of the teacher, are objects of change. Of course, good learners themselves are interested in change, as Postman and Weingartner say, 'changing the character of their minds is what good learners are interested in doing.'[3]

Given that education involves change, it is important that learners and teachers are able to identify change and to know when it has occurred, for it enables purposes in learning to be described so that learners and teachers can know when learning has been achieved. Learning can only be known through behaviour, so that if the learner wants to know whether he has learnt anything he must test himself in action. Similarly, if the teacher wants to know whether he has taught anything, he can perceive his success only in the behaviour of the learner. It is important to note that the word 'behaviour', as used here, denotes all the various kinds of response a person can make to his environment, and to his feelings and thoughts, and since human beings are meaning-making mechanisms, they cannot help but become different as experience enables them to think, to feel, to move, in new ways. Teachers, who by the very nature of their work facilitate the process of change in people, need to ask the question, 'what changes do I wish to facilitate in children, and how can I know that I have succeeded?'

In the field of educational drama the first part of the question is often answered in statements which suggest that drama leads to such things as the development of the whole person, self-confidence, awareness of others, emotional maturity, social awareness, growth of the imagination, sensitivity, leadership, clarity of thought, vitality of speech, etc. The second part of the question, which concerns evaluation, has generally not been asked with the determination which has led through to answers.

Most statements of aims in educational drama tend to be made in general terms such as these and it is, no doubt, reasonable to expect this kind of general statement of long-term aims. Unfortunately, these general statements are rarely made specific enough to be helpful in the day-to-day practice of drama in the classroom. For example, it would be useful to the teacher and learner to know how a person who is sensitive, or socially aware, or emotionally mature is different from the one who is not. The ability to describe characteristic behaviour of the sensitive, or socially aware, or emotionally mature, would enable the teacher to set objectives which both he and the learner could understand and work toward.

In this chapter I shall endeavour to suggest a method whereby teachers are able to define clearly the learning objectives they have for their pupils, so that they are able to structure their work purposefully, and gain feedback with regard to their effectiveness as teachers. The technique I shall suggest, though new to drama, has already been applied to other subject areas in connection with curriculum development. I am, of course, referring to the method of stating objectives in operational or behavioural terms.

In fulfilling his function the teacher needs to find answers to three questions.

1 What are my aims and objectives for my pupils in this school? That is, what do I want my pupils to learn? What differences in their behaviour do I wish to facilitate?
2 What strategies can I use in order to help pupils achieve these objectives?
3 How can I know when pupils have achieved these objectives?

From the other point of view, the learner needs to ask the following questions.

1 What do I want to learn?
2 What strategies do I need to employ in order to achieve that learning?
3 How can I know that I have learnt what I set out to learn?

There is an obvious link in both cases between questions 1 and 3 for if one has a clear picture of what one's destination is like then one is able to observe whether or not one has arrived. I am conscious of the objection that education is more than this, and that, to continue the metaphor, one is often pleasantly surprised at the nature of the destination. Of course, there is truth in this, as there is truth in the idea that education is a goal-directed process. What I am suggesting is that to a very large extent evaluation has ties with objectives and that the clearer the statements of objectives, the easier it is to evaluate effectiveness of both teaching and learning

Evaluation of learning is of enormous value to the learner in the ongoing process of learning, for it enables him to monitor his progress and with the help of the teacher to employ strategies which lead to effective learning. The assumptions are that the learner knows what he wants to learn and that evaluation is criterion-referenced. I think it true to say that the prime function of evaluation is to provide feedback to the learner. Unfortunately, in schools and colleges evaluation is a process whereby learners know how they are progressing only in relation to other learners, and not in relation to criteria which are clearly defined and open to both teachers and learners. There does seem to be a magnetic attraction to norm-reference testing where lists of names and grades predominate. No doubt this is a reflection of the comparative difficulty of criterion-referencing. What I am suggesting is that criteria of learning in drama be structured by teachers for and with their own pupils and that these criteria be stated in terms of what pupils should be able to *do*.

In order to do this in any curriculum 'subject,' it is essential to identify the nature of the subject, that is, the kinds of behaviour which are distinctive to that subject. One needs to ask, 'what do people *do* when they engage in this or that subject?' For subjects do not exist without behaviour. For example, astronomy is not the stars, it is a way of perceiving the stars, a way held in language, and to learn astronomy implies learning a language, a way of seeing the skies. It is in fact a human *activity*, and to talk of 'doing' history or 'doing' physics is more accurate than we sometimes think.

A further question concerns *why* people engage in activities which can be listed under curriculum subject-headings. The answer to the question why, in each case is, that meaning is being made of experience. Of course, the nature of the meaning will be different in each 'subject' and each subject will hold its meanings in its own set of symbols – its own language. To 'do' the subject means to manipulate the symbols in the process of thinking, and to use the symbols to express meaning in the process of communication.

However, in using the term 'subject', I do not want to give the impression that I perceive meaning to exist 'out there' and that the task of the learner is to absorb knowledge in order to replicate it. Rather, I see the learner engaging in the process of creating and generating meanings as he makes sense of his experience. In Esland's words, man is viewed as 'world-producer' rather than 'world-produced'[4]

Ultimately the school curriculum will be structured and perceived as a differentiated process, because this reflects the nature of man himself who perceives and creates meanings which are different in kind. Hirst and Peters suggest seven modes of knowledge and experience,[5] whereas Phenix suggests six realms of meaning.[6] The suggestion is that each of these areas has its own distinctive way of making meaning of experience, its own method of working, its own characteristic behaviour, so that, for example, one could say that when a pupil is engaging in mathematical studies he is perceiving the world in a particular way. It follows that in seeking to structure learning objectives in any of these areas, it is important to define relevant behaviour – what is a person doing when he is engaged in science, geography, history, art, drama? – for these behaviours lead to and arise from distinctive perceptions.

What Behaviours Are Distinctive to Drama?

The Schools Council Drama Project (10–16) team suggests that all activity which can be called drama has at its core 'acting-out':

> The essential and recurring feature of all school drama work is that it involves children, as participants, projecting into imagined or assumed roles or situations. We have called this process of projection 'acting-out'. It is the foundation of drama upon which the case for its place in education must first be built. What then are the essential characteristics of acting-out?

Acting-out involves the participants in accepting a shift in the conventions of behaviour towards each other.

1 There is an agreement to suspend the normal social roles with each other in identifying with the new imagined roles.
2 There is an agreement to make a different use of the environment. In this case a desk becomes a dining-table laden with food, a chalk box becomes a ciger box, and so on. This different use of the environment includes a shift in the conventions of time. Events may be telescoped to give them greater or less significance. The usual conventions of space and time may be suspended during acting-out.[7]

In more detail one can say that 'acting-out' involves the following elements.

1 *The will to participate.* In the same way as a game of football cannot take place without a volunteer spirit on the part of the players, so drama cannot take place without this element. The participant is willing to play the game according to the rules, treating a play situation seriously.
2 *Suspension of disbelief.* The participant in drama accepts that he has stepped out of the world of real consequences into a world of make-believe, that is, he has stepped into the world of play. He accepts the given circumstances as though they were true and responds accordingly. He is serious in his pretence.

3 *Concentration on the task.* The participant focusses his attention on the task as he perceives it and seeks to exclude intrusive thoughts, sounds, movement. He becomes absorbed within the imagined context.

4 *Use of imagination.* The participant, given a make-believe situation, recalls what he considers relevant ideas and attitudes, allowing these to guide his behaviour in the given circumstances. For example, when the given circumstances are that the participant is a crofter facing the soldiers at the time of the highland clearances, in the acting-out he recalls ideas and attitudes from his past experience, first or second-hand experience, and allows these to guide his behaviour.

5 *Imaginative action.* The participant links imaginative thought to action. He does not remain physically passive as in day-dreaming, or reading, or watching television. In the latter activities no doubt the day-dreamer, the reader, the viewer, do experience physical responses to their imaginative experience. These responses can be observed in small movements such as a tension of the body, a smile, a laugh. In acting-out, however, the participant can be observed actually to do what is imagined. For example, he can be observed to creep through a make-believe forest; or to make excuses for having broken a make-believe window; or to comfort a bereaved mother. Acting-out is imagination come alive, for instead of merely experiencing a flow of internal images, the participant allows these ideas to carry through into action.

6 *Receiving and giving stimuli.* The participant, willing to suspend disbelief, receives stimuli from his environment and responds to them. The stimulus might be the teacher's voice, a sound made by a percussion instrument, a piece of music, an article, another person, etc. Since he has taken the step of accepting the imaginative situation, he responds to the stimulus with action which he believes to be appropriate to the situation. The participant might also provide a stimulus to other participants. For example A as an old man might ask B, a boy, 'Why did you throw a stone through my window?' A's presentation of himself, together with the question, become a stimulus for B, and B's response, 'I never did', together with his presentation of himself, become in turn a stimulus for A. So long as both A and B are able to maintain their roles and the imaginative action, they are both givers and receivers of stimuli within the process of acting-out.

7 *Spontaneity.* The participant responds to stimuli in an unguarded manner, that is, he responds honestly and openly in the given context, being willing to suspend the responses of the real world in favour of the responses appropriate to the make-believe context.

8 *Working against something.* The participant recognizes opposition to his imaginative intentions and seeks to solve the problem in action, within the given circumstances. For example, it might be the problem of how to persuade another participant to help him in some way; or to

influence the decision-making of a local council; or to organize for survival in an alien environment.

These are behaviours which are relevant to acting-out and, at a deeper level, Brian Watkins suggests:

> The drama is a model of social interaction procedures; people's relationships under stress, requiring resolution or alleviation in a social context where decisions must affect others for better or worse. The play is a dynamic example of how a number of people are faced with a crisis which requires them to employ social values and agreed procedures to attempt to solve their problem. It deals with its own created reality and employs its own logic dependent upon the consensual framework created by the players.
> The way that the game operates is familiar to us all and proves a valuable concept when considering the drama. Indeed the terminology of the drama commemorates a time when the game and the drama were regarded as synonymous. It had a very specific function in the community, for though it worked in unreality, the drama both celebrated and challenged the values of that community; a reliable and manageable tool for examining the very basis of their social reality. It became, after its early magic and ritualistic beginnings, a game that employed language, conversational exchange, those 'socio-linguistic mechanisms that render behaviour intelligible' as Lymann and Scott describe it in 'The Sociology of the Absurd'. The players interact dynamically, moment to moment, within the framework of the formal verbal exchanges which preserve our recognition of social order. The conduct of the relationships is not only in words but employs other sense perceptions, excited not by the real occurrences as in life, but selectively recalled and applied in the game of drama.[8]

Thus it is possible to identify certain modes of behaviour which one could label dramatic, and further to say that in drama, and indeed in all 'subjects', two kinds of behaviour can be distinguished, namely, behaviours which are concerned with process, ways of doing things, and behaviours which arise because of the process. For example, scientific method, ways of doing things, leads to certain kinds of responses, either instrumentally leading to control over and change of environment, or alternatively, expressively, leading to explanations of perception.

In drama too we have behaviours which relate to process, and behaviours which arise because of the process, and it is in these two general areas that learning objectives can be sought. In more detail the writers of *Learning through Drama* making careful observation of what actually happened in drama classes, distinguished four kinds of behaviours:

1 learning to use the process;
2 understanding themes, topics and issues through acting-out;

3   participating in presentation;
4   interpretation and appreciation of dramatic statements by other people
    (that is, experiencing other people's drama).[9]

These four areas provide a clear framework which I shall use in seeking to outline kinds of learning for drama and ways of describing them, though I suspect that my definition, of each of the four areas might be rather different from those of the writers of *Learning through Drama*.

A Suggested Method for the Structuring of Learning Objectives in Drama

A learning objective can be defined as a statement which represents the kinds of change in behaviour which the teacher wishes to facilitate in the learner; it is a statement of how the learner will be different and describes what the learner will be doing to demonstrate this difference. For example, in physical education a teacher might think it appropriate for certain pupils to learn the skill in football of passing the ball accurately over 20 yards. After providing suitable experience, the teacher will want to know whether the pupils have learned the skill and might test by asking each pupil to attempt to pass the ball 20 times. The teacher might be satisfied when a pupil, out of 20 attempts, makes accurate passes.

A formula which the teacher can apply when constructing a learning objective is given by Mager:

To describe terminal behaviour (what the learner will be DOING):
(a)   Identify and name the over-all behaviour act.
(b)   Define the important conditions under which the behaviour is to occur (givens and/or restrictions and limitations).
(c)   Define the criterion of acceptable performance.[10]

Applying this formula to the PE objective given above it could be stated thus:

Name of behaviour	*Conditions under which it will occur*	*Criterion of acceptable performance*
Passing the ball	Having trapped the ball the player then immediately passes the ball along the ground to another player 20 yards away who has to run on to the ball	15 accurate passes out of a possible 20

Here is a clear statement of intent which is at once the aim of the teaching and the means of accurate assessment.

Learning objectives can be categorized under the three headings: cognitive, affective and psychomotor. The PE objective above is from the psychomotor area and is simple to construct. The category which causes most difficulty is the affective, and it could be that drama teachers would say that this is the area from which most of their learning objectives would derive.

I suggested earlier that drama objectives are to be sought in the four areas distinguished by the writers of *Learning through Drama*, namely, learning to use the process; understanding themes, topics and issues through acting-out; participating in presentation; and interpretation and appreciation of dramatic statements by other people. I now seek to define in more detail relevant kinds of learning, giving examples of learning objectives from each of the four areas. I make no attempt to define *the* learning aims and objectives for drama, but I do seek to argue that there are four distinct *kinds* of aims and objectives and that it is helpful to teachers and learners if these are defined in terms of behaviour. I seek to share with the reader my thoughts on what the four areas mean, and hope that because I have attempted to do this in behavioural terms that my meanings will be clearly understood.

Area 1. Learning to Use the Process

I think it useful here to think of learning *about* drama rather than learning *through* drama. It is like thinking about the elements of the process employed by the woodworker in making a table. He needs to be able to select timber, to measure and mark, to cut, to make joints, to polish. Having acquired sufficient skill in these elements he is able to employ them in the making of a table. In other words, there are specific behaviours he must master. The woodworker can learn the skills in two ways. Firstly, he can isolate a skill and practice it in exercises demanding only that skill. Secondly, he can set himself the task of making a useful object, and in the making of it exercise the skills because they are necessary to the making of the desired object. It may be that if he chooses the second alternative his lack of skill will be highlighted, and he will see the importance of mastery of a specific skill and end by combining both methods as they are appropriate.

In seeking to make meaning through drama, participants need to employ behaviours which facilitate their purposes. There are skills without which the exploration of meaning is hindered, and I believe that the clear identification of these skills is of great help to both teachers and learners. The kinds of behaviour which I consider to be important for the successful exploration of meaning are categorized below under four headings: improvisation; group dynamics; discussion skills; evaluation skills.

1 *Improvisation* Spontaneous improvisation is the basic tool employed by participants in their attempts to explore meaning through drama. Improvisation is a social event and makes great demands on participants as individuals and as groups. Some of the important behaviours necessary for successful improvisation, as I see them, are: the will to participate; suspension of

disbelief; concentration on the task; use of the imagination; imaginative action; receiving and giving stimuli; spontaneity; working against something (for definitions of these see above); the ability to sustain a role; divergent thinking; boldness of action (verbal and non-verbal); willingness to take personal risks of self-disclosure, embarrassment and failure; imaginative use of objects and space; avoidance of blocking as in, 'Yes you did', 'No I didn't;' sensitivity to initiatives in interaction, that is, perceiving ideas offered by other participants, and supportive of ideas offered by others; building on ideas offered by other participants; initiating ideas in interaction; knowing when to take a lead, and when to follow a lead; choosing appropriate ideas, and adequate means of representing them.

2 *Group dynamics*   Since drama is essentially a social event, the dynamics of the group are of great importance. Assuming that the overall task of the group is the negotiation of meaning, then the meaning which can be found is facilitated, or hindered, or determined by the relationships within the group. Recently, for example, two school pupils who were in competition for dominance within their class, and who each found himself a group leader in the acting-out activity, were totally unable to move progressively in the improvisation for they each brought their real-world relationships to bear on the acting-out situation.

I suggest that this field of group relationships should be of prime importance to the teacher using drama and that he be very conscious of behaviours which can be identified here. One could argue that this is equally true of all curriculum areas where pupils work in groups, and that such behaviours, since they are essential to the activity of the subject discipline, could be classed as learning objectives for that discipline. It would be perfectly reasonable for a science teacher to include as behaviours to be learned in, say, the first year of a five-year science course, behaviours concerned with group functioning and efficiency.

I believe that drama is the discipline which makes the greatest demands on pupils in terms of human relationships, and that the drama teacher needs to identify the interpersonal demands made by his discipline and to set specific objectives in this field for his pupils. Some examples of the kinds of behaviour I have in mind are:

a   that pupils are able to explain the kinds of interpersonal demands made on them. I suggest here a cognitive aim, where pupils know what is demanded of them. It involves the development of a vocabulary so that communication about group relationships can occur. Of course the vocabulary need not be exactly sociological; a group will understand its own terms for specific behaviours.

b   that pupils are able to work in acting-out, and other attendant activities with *all* members of the class group. Here I suggest that pupils might be called upon to exercise their wills. Not only should they be able to work in friendship groups, but they should also be able to will themselves to work with others whom they might not naturally get on with.

c that pupils are supportive of difference. I mean that the group can tolerate difference of ideas, wants, intentions and still function positively in the completion of its task.

d that pupils are able to share leadership functions so that the need for designated leadership is minimized.[11]

e that the group creates an atmosphere or tone which allows members to take risks. I mean by this that members of the group should feel at ease in each other's company, each feeling that the group is supportive, and that individual experiment in unfamiliar work is non-threatening.

These examples will, I hope, illustrate the *kinds* of behaviour I have in mind. They apply to acting-out and attendant activity.

3 *Discussion skills* Drama uses discussion more than any other school subject. Along with acting-out, discussion is the most frequently used teaching/ learning strategy. However, I feel that what is often termed 'discussion' at the end of many drama lessons is little more than a question/answer session with all initiatives coming from the teacher. The kind of discussion I have in mind is where participants engage in an open exchange of feelings and ideas, where channels of communication are broad, and where group relationships are such that each group member feels free to contribute without prompting. Examples are:

a consciousness of the importance of face-to-face encounter shown in the physical arrangements of groups. Here I am thinking of the way groups arrange themselves so that open communication is facilitated. For example, the levels on which people sit can underline dominance or withdrawal. Again, sitting in a square as a discussion group imposes different constraints than the use of a circle arrangement.

b the creation of an atmosphere which enables group members to be open to each other. By this I mean a situation where individuals feel no threat from the group, but on the contrary feel a supportive interest, an acceptance. In such an atmosphere there are no reluctant speakers.

c the ability to listen for understanding. Often in discussion the level of listening is very low. This is seen in speakers being interrupted, in irrelevancies, in a situation where speakers seek to win an argument rather than share meaning.

d the ability of a group to value silence, and to use it as an interval for thinking.

e the ability of individuals to function efficiently in discussion groups of various sizes.

f the ability of contributors to discussion to contribute audibly and confidently.

g   the ability to share leadership functions. This would mean that a group would take over those functions normally performed by designated leaders, for example, the functions of initiating, summarizing, informing, evaluating.

The kinds of demands I have outlined are not easy, but if, as I have suggested, discussion is a behaviour integral to drama work, the purposeful attempt to meet the demands is of prime importance.

4 *Evaluation skills*   Again, in drama more than in other subject disciplines, evaluation of the work is given to a considerable extent to the participants themselves. Often at the end of a lesson, or at appropriate points within it, the teacher might invite comments on the work. The comments can be about the ideas represented, or about the methods employed to represent them. Or again, the teacher might invite participants to evaluate their own work. I suggest that there are particular kinds of behaviour which facilitate the process of evaluation by participants, behaviours which can be learned and used in a positive way. As I have suggested earlier, the most important use of evaluation is to provide feedback to the learner. This is a delicate business which those who evaluate should handle with care and skill. The kinds of skills I have in mind are:

a   the ability to observe the behaviour of participants in an acting-out situation. The quality of the feedback depends on this. This involves a sensitivity on the part of the observer, an ability to perceive selectively and accurately. It demands concentration on detail both visual and aural.

b   the ability to give non-threatening feedback to other participants. This means that when pupils are asked to comment on the work of other pupils, they use descriptive rather than judgmental language, focussing on what happened rather than why it happened. It is easy to say that something is good or bad, and more difficult to act as a mirror enabling the participants to evaluate their own work.[12]

c   the ability of the individual to set goals for himself, and with the help of others to evaluate his own learning. For example, if a pupil constantly finds difficulty in maintaining seriousness of belief in acting-out, he can set himself the task of overcoming this difficulty, gaining support and feedback from other pupils and from the teacher.

d   the ability of the group to evaluate its own work in relation to agreed criteria, for example, the ability of the group to evaluate its own functioning in relation to shared leadership functions, or its own work in relation to choice of symbols in representing meaning. Here the task is to evaluate cooperative effort using criteria established probably with the help of the teacher. This is an area where the teacher needs to be careful to use non-threatening feedback procedures for the group. He is the one who is able to act as a mirror for them so that *they* make the judgments using the data supplied by the teacher/observer.

In theory one could argue that the kinds of skill I have suggested under the heading 'Evaluation' could equally apply to other subject disciplines. This is probably true, but in practice it seems to me that drama makes more demands in this area than any other school subject.

Under the heading, 'Area 1. Learning to Use the Process', I have given examples of the kinds of behaviour which I think are descriptive of the process. Acting-out is the core behaviour and is the behaviour which is distinctive to the discipline called drama. The attendant behaviours, like interpersonal relationships, discussion skills, evaluation technique, form a context in which, and through which, acting-out can lead through to meaning-making. Therefore, the contextual or attendant behaviours are as much part of the drama curriculum as acting-out, for *with* acting-out they facilitate particular kinds of perceptions. In other words, acting-out itself is not enough; the process is more complex.

Given that these are the kinds of behaviour which describe what people do when they engage in the work of a drama lesson in order to tackle problems of understanding, I now give some specific examples of learning objectives concerned with this area of process. These are examples of particular behaviours relevant to ways of doing things. I have attempted with some difficulty to present them along the lines of Mager's three-part model. I am thus illustrating an extreme procedure which I can recommend as a great clarifier of woolly thinking. The examples are in a sense check points in the learning process. Assuming that the teacher has developed aims for a group of pupils in the area of process, the kinds of statement I exemplify enable him and the pupils to evaluate progress towards the aims (see Table 1).

I have attempted to outline the kinds of behaviours relevant to the area of process in drama, ending with an attempt to describe some specific behaviours in operational terms. It might well be that readers would disagree with my definition of the process, but I hope I have made my thinking clear because I have talked about process in terms of behaviour. I now attempt to use the same approach to the second area.

Area 2. Understanding Themes, Topics through Acting-out

This is the area concerned with learning *through* drama rather than learning *about* drama, though in practice the two often overlap. It is the area in which teachers seek to use drama as a method of teaching/learning and can be seen in a variety of educational contexts from the free-flowing improvisation in the primary school to the highly structured role-playing in a management staff college. The common element is acting-out.

As Brian Watkins has said, 'The drama is a model of social interaction procedures; people's relationships under stress requiring resolution or alleviation in a social context where decisions must affect others for better or worse'.[13] Drama provides the means for the creation of models. It involves abstracting particular examples of human interaction and holding them as moving

Table 1.   Behaviours Relevant to the Area of Process in Drama

Name of behaviour	Givens/Restrictions/ Conditions	Criteria of acceptable performance
Maintaining the suspension of disbelief (seriousness)	Working in *pairs* in improvisation, in a naturalistic style	A continuous concentration on the action where the behaviour of each participant matches the situational context and roles, for example, if the interaction concerns a policeman and housewife over a lost child, the participants are seen to be acting continuously in relation to this idea and in these roles
Maintaining the suspension of disbelief (seriousness)	Working as a *class* where the teacher assumes a role	Pupils sustain their roles, initiating ideas and action relevant to the imaginative context, and making use of initiatives supplied by the teacher in role
Risk-taking	A group of teenagers new to drama and working through improvisation	(i) Each member of the group attempts the unusual nature of the work (ii) If improvisations break down, willing to take help from others and to continue to try to achieve purposes in improvisation (iii) Responding to the attempts of others in a supportive encouraging manner, thus trying to create a trusting environment.
Confidence in use of space and objects	Pupils working through improvisation in a drama room	Pupils do not huddle close together and simply talk to each other in role but they use space and objects as elements of the action, for example, (i) the use of rostra to underline the dominance of an authority figure; (ii) chairs used in the normal way, or used to represent other things, like mad dogs, safes, barriers
Team-work in improvisation	(i) Pupils work in a group of three. (ii) Pupils improvise from an initial stimulus	(i) Continuous 'belief' as in (i) above (ii) Avoidance of blocking as in 'No you can't' – 'Yes I can' (iii) Sensitivity as to when to give a lead, initiate a new idea or action, and when

		to follow a lead, building on an idea or action offered by others
Listening for understanding	(i) A group of five pupils (ii) Pupils are using discussion as part of their method of working (iii) Pupils sit in a circle	(i) Pupils look at the one who is speaking (ii) They frequently use some such phrase as, 'Do you mean . . . paraphrasing the speakers ideas (iii) They ask speakers to explain what they mean rather than assuming a meaning too quickly
Giving non-threatening feedback	Small groups of pupils presenting their work to the class, and then discussing the work with the class	(i) Pupils discuss in terms of description rather than judgment, for example, 'When John laughed in the serious bit, I couldn't believe in the situation any more', rather than, 'John spoiled it all by laughing' (ii) Pupils focus feedback on the sharing of ideas and information rather than giving advice (iii) Pupils avoid terms like 'good' and 'bad' and instead focus on 'more' or 'less', implying that behaviour falls along a continuum (iv) Pupils explore alternatives rather than supplying solutions

diagrams through the form of impersonation. The use of this method enables learning to take place in two ways. Firstly, the participants, challenged to think and feel from within the acted-out situation, and seeing the implications of their action, can through reflection on the experience gain an empathic insight. Obviously acting-out is not the only way of achieving this insight, as teachers of literature will be quick to point out. It is, however, a very powerful and direct method of creating the 'here and now' in areas where direct experience would be impossible. Acting-out enables the participants to get as close as possible to real experience in the present tense. The second way in which acting-out affords opportunities for learning is that it enables models of interaction to be set up for observation. Thus a group of learners can in a sense conduct experiments in human behaviour. The very reflection on the interaction and the feedback provided by observers can be a very fruitful means of learning. The use of this method could, for example, lead to improvement in interpersonal skills, including language skills, or it could lead to clarification of particular concepts in history or economics. What is important is that it works in the present tense, problem situations having to be faced and resolved in action; the consequences of the action being seen to take place.

Recently a class of primary schoolchildren aged 9+ were engaged in acting-out a drama concerning a group of gypsies who had been told to move on by an irate landowner. Pupils played the roles of the gypsy families and local councillors, and the teacher played the role of the landowner. In the acting-out the pupils became intellectually and emotionally involved with the problem situation. They had to think and speak from the points of view of their roles. Following the acting-out, the discussion activity was enhanced by the dramatic action, allowing perceptions to be refined through the sharing of feelings and thoughts.

Another example, drawn from a very different context will illustrate further how dramatic action can facilitate learning. The setting was a college of further education where a class of motor vehicle mechanics was following a management course. Their particular concern was garage/customer relationships, and specifically how to handle angry dissatisfied customers. Instead of merely reading and talking about the problem, or using case-study material for analysis, they set up dynamic models through the medium of acting-out. Here the students were placing themselves in the shoes of the people involved, challenged to perceive the problem from their points of view and to act in consequence of these perceptions. Attendant on the acting-out were other behaviours which enabled meaning to be created. Students made use of observation, discussion, feedback and evaluation. Ideas could be drawn from two directions: from the actors' points of view from inside the problem interaction, and from the observers' points of view from outside.

In both examples, the gypsy drama and the garage drama, the purpose was not to create plays for artistic reasons but to make use of the basic activity of acting-out in order to learn. Acting skills and theatrical conventions, though in a sense present, were not important. Models and diagrams can be effective though crude in form. However, basic improvisatory skills were employed, without which the acting-out could not work well enough to be useful in the learning process. The demands made on participants, and relevant behaviours required when using the process of drama in this way, I have already outlined under the heading 'Area 1. Learning to Use the Process'.

Other most interesting and detailed examples of the use of drama as an important strategy of teaching/learning are given in Fines and Verrier, *The Drama of History*. Here two teachers were concerned to facilitate learning in the area of history, and in their book describe how they made use of acting-out to this end. Of the possibilities of the use of drama as a strategy in the teaching of history they say:

> Perhaps the most important kind of historical learning and understanding drama can provide is the ability to feel what others felt – the power of empathy. We have observed three kinds of empathy resulting from dramatic work: a straight personal empathy in which a child

begins to feel a little of what a character or group under study felt; empathy for a situation in which children can feel the mesh of constraints that pulled once on a group; and finally a temporal empathy, whereby children re-living at life rate a particular situation can, as it were, 'hear the very clock tick' and understand the constraints that time itself puts upon history.[14]

Thinking now of learning objectives in this second area which is concerned with learning *through* drama, it will be clear that learning, that is, changes in behaviour, will be looked for not in the area of mastery over the medium, but rather in that area of outcomes resulting from the use of acting-out and its attendant activities. It is like using the skills of reading to acquire knowledge; like using the skills of map-reading and driving to win a car rally.

Example 1 The following objectives are derived from a study of the use of language such as that suggested by Seely in *In Context*.[15] Here major concerns are with helping pupils understand the demands made on people in acts of communication, and with helping pupils to behave appropriately in many communication contexts. Two specific learnings which help in the achievement of the aims are as follows:

1 Given that pupils observe interactions played out by small groups in class, they make notes in which they identify:
   (a) the social roles and role relationships of participants;
   (b) the linguistic roles, that is, the primary intentions of participants;
   (c) the styles of language used.

I have assumed that previous work by the teacher and pupils has clearly established the meanings of (a), (b) and (c) so that the observations would be judged against this common knowledge.

2 Given that pupils are asked to act-out interpersonal interactions, each with its own communication demands, pupils exhibit a flexibility shown in their ability to employ appropriate linguistic roles, registers and styles, according to the various contextual demands.

Here drama is used as a means of testing learning and, of course, along with other activities, would be of great help in the work leading up to the ability to behave in this way.

These examples might well be said to be part of the work by the teacher of English, and teachers of other subject disciplines might also make use of acting-out so that pupils achieve particular kinds of learning. But what about the work of the drama specialist teacher concerned with learning beyond mastery of technique? What about learning in the area of negotiation of meaning through symbolic representation in drama?

In the primary school, the teacher, responsible for the whole curriculum for his class of children, is able to use acting-out, the creation of social models, within a complete context of learning. The acting-out activity derives its purpose from the need to make meaning of a topic or theme. It is only one of a number of strategies in the teaching/learning process and feeds on the work of the classroom. In turn, the drama provides resources which feed further classroom work. In a sense the whole topic study is a negotiation of meaning, where learners interact with varied learning resources – people, places, things, ideas.

Like the teacher of English or geography or history, where drama is used as a method of working, the primary school teacher is using drama in a context. However, in secondary schools, the specialist drama teacher rarely enjoys the luxury of using it in this way where he can be sure of a rich context. Sometimes informal links with other disciplines are formed over coffee in the staffroom, but because of the lack of disciplined preparation underlined by haphazard communication the work is often in danger of losing its impetus and direction.

Given that specialist drama teachers lack this kind of contextual framework, where there is a purposeful continuing multi-resourced programme of learning, they may feel forced into a position of finding acting-out activities which rely on the current information, attitudes and interest of the pupils. The improvisations feed on what the pupils bring to the lesson; there can be little certainty of what pupils know of a topic before they come to drama. In this situation the teacher might decide to supply concepts by providing resources such as photographs, printed material and tape recordings. Alternatively, the teacher can choose topics for acting-out which touch strong feelings, and the drama can be alive in its action, but unhelpful as a model because of a lack of ideas leading to superficial responses. However, given that the teacher wishes to use drama as part of an investigative process, what kinds of learning objectives can he structure which are to do with outcomes other than those concerned with the process, ways of working? I propose now to take a topic and suggest some aims and relevant learning objectives.

In formulating the topic title, I think it is helpful to hold the idea in the form of a question, so that pupils perceive the topic as a problem-solving event rather than as an information-collecting event, though in seeking to solve problems information is often important.

Topic: What are the social implications of urban renewal?
Pupils: a mixed class of 15-year-olds
Aims: that in observing/experiencing urban change in their immediate environment pupils (i) understand how it occurs (ii) have an empathic understanding of what it means in terms of the experience of people; (iii) are better able in their own lives to tolerate the demands of a society which continually imposes change.

Learning Objectives

1 *Administration:* that pupils are able to describe the administrative process in terms of: decision-making; legal requirements in implementing change; communications procedures;

2 *Empathic understanding:* given a profile of a hypothetical area and the proposed changes for it, that (i) pupils are able to describe the likely difficulties from the point of view of the administrators, illustrating their answers with specific examples from the profile; (ii) pupils are able to describe (possibly through role-play) the likely responses to the proposed changes from (a) particular individuals from the profile; (b) particular groups from the profile; (iii) pupils imagining that they are members of the administration outline a method of implementation of the changes showing consideration of: (a) the need for change; (b) minimized unhappiness and disturbance; (c) the need for consultation and honesty; (d) equal regard for all people involved;

3 *Decision-making:* given that pupils serve on various committees in the acting-out situations that they are able to: (a) use accepted conventions of meeting procedures; (b) when decisions have been reached, be able to evaluate them with reference to the values that informed the decisions;

4 *Responses to real problem situations:* when pupils are faced with problem situations in their own lives that they respond to the problems in a feeling, thinking *THEN* acting sequence, acting in the light of considered consequences.

This topic is of particular relevance to many of the children in our city schools, and it seems to me that the learnings I have suggested are important. If the reader does not agree with the learnings I have suggested, I trust that at least he is able to understand what my statements mean. Of course, it will not be possible to observe whether pupils are able to behave in the manner described in 4, but the fact that the teacher has made the statement will, I believe, have an effect on his teaching methods.

These statements of objectives are statements of what pupils should be able to do *because* they have experienced particular learning situations. In a sense it is formulating the examination questions before the teaching begins. In this particular topic many teaching/learning strategies would need to be employed, *one* of which would be acting-out. I consider that acting-out could form the basis of the work, providing involvement and the motivation to engage with other learning resources.

Obviously these are not the only learning objectives concerning this topic, for there could be others in the area of process, where pupils are learning how to learn, or yet others in the area of information and fact. The teacher, in the light of his own situation – himself, his own interests and abilities; the pupils, their interests, abilities, knowledge; the school, its physical provision, time, attitudes – needs to judge what learning is relevant and possible. It must be remembered that a given learning situation can lead to different kinds of learning, and that much learning takes place which the teacher is unaware of. However, I suggest that having a map and a compass is useful when embarking on a journey in difficult country.

Under the heading, 'Area 2. Understanding Themes, Topics through Acting-out', I have attempted to define the area in terms of kinds of learnings suggesting that acting-out as a teaching/learning strategy has wide applications and that acting-out alone is not enough to facilitate worthwhile learning, for without the attendant behaviours there is a danger that acting-out becomes mere self-indulgence.

Area 3. Participating in Presentation

This area is concerned with theatre, when pupils communicate to an audience through the medium of acting-out. The possibilities for pupil involvement here range along a continuum from small groups sharing their work with other pupils in their class to the full-scale public production with a paying audience. The latter is often highly valued by teachers and headteachers, for the school play is seen as a respectable activity, clearly an art form, and affording the school the opportunity of presenting itself to parents and the public at large as a 'cultural' institution – provided that the play is respectable.

However, in the world of drama in education there has been a general acceptance of the view that presentation is not vital to a drama syllabus, and that, for example, to offer a theatre studies mode 3 CSE examination is the easy way out and is doing less than justice to drama and to the pupils. Nevertheless, theatre studies feature frequently in such examinations. Is this because it has been difficult for teachers to think of what it is possible to examine in 'drama'? I think there have not been clear enough definitions concerning what it is that pupils learn in drama classes. Certainly, one area for examination is the area of process – can pupils use the process to negotiate meaning? The other area concerning what can be learned *through* drama is less easy to define. The content of what is learned could well be attitudes, concepts, skills, not directly drama-related. Drama teachers sometimes say that the content of drama is life itself – whatever that may mean.

As drama teachers, we tend to undervalue the art of theatre which has a long tradition, as a medium through which mankind has expressed and found meaning. It is an art form which shares meaning through the presentation of social models, and offers enormous enjoyment and satisfaction to the participants. There is magic in the words 'let's put on a play' reflected in the interest and enthusiasm which the activity generates. More fundamental than the enjoyment derived from working in the art form is the basic human drive to communicate. Works, of art in general are not, in the end, private events. Painters, sculptors, writers and musicians need audiences. Obviously, the first act of communication is from the artist through interaction with the medium to the self; it is an expressive event and self-enhancing. Though the artist might create work which is not appreciated by others, and though he might continue to work along the same lines in spite of this lack of appreciation, the approval of significant others is highly valued.

In the performing arts the audience is an essential element, influencing the act of performance in subtle and sometimes not so subtle ways. More often than not the performer acts as interpreter rather than original creator, and it might be this which leads drama teachers to value theatre less than improvised drama. It might be argued that 'drama' is more expressive for it allows the participants to represent their own ideas rather than someone else's. Certainly drama does facilitate expression in this sense but it can also lead through to a *sharing* of ideas found through improvisation. The desire to share ideas with an audience makes new demands in terms of refinement and precision. There is no doubt that for many children the drive to communicate to an audience is strong.

Two kinds of theatrical communication are open to pupils, namely, that which is developed by the participants themselves through group interaction towards the development of ideas and ways of presenting them, and that which seeks to interpret ideas ordered by the playwright. Both approaches offer different challenges and can be equally creative, though it does seem at first glance that group playmaking is the more creative of the two because it works from perception, through feeling, to interaction with the medium, to form. One difference between group playmaking and the work of the playwright is that in group work the level of work achieved in respect of ideas tends to be that of group consensus, whereas the work of the playwright is his alone. There is great value in the attempt to understand and interpret the works of great playwrights for their expressive work is more profound than could ever be achieved by group consensus. The challenge is to find meaning in the script, to interact with the medium and to arrive at form.

The basic behaviour in the area of presentation is acting-out, supported by behaviours in the area of process, and incorporating elements of other art forms. Learning to present ideas in theatrical terms involves more than learning how to act-out; the demands flow into the fields of music and the visual and plastic arts. The demands of theatre are many and varied and need no apology for inclusion in the school drama curriculum, for at least theatre arts provide a worthwhile way of using leisure time, and at best provide opportunities for self-expression and creativity of the highest order.

Within this area particular kinds of activity can be identified, and within these broad classifications specific behaviours can be described. The broad classifications might be:

(a) *Acting.* Here one would look for behaviours in movement, voice and speech, ability to interpret a script, characterization, team-work, flexibility in styles of acting, etc. Obviously one could classify so that one ended up with something very much like the syllabus of an acting school. Though this may seem absurd in relation to a school syllabus, the drama school statement does provide a description of the field. The drama teacher in school must decide for himself what is relevant to his pupils. However, if the teacher does consider that theatrical presentation is legitimately his concern, then relevant learnings will be like those of actors in training; any difference will be in degree rather than kind.

(b) *Technical aspects.* These supportive activities can be classified as costume, make-up, lighting, sound, props, setting, stage management. Many pupils develop an interest in this field and find great satisfaction in meeting challenges here.

(c) *Production.* It is likely that the teacher will undertake most of the work in production of presentations, but there is no reason why pupils who are interested should not learn. The learning involved is complex, for production demands a maturity and a broad knowledge of theatre to be effective at the level of public performance. However, pupils given limited objectives should be able, through experiment, to acquire some expertise in this field. Kinds of learning are: interpersonal skills – ways of handling people; rehearsal technique, ways of helping actors find meaning in the script; the demands of style; ways of staging.

(d) *Administration.* Here the demands lie in that whole supportive organization which enables the performance to be smooth and successful. I include such things as advertizing, ticket sales, public relations, and front of house management.

These sub-headings are helpful in thinking about the kinds of learning within the area 'Presentation'. I now give some examples of specific learning objectives which illustrate the kinds of statement which teachers can make as they plan work for specific groups of pupils. The examples form no coherent pattern because I am not attempting to write a syllabus; I merely seek to exemplify a way of making statements about teaching/learning intentions. Syllabuses can be written only in relation to particular groups of children.

Example 1   This example is given from the sub-section 'Acting' and shows one of the objectives a teacher might have in mind for his pupils. It would be helpful if pupils also know what the learning objective is. The learning objective has a direct bearing on the work done in class; the objective gives purpose to the work. I imagine that the following objective could provide the underlying purpose of the work for a term.

Performance of a Duologue.   Pupils aged 15+ work in pairs; they are given six hours class time for rehearsal when the teacher is available for advice, and perform a five-minute excerpt from a naturalistic script to remainder of classmates. Following the performance there will be a questioning and feedback session with class and teacher.

Criteria: (a) In acting and discussion pupils show an understanding of the subtext, speaking in terms of motivation and intentions.

(b) Pupils display characters which the audience can believe in, and can explain how the characterization was developed, giving evidence of clues from the text and any relevant information, such as observations from real life or descriptions of work in improvisation.

   Here the objective is limited to characterization and subtext, two closely related concepts. No particular attention is paid to the tempo of the scene or to movement. At this stage only two kinds of behaviours are being tested, though obviously there will be evidence of other behaviours too.

In order to help pupils achieve this objective, the teacher will spend time in structuring learning situations for them. He might ask pupils to invent a character suggested by a photograph, or again, given minimum evidence, to invent a fully rounded person. As a smaller learning objective leading to the major one, he might ask pupils when they have been given time to develop a character to answer any question about that character which other pupils might ask, whilst at the same time staying in character. Similarly, he will work with pupils on ways of analyzing a script, or on exercises which concentrate attention on motivation and intention. It will be necessary to develop another small learning objective here which will establish when pupils have acquired sufficient skills in handling the text. When the teacher and pupils have done the relevant work, they can test themselves against the major objective and, of course, the feedback gained from the test can guide decisions about future work.

It is likely that there would be other learning objectives associated with the work, which could be thought of as ongoing objectives. These would probably be in the field of interpersonal relationships and communication skills, especially those of discussion, and evaluation skills (see 'Area 1. Learning to Use the Process').

Example 2   This example is from that area of a drama curriculum which might well seek to help pupils make use of the documentary style of theatre. The aims of the work could be to enable pupils to understand the nature of documentary theatre, and to help them to discover ways of working in this style. One particular behaviour which would help towards the achievement of the overall aim might be that pupils become flexible in their experimental work as they seek to find expressive form. In this case the particular learning objective could be stated thus.

Flexible approach to finding form.   Pupils aged 16+ work in groups of fives; the group is given a piece of factual information, for example, the minutes of a council meeting concerning the decision to close a youth club, and asked to make a short statement in dramatic terms using only the information supplied. *Criteria:* In their exploratory work pupils employ a variety of forms of presentation before reaching a final decision on form for example, a naturalistic scene; an absurdist scene; the use of voice only; the use of movement only.

Example 3   Often the needs of performance make demands on technical expertise, and it is from this technical side of presentation that the next example is taken.

Preparation of a lighting plot.   Pupils aged 16+ are given: (i) a scripted scene requiring three lighting changes; (ii) a Mini T-12 control desk; twelve 1000-watt outlet sockets; fifteen 500-watt fresnel spots; ten 500-watt profile spots; (iii) a pros. arch stage with a 20ft. opening, and 16ft. deep, three bars + FOH. They are asked to devise (a) a hanging plot; (b) a lighting plot; (c) a lighting operator's plot.

Criteria: (a) orderly systematic presentation of ideas, including diagrams, easily interpreted from the page into action, and all necessary cues accounted for;

(a) within the limitations of stage and available equipment, optimum hanging and focussing of lanterns so that actors are clearly lit;

(c) all cues, changes and resettings clearly indicated so that a lighting operator would work efficiently.

This is a limited objective only; no mention has been made of artistic interpretation arising from the script, or of the use of colour. These might be learning objectives which come later, and earlier learning objectives might simply have been concerned with the pupil's ability to discriminate between profile and fresnel spots and their uses. I have given an example of just one of a series of objectives within this technical field.

I am sure that readers will have clear notions themselves of the demands of this area of presentation. What is important is that in making decisions about presentation teachers are conscious of what learnings are possible in this area, and that their choices of intentions are in terms of what pupils should be able to do.

Area 4. Interpretation and Appreciation of Dramatic Statements by Other People

I include in this area the ability of the pupil to appreciate a play as a member of an audience, and to appreciate a play through study of the dramatic text. Within these two general aims I see the following as examples of relevant kinds of learning, and it might be that the teacher of English would claim that part of his work falls within this province, for he has traditionally been the one who helps pupils to an understanding of plays. Because of this link with English teaching, the study of plays has in general been less than it ought to be, for the English teacher's concern is with the text as a piece of literature rather than as a blueprint for action. The drama teacher in a secondary school is underused if he is not given the opportunity to harness his expertise to the attempts to open up scripts as working blueprints for practice.

Within these two general aims I see the following as examples of relevant kinds of learning:

1 that pupils are able to analyze a performance in terms of acting ability, appropriateness of setting, costume, lighting, movement, pace, imagery, style;
2 that pupils can place the play in the context of genre, socio-political background, playwright's development;

3 that pupils can identify and describe different styles of theatre, for example, naturalistic, poetic, absurdist, Brechtian;

4 that pupils can outline the contribution to theatre made by outstanding figures, such as Stainslavsky, Craig, Appia, Brecht, Brook;

5 that pupils are able to read a play and to understand the practical implications of staging it;

6 when pupils are studying play scripts for, say, English examination purposes, that they are able to work together in ways which rely on their practical involvement, discovering meaning through practical exploration (I am thinking of approaches suggested by Hodgson and Richards in *Improvisation*[16]);

7 that pupils are able to describe the social functions of theatre in our society, taking into account the live theatre, TV drama and film;

8 that pupils develop a continuing and discriminating interest in theatre of all forms, being able to tolerate the unfamiliar and to make reasoned judgments from a personal point of view.

Here again are examples of learnings which to my mind are relevant to the whole area. I am not suggesting that they are relevant for all schools or all pupils but that any of them could legitimately be placed in a drama curriculum, and that the trained drama teacher is the best person to work in this area.

The following are examples of specific learning objectives in this area.

Example 1   This example is to do with the application of skills of analysis in connection with a live performance, and the ability to use the skills in a shared experience in discussion. The teacher is looking for the ability of the individual to apply skills of analysis, and he is also evaluating the ability of the group to function effectively.

Reasoned group evaluation of a play.   Pupils visit a theatre to see a play; as a group of ten with a designated leader, they are asked to evaluate the performance; the group sits in a circle.

Criteria: (i) Pupils employ good discussion skills (see above 'Discussion Skills').

(ii)   The group employs a systematic approach so that the discussion is progressive, for example, (a) sharing the general feeling response of the group; (b) what does the group think was the playwright's intention? (c) was the intention achieved? (d) how was this facilitated or hindered? (e) given the present social context, was this a good choice of play?

(iii)   Each group member contributes to discussion.

To be able to function well in this way is not easy, and the level of ideas will depend on the particular group of people. If they have had a rich background of experience, the teacher's expectations will be high. The teacher as observer of this behaviour will know whether a particular group or individual member of it is meeting his expectations at the congnitive level.

Example 2 The second example is in connection with helping pupils to understand a particular play. Suppose that fifth or sixth-year pupils in a secondary school are studying the play 'Mother Courage'. The teacher needs to ask what pupils should be able to do at the end of a block of teaching/learning, which they could not do at the beginning. It is likely that answers would be something like:

(i) to outline the plot of the play;

(ii) to be able to describe the structure of the play and to contrast it with the structure of a play by Chekov;

(iii) to outline the social message of the play;

(iv) to describe the staging requirements of the play;

(v) to explain, giving illustrations from the play, Brecht's theory of alienation.

These are statements in terms of pupil behaviour and as such can be useful to teacher and to learner. They tend, however, to be rather general statements of intent and for the most part it is not easy to see precisely what pupils will be expected to do as a result of the course work. To make the intentions more exact requires a more detailed statement such as the one given below.

Application of principles of staging. Given a particular set of constraints – the school stage, or drama studio – the pupil is asked to imagine that he is the producer of the play and to describe, using diagrams, how he would stage the play, that is, shape of stage, setting, audience seating in relation to stage. *Criteria:* due consideration to be given to at least the following: physical constraints of space; the relationship of actor to audience; the structure of the play; the intention of the play; Brecht's theory of alienation; practical possibilities for actors and technicians.

This test of learning would come at the end of a particular set of learning situations which would probably include practical work, reading, discussion, examination of drawings and photographs, model making, writing.

The fourth area, 'Interpretation and Appreciation of Dramatic Statements by Other People', is enormous and complex. Drama teachers are not likely to have enough time to do much work in this area on their own account, but I see no fundamental reason why they should not contribute to the work of the English department, either by teaching complete modules, or by working in drama classes on texts being used in English classes. In whichever way drama teachers are involved, however, in doing this work they will be fulfilling their function as drama teachers: they *are* teaching drama.

Conclusion

At the beginning of this chapter I suggested that it is important for both teachers and learners to be able to identify learnings, that is, changes in behaviour, so that they can know when learning has been achieved. In concluding, I should like to stay with this thought, for it seems to me to be of the utmost significance for the process of education.

Lack of motivation in learners is the central problem in schools today. Many pupils have little commitment to their own learning and teachers, especially those who work in secondary schools are compelled to be involved in controlling reluctant learners, rather than in controlling learning. This arises largely because schools as institutions tend to establish and maintain dependent relationships, where pupils perceive schooling as something that happens *to* them, rather than as a process which they are engaged in creating. In Esland's terms, they are 'World-produced' rather than 'World-producing[17]. Teachers make decisions about what is to be taught, refrain from communicating their intentions to pupils, and then attempt to engage pupils in activities which are designed to lead through to learning. It is no surprise that pupils fail to be involved with the teacher's agenda, unless by some happy accident the teacher's intentions match the pupils' interests.

There is no doubt that learners learn best when they have learning goals which they own as significant for them. When this obtains the job of the teacher is straightforward. Schools, that is, teachers, would do well to centre their attention on creating situations which enable pupils to perceive and hold learning goals. In doing this they would move significantly towards changing the traditional dependency relationship. Obviously learners would still depend on teachers for help in the learning process, but the nature of the dependence would be changed from that of passive dependence, where the teacher is seen to be *in* authority, to an active dynamic dependence, where the teacher is seen to be *an* authority.

Clearly one of the first steps towards the achievement of this new relationship of the learner to learning is a degree of precision in the identification of what can be learned in a given 'realm of meaning'.[18] This paper has been an attempt to delineate the approximate boundaries of drama as a way of knowing but, more specifically, to suggest a way of talking about learning in drama which makes for clarity of thinking and communication.

I am conscious of the fear that the use of behavioural objectives imposes too narrow a view of learning; that persons are processes rather than measurable objects; that learning never stops; that the only terminal behaviour is death itself. Nevertheless, underlying the process of education is the assumption that it is a purposeful activity which manifests itself through the intervention of teachers in the lives and development of learners. The fundamental question for the individual teacher is: how should children be different because they have worked with me; what thinking, what feeling, what skills have I facilitated?

Notes

1 McGregor, L., Tate, M. and Robinson K. (1977) *Learning through Drama*, Heinemann Educational Books, p. 171.
2 Mager, R.F. (1975) *Preparing Instructional Objectives*, Fearon.
3 Postman, N. and Weingartner, C. (1969) *Teaching as a Subversive Activity*, DePacorte. p. 42.
4 Esland, G.M. (1971) 'Teaching and learning as the organization of knowledge', in Young, M.F.D. (Ed.) (1971) *Knowledge and Control*, Collier-Macmillan, p. 76.
5 Hirst P.H. and Peters, R.S. (1970) *The Logic of Education*, Routledge and Kegan Paul.
6 Phenix, P.H. (1964) *Realms of Meaning*, McGraw-Hill.
7 McGregor *et al.*, *op. cit.*, pp. 10–12.
8 Watkins, B. (1972) 'Facing up to the problem: A reappraisal of the aims and methods of teaching drama', unpublished mimeo.
9 McGregor *et al.*, *op. cit.*
10 Mager, *op. cit.*, p. 53.
11 For details of this demand on groups, see Miles, M. (1959) *Learning to Work in Groups*, New York.
12 For more on this approach to feedback, although in a different context, see Johnson, D.W. (1972) *Reaching Out*, Prentice Hall.
13 Watkins, *op. cit.*
14 Fines, J. and Verrier, R. (1974) *The Drama of History*, New University. Education p. 89.
15 Seely, J. (1976) *In Context: Language and Drama in the Secondary School*, Oxford University Press.
16 Hodgson, J. and Richards, I. (1966) *Improvisation*, Methuen.
17 Esland, *op. cit.*
18 Phenix, *op. cit.*

8   Standards in Drama: Some Issues

Lyn McGregor

In this chapter, McGregor deals with the difficult issue of standards in drama. She asks the questions: 'Drama for what?' and 'Drama for whom?' In attempting to answer she touches on many of the issues of purposes of drama and evaluation of drama raised in earlier chapters. Like O'Neill, she believes that it is the clusters of knowledge and skills that may be acquired in drama itself which must be evaluated; like Robinson, she is concerned that understanding of and standards in drama may be affected by examinations in drama, though she is more sanguine; and, like Day, she identifies the continuing necessity for teachers of drama to clarify their intentions and practices. The prime importance of this chapter, however, lies in the assertion by the author that criteria for judgments of drama work are governed by prevailing trends and existing knowledge about and attitudes to children and learning. They are, therefore, complex and, by implication, need to be approached with care.

This discussion concerning standards in drama teaching is based on three years of observing teachers in their classrooms and a further two years of running courses and conferences for teachers all over the country. But before elaborating on what my impressions were, I feel that any discussion concerning the question of standards should look more closely at what is meant by standards in the first place.

Like any other aspect of education the issue of 'standards' should be seen in its wide 'political' context. Apart from the universal all-time complaint that 'standards' are not good enough and could always be improved, nothing about the word can be taken for granted. Standards for what? For whom? are central questions to be asked. These will be bound up with the value systems of those talking about standards and the reasons why the achievement of certain standards are felt to be meaningful.

In the last few years, banners displaying the bold words of 'standards' have been waved by a number of different camps. Exponents of *Black Papers* criticize the falling of standards due to progressive methods of teaching[1] in spite of the fact that there are no conclusive figures to prove or disprove the claim. Mr Callaghan, then Prime Minister, heralded the DES Green Paper on Education[2] by making a number of statements about standards. 'In to-day's world higher standards are demanded than were required yesterday and there are simply fewer jobs for those without skills. Therefore more is demanded from our schools, than in our grandparents day.'[3] Unfortunately, both the PM's speech and the Green Paper were misrepresented in sections of the press as criticizing present methods, and this resulted in many people becoming defensive and returning to traditional forms of teaching and testing.

What was actually said was that 'there are signs that it is becoming more widely understood that the new approaches do demand rigour and some recognition of the widely varying capabilities of individual teachers. The challenge is to restore the rigour without damaging the real benefits of the child's centred development.' The Green Paper, along with later DES documents on standards in schools and different subjects,[4] was part of a general trend in education, caused by two main factors. The first is that the ideology and practice of child-centred subjects had been thought for some time as being worthwhile, but no specific detailed questions had been asked about what was actually being achieved. It was only natural that as development occurred more sophisticated questions should be asked about aims, objectives and assessment. The second factor was that for the first time in many years educational expenditure was cut. The time for expansion was over. The age of accountability had begun. Should certain subjects be given priority in the timetable? Should there be a core curriculum? How could each subject justify its existence on a timetable?

It is within this context that a consideration of present standards in drama teaching needs to be made. In ten years' time the issues may be different. The brief of the Schools Council Drama Project was 'to clarify the aims and objectives of drama teaching; to develop methods of assessing outcomes and to suggest ways of developing drama in the curriculum.' This was indicative of the current educational climate. For the first time a large sum of money was allocated for a systematic attempt to define and describe 'standards' in drama teaching.[5]

I would like to go back to my initial question. Standards for what and for whom? To my mind there are three interrelated areas to be examined:

1 standards in drama work;
2 standards for selection;
3 standards in teaching drama.

The first is concerned with what standards of work are being achieved in the classroom. The second is about the issues involved and the relevance of the kinds of standard required with examinations in mind. It is important to discuss this last area as the examination system dominates much of what is done in schools. Pieces of paper representing academic attainment are still a passport to the future. The third area relates to what is expected of teachers if high standards of drama are to be achieved.

(1)   Standards in Drama Work

A few pupils have told me that they did not like drama because they were 'not good at it'. Unlike a number of teachers they recognized that there are forms of achievement in drama and that for various reasons some pupils are better than others. This is not to say that all pupils cannot do drama. They can. But the quality of work each class and each pupil will produce will be different. What then are the standards that should be achieved in drama work?

In the early days of 'speech and drama', standards of elocution and received pronunciation loomed large in the assessment of drama. These were super-ceded by standards of spontaneity and extended play[6] and in turn, by a stress on group development.[7] Many practitioners now stress that drama should be used to challenge children's preconceptions[8] or (more eclectically) that children should achieve standards of work over the whole field of drama.[9] The point is that the criteria used to judge the standards of any work in drama (and education) will depend on prevalent trends and existing knowledge about and attitudes to children and learning. For instance, those who believed that 'children were empty vessels to be filled with knowledge' would be shocked by a child-centred approach to education. Changing attitudes to authority and democracy are also reflected in the expectations teachers have of children's performances. Teachers who encourage children to make decisions about their work and evaluate the standard of work in those terms are expressing certain sets of value assumptions. In the sense that drama has to do with the emotional and intellectual involvement in exploring peoples' attitudes, behaviour and feelings, the political/moral undercurrent of what is being explored cannot be ignored.

How does this relate to the original question concerning standards? It relates in the sense that '*what*' standards are being assessed, will change from time to time. Sometimes confusion occurs because teachers use. inappropriate standards to assess new ways of working. For instance, criticism of a piece of work pupils have done on exploring feelings of conflict may be in terms of 'you all spoke at the same time', instead of the teacher trying to judge the work according to what pupils were trying to do.

If there are no fixed standards concerning drama work, how does one go about assessing standards at all and for what purposes? I would suggest that there are common factors that could be discussed concerning the achievement of any work. On the assumption that there are different levels of assessment I have distinguished at least two levels:

(1)   standards of achievement over a long period of time;
(2)   standards related to specific tasks/projects over a given period of time.

The scope and complexity of many subjects and processes means that over a number of years children will develop understanding and skills by experien-cing a range of activities. What is taught in the classroom should be regarded as laying the foundation for an accumulation of skills that the child should be able to use when relevant. In my experience the effects are sometimes not evident until some time after learning has occurred. One example is of a teacher who taught a class formal debating procedures. Two terms later, when working on a local election campaign, the children, without being reminded, used the procedures as part of the drama.[10] What is being accumulated are clusters of skills and areas of knowledge. Take, for instance, the Bullock Report's recommendations of what the reading demands of the later years might be:

(1) the pupil needs to be able to cope with the reading required in each part of the curriculum;

(2) he should acquire a level of competence which will enable him to meet his needs as an adult in society when he leaves school;

(3) he should regard reading as a source of pleasure and personal development which will continue to be a rewarding activity throughout life.[11]

The same claims could be made for drama, with one difference. The functional value of reading is commonly accepted as having direct relevance for the child. It is also easy to expose children to a range of literature and to devise ways of monitoring pupils' ability to understand and handle the material. With 'drama' it is not so easy.

How, then, can one tell how a child is coping with demands put upon him in drama – especially if he is required to do drama in English, history and RE, as well as something in its own right? In what ways can drama help the child meet adult needs when he leaves school? What levels of competence of what skills should be required? When some teachers were asked what children should achieve through drama the following answers were given: drama helps the child to develop his full potential; it helps children to learn to express themselves, to develop sensitivity to others and it encourages them to learn to make decisions. These teachers missed the point, which is that, first and foremost, standards concerning drama teaching should be concerned with *drama*. In other words, what children gain through drama should arise both from their ability to do drama better and to appreciate other people's drama.

This is fundamentally related to the developing capacity to project into social situations and to identify with the deep structures of meaning expressed through roles being played. When we respond to Hamlet's 'to be or not to be', it is because we recognize similar impulses in each of us. Understanding of that emotion is heightened through the particular problems Hamlet encounters. Drama gives us the possibility of coming to deeper understandings of ourselves and others. 'Doing drama better', therefore, means a continual striving by the individual to create and develop imagined roles and characters within the dramatic context so that they are plausible. Plausibility can happen at two levels. The first is that for the actor the role he is playing must be an external manifestation of an inner understanding and feeling he has about the nature of the character he is playing. For instance, the child acting out a situation in which as a lonely old pensioner having to give up a much loved pet in a council house, would find it difficult to make the role plausible without a great deal of preparation. He would need to understand the implications of age and loneliness which could be built up only by creation of and detailed attention to the imagined physical environment and life-style of the pensioner and his relationship to the pet. Only when this was internalized would the experience become relevant to the child. Not many achieve a great measure of identification. However, this is what working towards greater competence at drama should be about. The second level, already mentioned, has to do with whether a form of dramatic expression approximates adequately to a perception of the truth. An example of this is a humorous mime done by a group of 12-year-old boys who mimed a hunter pretending to be extremely brave. He was terrified by the size of an elephant, which turned out to be tame. Having confused his fear of size, he boastfully refused to bother about smaller matters and allowed himself to be stung by a mosquito which killed him. What the boys were trying to express is that what appears superficially to be dangerous is not necessarily what may destroy an individual. (See also Bolton's article.)

Getting better at drama means being able to use drama to penetrate reality and then to find ways of symbolizing, through roles and situations, an interpretation of that reality. Being able to appreciate other people's drama means being able to understand the meaning behind the drama and whether it has been adequately done.

Every child ought to be working towards being able to use drama so that it is a meaningful, not superficial experience. By the time a pupil is 16 and has had a number of years of experience, he should be closer to an understanding of what drama can be about. He should have acquired various skills and attributes which could enable him to be competent at the business of exploring roles and situations through drama. He should be able to draw on a wide range of experiences at three main levels.

1 *At the practical level:* having sufficient physical and verbal skills to create roles and characters; being able to use different dramatic conventions – caricature, naturalism, mime or speech – in determining which dramatic modes may be most fitting for a particular piece of work. He should also be able to make use of space, light, objects, etc. to create effective contexts for the drama.

2 At the cognitive and affective level: the pupil should be able to choose an idea and explore it through the creation and development of roles within situations. He should be able, while picking up cues from fellow participants, not only to develop his own character, but also to help develop other characters through his responses. He should be able to analyze the success or failure of an effort, to explain the difficulty and suggest developments. A pupil should, therefore, be able to step out of role and back into role without losing any emotional or intellectual commitment to the role or situation. He should be able to deepen the experience by being critically aware of the standard of work being

produced. He should be able to apply his experience to being critically appreciative of other people's drama.

Pupils should be able to shape their ideas into coherent dramatic structures. The more competent, the more able they should be in working quickly. They should be able to perform either their own or other people's plays in such a way that they communicate their understanding of the play to others. This involves the ability to interpret texts, to translate them into action and then to communicate with commitment and clarity.

3   *At the social level:* the pupil should be competent in two ways: at a real level, he should be able to negotiate and work out ideas with others – to give and receive ideas and at a symbolic level as mentioned above. By the time pupils are 16, they should have been exposed to a range of imagined social roles and situations. They should be flexible enough to pick up nuances of meaning and respond to a variety of types of people and circumstances in drama.

This means that pupils should be able to decide what they want to explore and develop drama which is plausible both to them and observers. They should be able to present ideas and to play credible roles, and to discuss other people's performances critically.

The problem in evaluating drama work is to establish the level of under-standing at which adolescents could be operating. It is impossible to give standardized expectations about maturity, especially in cases where pupils have had limited experience of the world. However, I would expect them to be able to recognize the limitations of stereotypes and to display in their acting a growing awareness of the complexities of human nature. For instance, their characters should have personalities, attitudes and reasons for being motivated to act in certain ways. If characters have social or occupational roles, pupils should be able to find out what the implications of those roles are so that they may become more plausible. This means, for example, that an interviewer interviewing candidates for social welfare work, should know enough to be able to decide what qualities were needed so that intelligent questions could be asked.

I hope by now it has become evident that the kind of standards required should relate strictly to the drama experience.

To return to some of the questions about long-term objectives for setting standards, I would argue that high standards occur when children are sufficiently in control of working through drama to use it as a vehicle for meaningful exploration and expression. All the skills suggested above are indicators of how children can cope with various demands in drama. If children have had specialist training in drama, they should be able to explore other subjects through drama without difficulty. For instance, if a history teacher wants pupils to explore the events leading up to the French Revolution, he could give pupils the relevant details and some suggestions and the pupils ought to be able to explore the events concerned either by trying to put themselves in the place of a pre-revolutionary or by taking an issue, exploring it through contemporary situations and relating it to the historical period.

When it comes to considering whether experience in drama directly relates to the demands of an adult society, a number of factors need to be taken into account.[14] The first is that there is no conclusive evidence for any aspect of education or whether there is direct transference between what is learnt in school and how a person performs in adult society. It is, however, possible to give pupils certain kinds of experience which may he helpful in later life. For instance, it may be possible to say that drama experience in schools enables children to be critically appreciative of drama on the mass media. One hopes that, if children have practice in projecting into other roles and characters, they would find it easier to sympathize with others and to appreciate and respond to other people's viewpoints. It is also possible to set up exercises to test pupils' responses, to, for instance, their ability to use language flexibly in a variety of social situations. Exercises like these may be diagnostically useful in gauging the standards of pupil performances, as can be seen in the increasing proliferation of methods of examining practical drama.

Although I would argue that any discussion concerning drama standards ought to be seen mainly in terms of competence in drama, the problems of transference into adult life should not be overlooked. I have suggested that the answer to the question 'what standards?' mainly depends on the value systems of the times. These might apply across the curriculum, for example, it is as possible to say that a certain approach to science encourages children to develop techniques of independent enquiry. The same claims could be made for drama. If this is so, a case could be made for two systems of monitoring at the end of a school career. The first would attempt to find out how much knowledge and skills have been achieved within any one discipline, including drama. The other should be seen as a means of monitoring general learning techniques and approaches across the curriculum. This could apply to, for example, the ability to apply research skills on any topic, decision-making, both individual and group, and the ability to understand and express opinions about a range of subject-matter. More work needs to be done on building up an explicit range of criteria, such as those which should take into account an individual's overall achievement by the time he leaves school. Drama, because many subject areas can be explored through it, and because it offers opportunities for individual and group initiatives, could have a major role to play in this area. If profiles on individual pupils could go beyond examination results, it should be easier for future employers to have a wider view of a pupil's potential than is currently given.

Unfortunately, it is mainly through low status subjects such as drama that children are encouraged to learn to experiment with ideas on a number of levels – emotional, social and intellectual. Those subjects mainly geared towards the examination system make demands on pupils in which stress is laid on learning ways of answering certain kinds of examination paper so that

A good drama teacher, like any other good teacher, needs to function well on both intellectual and practical levels. He needs to be able to relate his academic knowledge of, for example, developmental psychology to the way he actually relates to children in the classroom. He needs to be able to work both diagnostically and developmentally. By diagnostically, I mean the ability to detect particular learning needs and difficulties of specific age and ability groups. By developmentally, I mean that he needs to know what areas of learning he wants to develop and to be able to devise ways of monitoring progress. He needs to be able to evaluate both the children's and his own work. He needs to be aware of the signs and signals given to him by the children about their attitudes, stages of development and ability to cope or need to be stretched. He needs to be able to seize learning opportunities as they occur and to exploit possibilities. To do this he needs to have a range of activities and strategies and to know when to initiate ideas, when to intervene or to do nothing.

Drama is a complex developmental process involving many activities for many purposes. The teacher needs to have an academic knowledge of all facets of the process – creative, asthetic, social – drama in performance and dramatic criticism. He needs to be clear about what aspects he is teaching and what stages of development his pupils should reach in practical terms. However, in training, teachers need to have experience in using drama at their own level (in addition to an academic understanding) and then to learn how to teach the process. This can only be done developmentally and over a sustained period. Teaching teachers to teach is not easy. It is a complex process which should involve in-service training as a continuation and development of initial training. The problem is that the ethos of academic attainment coupled with the attitude that 'those who can, practice, and those who can't, teach' means that the art of teaching, or indeed learning, is not taken seriously enough.

In 1967 John Allen felt that there was a need to define aims and objectives in drama: 'the need for clarification is strong and since quantity of work is far outstripping quality, urgent.'[16] Standards are higher in the 1980s although there is still room for improvement. Although there is cause to be generally optimistic about improving standards in drama work and teaching, it is also important to examine the topic realistically in the general educational context. In our present system we are still mainly obsessed with standards for passing academic examinations and standards for selection. De facto this is happening, in spite of wider issues raised in the current debate. Ironically, however, the trend towards rationalization is positive in the sense that teachers have to clarify their aims and think more deeply about standards. However, in a climate where academic achievement in increasingly emphasized and there is a return to conventional forms of education, as seen in increasing demands for private education,[17] exponents of drama in education cannot be complacent.

Any debate about education comes back to the question: standards for what? The answers are inevitably ideological. What we should be fighting for is an improvement in the quality of the lives we lead. In this drama and the other arts have a great deal to offer.

Notes

1 For example COX, C. and DYSON, A. W. (1970) *Black Paper 2*, London Critical Quarterly Society.

2 *Education in Schools: A Consultative Document* (1977) HMSO.

3 Prime Minister's Speech at Ruskin College, *The Guardian*, 18 October 1976.

4 *Curriculum 11–16* (1977) HMSO.

5 McGREGOR, L., TATE, M. and ROBINSON, K. (1977) *Learning through Drama*, Heinemann Education Books.

6 SLADE, PETER (1968) *Experience of Spontaneity*, Longmans.

7 WAY, B. (1967) *Development through Drama*, Longmans.

8 HEATHCOTE, D. 'Drama and Education' Subject or System', in DODD, N. and HICKSON, W. (Eds) (1971) *Drama and Theatre in Education*, Heinemann Educational Books.

9 McGREGOR *et al., op. cit.*

10 McGREGOR, L. (1976) *Developments in Drama Teaching*, Open Books.

11 *A Language for Life* (1975) HMSO, p. 115.

12 *Actors in School* (1976) Education Survey 22, HMSO.

13 For examples, see 9 and 10.

14 McGREGOR, L. (1977) 'Assessing drama, some implications', in *Education Review*, November.

15 DORE, R. (1976) *The Diploma Disease*, Unwin Educational Books.

16 *Drama Education Survey* (1967) HMSO.

17 Survey by the Independent Schools Information Agency, 1978.

9   A Plea for Self-Evaluation

Michael Vernon

Vernon presents a depressing picture of the response of (a sample of) drama teachers to the notion of evaluation. His findings suggest that despite the growing concern with the need to design more effective assessment and evaluation procedures – as expressed in the literature over a number of years – drama teachers remain firmly at the intuitive stage in making judgments about both their own and their pupils' work (see Bolton's article). Communication between drama teachers and colleagues, parents, etc. about purposes and content of drama would appear to need considerable improvement. Vernon calls to those involved in training teachers to carry out the basic tasks of self-evaluation and 'jargon-free explanation and justification'.

This chapter is an initial exploration of how drama teachers evaluate themselves and how they explain what they do to 'the world' in terms which 'the world' can understand. More precisely, it is about the problems of self-assessment and the drama teacher's perceptions of his role in the current debate about accountability.

I have tried to keep one foot on the ground by basing my comments on the results of a micro-project which I have recently completed in the north-west. The core of the chapter is a descriptive analysis of what *is* (at least in the eyes of the author). I am encouraged in this approach by the comments of many teachers who have picked glumly through the openly (but rarely helpful) prescriptive 'theorizing' of the obligatory 'philosophical' introductions to money-spinning 'tips for instant drama' books. It must be said, however, that these teachers also include in their ranks many who were deeply offended by Clegg[1] and even by *Education Survey 2: Drama*,[2] which seemed to them to be letting the side down just when all their hard work to get drama established seemed to be having some positive results.

The micro-project was based on selected schools in a Metropolitan Borough of Greater Manchester, using teachers belonging to the local Association of Drama Teachers, one of the largest and most active of such groups in the country. Teachers from a wide variety of backgrounds (of both training and experience) were interviewed, as was the Drama Adviser for the area. The project does not make any claims to completeness and is at most a subjective appraisal of attitudes to evaluation and accountability prevailing in a small corner of England.

In his report of the Third International Curriculum Conference, *Curriculum Innovation in Practice*,[3] McLure notes Tyler's comments to the effect that systematic evaluation was 'the only way to sort out worthwhile curriculum development from a succession of fads and fashions' (p. 37). The Americans, of course, have been 'into' systematic (that is, objective behaviour) evaluation for some time, and Tyler's comments are neatly contrasted with McLure's report of the Expressive and Creative Arts Seminar. Whereas the modern linguists 'conducted their dialogue at a sophisticated technical level, having already established definitions and a working vocabulary ... a splendid anarchy reigned in the "Creative and Expressive Arts".' This group was caught up arguing the case and convincing people and 'it was significant that till they had established this and a rationale by which it could be expressed, they were reluctant to discuss detailed aspects of curriculum reform in their discipline' (pp. 49–50). Of even greater significance for the future was McLure's observation that 'in terms of curriculum innovation ... the English – with important individual exceptions – were impatient of theory and intensely pragmatic in their approach. They doubted the value of wasting much time discussing the aims of education' (p. 3).

'Aims and objectives', this magical key to the future was tried in many previously unlocked doors at the end of the 1960s but some individuals began to question the validity of at least the interpretation of aims and objectives in behavioural terms when applied to arts teaching. 'The formulation of educational means is never a neutral act. The tools employed and the metaphors used to describe education lead to actions which are not without consequences with respect to value ... under the rug of technique lies an image of man.'[4] Eisner, the author of this statement, attempted to break out of the behavioural straight-jacket by proposing two types of objective, 'instrumental' and 'expressive'. Whereas the former involves the learning of codes appropriate for life in our culture – the basic skills of reading, writing, and numeracy – 'expressive' objectives 'enable children to *contribute* to the culture and re-interpret *given* definitions and material' (p. 14). Unfortunately, his view of evaluation of outcomes of expressive objectives is essentially 'product'-based, and his comment that the expressive objectives are really about 'specifying the kind of encounter which is likely to yield it' is ultimately not very helpful.

In 1973 Crompton started an intense and protracted debate by confronting drama teachers with what he saw as their sloppy thinking.[5] He was one of the first to challenge the keystone of what passed for evaluation – 'intuition'. 'Drama teachers do their own things; they work out their solo styles and personalities and tend to believe that their teaching, to be 'effective' or 'worthwhile', must depend on the idiosyncracies and nature of their own experiences and approaches to their subject and their pupils' (p. 145). This call to action was accompanied by a suggested syllabus which even by the standards of the day, and before the full reaction against Slade had set in, was rather simplistic. The first public response to Crompton was by Byron,[6] who rejected the syllabus out of hand. He didn't offer much in its place but he did put his finger on what was to become a key theme, the inadequacy of teacher training with respect to drama. Spalding, who took up the argument in 1974,[7] started by rejecting the notion that 'it is possible or desirable to have "a coherent philosophy of drama"' (p. 74). His reason was the 'intuitive' basis of the activity. His comments are worth quoting in full:

> The discipline remains intuitive. I try to do two things simultaneously; to get to know each group through the drama activities we share and to provide them with appropriate techniques of their use when they go into their first, middle, or even secondary schools as teachers, not *of* drama, but of anything they like through drama ... this very readiness and the enjoyment that pupils find in drama makes it difficult for the teacher to assess his work. I frequently ask, having seen a student at work with a class: 'All right, so they enjoyed it, but what did they learn? Were you teaching drama or history? Did you set out to implant a skill, instil a fact, or suggest an attitude?' Sometimes the truthful answer is 'I don't know. I set out to do one thing, but what happened was better.' Sometimes it is, equally truthfully, 'Nothing at all.' Sometimes it is, rarely but enough to be encouraging: 'All of it. History, drama, skills, facts, attitudes.' (p. 77)

In 1967 Eisner had noted this general reluctance of teachers to take objectives seriously,[8] and went on to ask some important questions about the role and function of objectives in evaluation: If teachers are to have educational objectives how many and under what conditions are they to be formulated? How should one move from a statement of educational objectives to the selection of content and the determination of teaching procedure? What constraints, if any, do educational objectives place upon teachers' behaviour? What effect, if any, do educational objectives have in homogenizing student behaviour? What normative conceptions of education underlie alternative positions regarding the importance and function of educational objectives? (p. 281). In 1975 Hoetker[9] attempted to suggest a more flexible approach to the problem of aims and objectives than the more 'scientific' behaviour approach which Davies had proposed in 1976[10] and again in this volume. Hoetker in fact suggested a way beyond aims and objectives as such, a means of helping teachers to monitor the relative success or failure of their attempts to make teaching and learning through drama more effective. He first adopted the distinction between 'formative' evaluation (addressed to an audience concerned primarily with 'what is happening') and a 'summative' evaluation (addressed to those who want to know 'what happened', that is, those not actually involved in the teaching programme). The function of the former is to provide information for the purpose of helping to improve the ongoing programme and both forms of evaluation really need an 'outside' evaluator. (That this presents difficulties in schools is obvious but it is certainly an area in which the colleges could help.) Hoetker identifies two general strategies open to the evaluator:

On the one hand the investigator could ascertain the teacher's objectives and then devise ways to gather data to establish the extent to which the objectives were attained . . . the evaluator's main contribution, in such a situation, might be to identify those students who were or were not indeed having the desired experiences and perhaps further to provide observations about the problems or positive and negative contributions of particular students during the experiences – information it is not always possible for the teacher himself to gather at the right time or in sufficient detail. . . . 'On the other hand, the evaluator might be given no information at all about the objectives or the intentions of the teacher, but would simply be invited to observe and participate. The evaluator's report would then consist of an account of what he thought he had seen happening and his inferences about who was learning what. The crucial issue in such a 'goal-free evaluation' would be the extent to which the evaluator's matched the teacher's intentions – the extent to which the drama had the same meaning to both.[11]

Five years before Griffiths had suggested that the Drama Adviser should have a role in this sort of evaluation,[12] and the signs are that the growing number of advisory teacher groups working closely with teachers *in the schools* are beginning to exploit their 'unique opportunity to assess the effectiveness of teachers work in drama' (Griffiths, p. 71). On a more ominous note, Griffiths also reported that 'many advisers are of the opinion that Colleges of Education do not yet train sufficient teachers in the use of creative drama' (p. 71). One such group of drama advisory teachers working for ILEA produced a statement of the objectives of drama teaching in 1976. *Drama Guidelines* reflects the growing concern with the necessity of analysis and evaluation.[13] It contains short sections on analysis, evaluation, and objectives in drama, the first of these being a useful adaptation of a list of post-lesson questions prepared by Dorothy Heathcote for her students at Newcastle. The section on evaluation, however, is hazy and unhelpful, focussing as it does on the difficulties of assessing an 'inner experience'.

By 1977, 24 years after the first appearance of *Child Drama*, teachers were *aware* of the pressures on them to evaluate but were not much nearer to mastering the ability to monitor and assess themselves as drama teachers. Many had found Witkin's *The Intelligence of Feeling* hard going and were waiting for *Learning through Drama*, on which the former book had such a profound influence. McGregor, Tate, and Robinson's book was greeted with wide and justifiable acclaim, but now it is reasonable to ask what help the book has been to the teacher in the fundamental activity of self-assessment. The relevant part is Chapter 5, 'Can Drama be Assessed?' The authors note the genuine doubts about assessment which concerns value judgments round expressions of feeling, but do not swerve from stating the obvious – that teachers *do* in fact make judgments all the time and imply that while such judgments remain at the intuitive level the development of both teachers and pupils will be very much a matter of hit and miss. The bulk of the chapter is taken up with the analysis of three drama lessons. This analysis is taken from the point of view of questions which the teacher might ask of himself before and after the lesson and as such is a very useful model of ongoing assessment. McGregor's other foray into the world of assessment is less immediately helpful at the practical level, although she does again identify the four main components which could provide a useful basis for assessment: content, media, forms of expression, and social interaction, the relative emphasis on components depending on the kinds of learning to be encouraged.[14] In an uncharacteristic slip into haziness, however, she suggests that, 'teachers could assess how work was going both through signs and signals given out by pupils and by discussion and other forms of reflection' (p. 269).

The area of assessment and evaluation in drama is riddled with complexity. Most emphasis at the moment is on the more thoughtful structuring of the drama experience and evaluation of the relative success or failure of the drama lesson as a whole with respect to the identified aims and objectives. This is natural enough in the present educational climates with pressures for more rigorous curriculum evaluation. There is, however, as yet, little emphasis on the way teachers evaluate their own performance, although lesson evaluation and teacher evaluation are so obviously interlinked. I have presented evidence of the growing concern with assessment and evaluation above, but in many ways this only serves to underline the continuing gulf between theory and practice which is reflected in a number of ways. The first indication is the depressingly large number of teachers who are aware of the Schools Council Project but who even now have not yet bothered to *read Learning through Drama*. A second and ultimately more important one is the general lack of *real* (as opposed to *professional*) interest in problems of assessment and evaluation; a recent Association of Drama Tutors conference on the assessment of practical work had to be cancelled because of lack of interest. If teachers working in higher education are not interested, then how can we expect our students and colleagues in schools to be? Another stumbling block is the continuing power of 'intuition' in the drama teacher's thinking about his role. (Ironically enough this is used in defence when in a stricter sense it could be used in attack. That however is another article.) Dorothy Heathcote herself (again ironically be-cause she is considered to be one of the greatest 'intuitive' teachers) has spoken out against the cult: 'I should like to explode this as a myth because I believe that much of these so-called talents and flairs can in fact be taught, and that all teachers can in some degree learn what they are, and also how to apply them through their own teaching personality, in their own conditions and circumstances.'[15]

In my interviews with teachers 'intuition' was generally explained in terms of 'sensitivity', and 'feeling in the bones', both the products of experience. This, I think, is the key. Intuition *can* involve creative leaps and be the source of the necessary flexibility, the necessary ability to make connections, the ability to feel the 'rightness' and 'wrongness' of potential courses of action, but only, and then to a limited degree, in teachers of wide and high quality experience. The inexperienced teacher, on the other hand, has nothing on which to base intuition apart from some degree of sensitivity to group dynamics borne of his work as a student, and is therefore at a loss from the start. He may be lucky and be apprenticed to a thriving department where true in-service training can take place, but if not he will often find himself as the only drama teacher, expected to teach successfully *and* to innovate at the same time. His models will be (if he has been lucky in his training) 'intuitive' teachers of great ability, but once in school he will be left like Witkin's teacher (Witkin, pp. 89–90), unable to create conditions for the achievement of reflexive control of the media and, therefore, in no position to move on from the crude evaluative point of 'it worked because they enjoyed it' or 'it didn't work because they were bored.' The long-term need in such a situation is a radical restructuring of curriculum courses in drama as offered by the colleges, polytechnics, and universities. Such restructuring is made all the more difficult by falling applications for specialist drama teaching courses. In some colleges, the small numbers involved necessitate teaching BEd students alongside BA drama students and curriculum content tends to go by the board. A more immediate need is the creation of 'bridging' material between frameworks for assessment and evaluation to its realization in practice. This might be provided in the form of case study material such as that provided in parts of *Learning through Drama*, backed up by commercially produced and easily available video-tape and film material. (A more fully elaborated and supported version of the Schools Council Drama Project's *Take Three* provides a useful model.)

One cannot, obviously, separate the pressures on teachers to evaluate their work and performance from the issue of accountability in general. Increasingly the drama teacher finds himself having to explain what he is doing to the various significant others who constitute his 'world': other teachers, interview panels, LEA Advisers, headteachers, parents, and pupils. Whether he likes it or not he is becoming accountable. Now, as Elliott so clearly argues,[16] one of the most important conditions of public accountability is the presupposition that teachers are able to consciously self-monitor (and therefore evaluate) their activities. As I have tried to indicate above, this is not always or entirely the case; Elliott is slightly more generous but his point remains the same:

> This ability is an essential component of accountability, and from my experience of trying to help teachers self monitor, I would assert that it is not a very highly developed ability within the profession. . . . It is not

so much the potential in teachers which is lacking here as the institutional contents in which they work. Few schools in my experience give much priority to supporting self monitoring in classrooms. This is reflected in the lack of time available and the lack of rewards given for systematic reflection on classroom practice. As a result much of what teachers do in classrooms is habitual, routine and unconscious. (p. 103)

In 1976 Elliott produced a major article on accountability,[17] designed to help the teacher become aware of' any discrepancies between his conception of his responsibilities as a teacher and the consequences of his actions'. From the ability to recognize his accountability to his pupils the teacher should eventually have the confidence to expose and explain his work to a range of increasingly pressing audiences (fellow teachers, inspectors, parents, etc.).

One of the most important moments of 'explanation' in a drama teacher's career has traditionally been the audience with the headmaster. Sadly, in some places the obligatory essay on 'justifying the place of drama in the curriculum to the head' continues to be set, and here I cannot resist the temptation to reproduce a marvellous example of the genre which, though not a little tinged with satire, still remains 'true'.

ACT I.   Scene I.

A Secondary Head's Office

Enter Stuart Dent, a student

HM   Mr Dent, in your prospective TP timetable you have put down a period per day of [*looks at timetable*] ah, yes – drama for every class you teach.

SD   Yes?

HM   Well, Mr Dent, I feel this is somewhat excessive in view of the amount of PT they do already. 'Mens sana in corpore sano' by all means, but –

SD   But this isn't just physical exercise, drama is a means of expression, it's a release of tension, its a cleansing experience.

HM   It sounds like a laxative, Mr Dent. To be serious, English is a means of expression, PT provides a release of tension and RI is a cleansing experience. Why should we do drama?

SD   To be completely frank Mr HM, don't you ever feel the urge to dress up, don't you ever go to fancy dress parties?

HM   Yes, of course! But if you are going to teach drama just to indulge fantasies you can forget it!

SD   But its not a fantasy, its a very basic human feeling. When you dress up you are putting yourself aside, and becoming another. There is a disguise you can wear and so you can put all those characteristics of yourself, that you like best, forward.

HM   So you mean drama is being other people.

SD   Yes, almost. It's more like being yourself, but appearing to be someone else.

HM   Acting behind a disguise you feel safe to bring out those more vulnerable parts of yourself.

SD   Yes. Yes. [*nodding*] That is what I think drama appeals to, this instinct. The experience is cathartic.

HM   And how do you implement this in practice. Hand out masks and fancy dress and say 'be yourself'?

SD   The teacher need never say that to any child in so many words. Nor could he start straight away, even assuming that what I have said could be practised just like that. With drama you have to start at the bottom. You can't do fascinating exoiting things with a class of 39 isolates, and that's what children are really, especially adolescents and children who've just arrived here from primary school. First of all, the teacher can foster a feeling of 'groupness', a kind of –

HM   Team spirit?

SD   Yes sir, just that. In a class there are those that need to be 'brought in' to the action and they all want to belong. Take it from me, drama can unify children.

HM   So can rugby.

SD   Rugby has to be played brilliantly well before it can be said to be a 'team' game and not 30 individuals, every boy out to score a try for himself. Drama at times makes it impossible not to cooperate.

HM   I can understand that this drama *can* provide this group confidence, but how?

SD   Not immediately, of course. Self-confidence, or at least a modicum of it, comes first, which is why a teacher might spend months with the children working with them as a whole group.

HM   Puppeteering.

SD   Could be, if the teacher isn't sensitive. But drama lessons and curricula are open-ended enough in practice to allow for feedback from the children influencing, in fact controlling, what comes next. We move at the children's pace, not at the pace of the syllabus.

HM   Flexibility is the keynote of the dramatic syllabus [*with the air of Chairman Mao venting a thought*].

SD   Should be engraved on every drama teacher's heart.

HM   So you allow them a period of adjustment to the new experiences, and then what Mr Dent?

SD   Well, it's more than that, pairs and group work is the logical progression, but the child 'happening' on his own is it. It's what goes on up here that counts [*taps head*]. I believe you can open their eyes to what they do. Encourage a little self-criticism, a little, and please God a lot, of awareness. Could you drink a cup of tea without the cup of tea?

HM   Ha! Hm! Well in the interests of science [*he attempts to mime tea drinking*].

SD   Pardon me for saying so HM, but how big was the saucer? You appeared to be holding a dinner plate and a soup tureen, not cup and saucer.

HM   *[laughs]* Quite so! Quite so! I have always drunk tea but never paid sufficient attention to how I do it. You are assuming an extension of this to the rest of life.

SD   By and large.

HM   About 'group and pairs' work?

SD   Pairs work is a stage in interdependence. One can set exercises that can only be solved by two working together and so on into groups.

HM   What about their lines.

SD   Lines?

HM   What they say?

SD   Well they don't *have* to say anything at all. It's not easy to do speech improvisations. I should be happy to arrive this TP at pairs work speech. There's a nice exercise for encouraging concentration.

HM   Now *that* I *can* see some point in. Sorry, do go on.

SD   Well there's more than one, and such things as speech flow, and space awareness.

HM   Jargonese to me, I'm afraid.

SD   Meaningful jargon though. All concerned with making the child aware of how much is in himself and how much is of others; of how much space he occupies; of how he moves; why certain feelings can be more emotive than others.

HM   Mr Dent, I'm not convinced, but I'm prepared to let you have a go with the lower classes.

SD   But what I've said applies to them all, they all need, or would benefit from, drama.

HM   Patience, Mr Dent, Rome wasn't built in a day. Convince me with some small successes and I'll reconsider.

SD   Well, thank-you.

HM   Good day, send in the other student will you. Good luck.

    [Exit student; enter another student]

HM   Mr Chippie, what makes you put one period of woodwork per day for every class you teach?

C   Ah! Yes.[18]

The tutor who set this essay was, in fact, conducting an interesting experiment. One group of students had to justify educational drama in schools without using any of the 'in-terms' then available, while the other group had a free hand. His comments on the results are interesting and relevant. The former group was a lot clearer and far more cogent, while the latter soon became bogged down in jargon. 'The implication is that the subject is a great deal better understood than the terminology of the subject.... Some answers read like mystical incantations of magic words, as if a spell was being cast to petrify the reader into amazed immobility' (p. 7). My interviews with teachers nearly ten years later confirm that this is still a viable interpretation. In their explanations of both what they do and how they do it, many teachers are trapped by the 'official' language of drama, and there is a great and ironical danger that the language of *Learning through Drama* will become the new orthodoxy with 'process', 'symbolization' and the 'negotiation of meaning' replacing Sladeian 'concentration', 'inflow' and 'outflow' in the working vocabulary *without necessarily being fully understood*. What seems to be happening is a change in the rhetoric which masks the 'business-as-usual' reality of the classroom.

In my interviews with teachers I was particularly interested in exploring their perceptions of the influences on them in respect of evaluation and accountability. Various factors emerged: initial training, type and ethos of school, age and ability of pupils, type of drama already existing, the range and extent of external pressures, and exposure to current relevant developments in education. Time and again the fundamental problem of the inadequacy of initial training reared its head. Almost unanimously, teachers felt that there had been very little, if any, consideration of the many-sided issue of evaluation in their training. They were left feeling (and sometimes believing) that the whole thing was magically 'intuitive' and dependent purely on experience. Some felt that while most student teachers, of all subjects, effectively had to retrain to meet the reality of school anyway, the problem in drama teaching was more acute since the tendency of what passed for 'experience' to reinforce 'bad' habits had more pronounced negative effects in arts teaching.

In answer to the question of how they explained themselves to 'the world' in terms which 'the world' could understand, they were at pains to point out that much depended on the extent to which they were forced to identify the various elements (other teachers, parents, etc), and the relative importance they were bound (by the ethos of the school) to give to these. From their replies it was obvious that the process of 'explanation' involves a prior perception of what 'the world' *will* understand and entails decisions regarding what the drama teacher wants the world to understand.

Teachers also brought up the interesting point of staffing policy (of both the school and department) since the school as a whole is also involved in the business of explaining itself.

At this point I would like to present a selection of case students. Teacher *A* is the head of drama at an academically minded comprehensive high school. He was college of education trained (BEd) and has four years of teaching experience in this his first school. The school is streamed and at the end of the first year the top stream starts Latin ... and the rest do drama. In terms of his career he sees drama as possibly a dead end in itself and preserves his link with English. He claims to have ceased to think in terms of 'aims and objectives' in any real way, mainly as a reaction against academic waffle! He realizes that 'enjoyment' is only part of the answer and worries about whether his pupils have crossed from 'enjoyment'/'play' to 'drama'. The 'production' model is his tool of evaluation – 'if they do it well, they must have developed through practical work.' His position is both intuitive and sceptical: 'In the end it simply comes down to a feeling of whether you think a particular child or group has succeeded in what they were doing.... There's no structure to *a* drama lesson.... There's no way at all of evaluating it at specific stages. There's no way of evaluating each child.... It's not a concrete subject.... If you do try to apply structure to them I think in many ways you're destroying what you're initially setting out to create.' As head of department he is aware that he is the spokesman for drama in the school and his long-term objective is 'to convince staff and pupils of the importance of drama'. Where parents are concerned, he tends to say, 'Come back in five years time and notice the difference in your child having done drama.' He is aware of the dangers of mystification and tries to use such terms as 'imagination', 'communication with people', 'talking', 'skills' and 'confidence'. He moves if anything towards simplification, 'even if it means doing a disservice to the subject.' Like many teachers he believes that to get parents and teachers to come to productions and workshops is the best form of 'explanation'. With other teachers he tends to beware of going beyond explanation to defence and considers that the pupils provide valuable informal feedback to other teachers.

Teacher *B* is second in the same department, has a degree in English with subsidiary drama, and a postgraduate teaching certificate in drama and English. She sees herself as 'an English teacher with an interest in drama', and considers the syllabus prepared by teacher *A* to be important mainly from the point of view of continuity. Her main problem in evaluating both herself and the lesson is 'how much help you ought to give them'. Production is also her evaluative tool: 'How do you evaluate something without seeing it in a finished production?' The presence of an O/A-level drama course has not affected her attitude to evaluation since the course is 'almost seen as an offshoot of English'. She is worried about 'very extrovert drama teachers, waving their arms about' and wonders how many of them upset the children and 'tell them what to do'. Here she touches on an important point – the unconscious level of 'explanation' which is interpreted by others in terms of such 'incidentals' as dress, behaviour, and relationships with children. With parents she tends to emphasize 'end-product' and long-term objectives related to the development of imagination and creativity. Alone amongst those interviewed, she gave more importance to this aspect of 'learning through drama' than the more usual social education justification. With other teachers she emphasizes drama's value in enabling lower stream pupils to succeed, but feels hampered by the prevailing identification of drama with 'productions'.

Teacher *C* is college trained (BEd English and history), her drama experience being derived from work with the Liverpool Everyman Youth Theatre TIE team, and study for a national in-service teaching qualification. She teaches in a middle school and is effectively head of department. Her work is theme-based and always ends in a 'product' – film, tape or presentation. In answer to a question about aims and objectives, her reply was simply, 'I do what I know they can do.' What does she evaluate? Originality, quality and extent of communication, and ability of the children to work together. How does she evaluate? 'I don't think I can ... as I'm watching them it happens.' On productions: 'It doesn't matter whether it's a flop, good or bad, if they enjoy it that's enough because it's their time and work.' In her contact with other members of staff she believes that they find it difficult to understand drama apart from the point of view of texts and the 'school play'. On the other hand, she has always been independent of other departments and feels that this gives her freedom to negotiate with the head directly. When asked by parents, she explains that drama is 'like a sociology course ... one of the most practical ways of getting people to communicate, to talk to each other, to listen and to work together ... if it does that then it's good.' She tries to get them away from the idea that drama equals classics and texts using the model of medieval and street theatre to reveal that 'it's entertainment as well. 'Her emphasis is also on the use of the imagination and drama as an approach to different types of content (for example, history). As far as other teachers are concerned, she tries to let her work speak for itself. She is nothing if not forthright. 'Somebody asked me once if they [her class] were being trees. I said, "No, they're being people".' She gives a standing invitation, 'Come in and see what we're doing.' This is rarely taken up by teachers in the school, although the LEA Adviser regularly sends people along. She also revealed that she is soon to be required to produce an explanation and justification of drama to be presented to the school governors.

Teacher D is the LEA Adviser. He is college trained (Certificate) and gained extra experience with the Liverpool Everyman and participation in the ADB (Ed). He still claims to be essentially intuitive and doesn't write evaluations unless something goes either very well or very wrong. In general he follows Witkin and admits to having difficulties in running 'aims and objectives' courses for teachers who really want tips and ideas. He does, however, make the point that drama teachers rarely go to 'sit down and talk' courses, so perhaps there is room for them. In terms of accountability, he also points out that in secondary schools the specialist nature of subjects tends to protect the drama teacher from criticism and comment in general from other members of staff. Where parents are concerned, he stresses confidence and communication and weights the social aspect 'very, very heavily'. Drama provides the 'tools for living' and he plays down preconceptions about 'acting' and 'theatre'. Like teacher A he is aware of the dangers of mystification and tries to avoid a specialist vocabulary with parents. On the other hand, he occasionally uses such a vocabulary with colleagues, mainly for status reinforcement. Again, like teacher A, he aims for simplicity, illustrating such concepts as 'confidence' and 'communication' with concrete examples of work culled from various sources.

It is ultimately very difficult to determine exactly *how* teachers evaluate themselves, especially in the light of the continuing anti-theoretical bias of arts teachers in general. Their evaluation of both their own performance and the drama lesson itself is hindered by the reluctance to derive more specific objectives from general aims. This is all the more remarkable in the light of the uniformity in the statement of long-term aims with only the occasional shift of emphasis.

Confusion still reigns in certain quarters, as is shown by the following extract from a drama syllabus: 'to be communicated to other potential teachers of drama'; 'Drama periods should be looked upon as sessions as drama as such cannot be taught and is therefore not as such a lesson. This, however, is no excuse for ill-constructed sessions.' [!] All the syllabus outlines I have read have been designed not only to help young or inexperienced teachers but also to 'justify' drama to senior decision-makers in the school. Such 'explanations of drama' tend to emanate from secondary specialists who are attempting to define drama as a *subject* in order to be able to fight from a position of strength. This strong subject definition is achieved at the expense of the 'drama as method' model, and many non-drama teachers are beginning to realize that many drama teachers are only paying lip-service to ideas of integration. In line with this strong emphasis on drama as a subject in its own right is the move in certain quarters to explore the possibilities of 'explaining' drama in terms of instrumental objectives which carry higher status than expressive objectives. This is revealed by the interest in behavioural objectives as applied to 'social drama'. As Witkin notes, the social adjustment theme expressed through the emphasis on analysis and discussion is rapidly becoming a major justification for drama in schools. This interest is paralleled by the flight from, or the playing down of, the emotional content of the drama experience.[19]

Some years ago John Pick said, 'Too easily in the present climate we can do what we know passes an hour or two with the children and explain to all interested that we are "developing the personality", "teaching self-awareness", "letting the child work out his emotional problems", or any of a dozen other half-baked pieces of modish nonsense.'[20] Is it too much to ask, after the initiatives of Witkin and McGregor *et al.*, that the colleges, polytechnics and universities get to grips with what will be a major stumbling block in the next few years and provide teachers with the necessary tools to carry out the basic tasks of self-evaluation and jargon-free explanation and justification?

Notes

1 CLEGG, D. (1973) 'The dilemma of drama in education', in *Theatre Quarterly*, 3, 9, pp. 31–42.
2 DES (1968) *Education Survey 2: Drama*, HMSO.
3 McLURE, J.S. (1968) *Curriculum Innovation in Practice*, HMSO.
4 EISNER, E.W. (1969) 'Instructional and expressive educational objectives: Their formulation and use in curriculum', in POPHAM, W.J. (Ed.) *Instructional Objectives*, Chicago, pp. 1–31.
5 CROMPTON, J. (1973) 'A syllabus for drama?', in *Young Drama 3*, October, pp. 145–8.
6 BYRON, K. (1974) 'Drama – subject of method?', in *Young Drama*, February, pp. 29–33, 43.

7   SPALDING, P. (1974) 'Drama – subject and method,' in *Young Drama*, June, pp. 74–7.
8   EISNER, E.W. (1967) 'Educational objectives. Help or hindrance?', in *School Review*, 75, pp. 250–82.
9   HOETKER, J. (1975) 'Researching drama: An American view', in STEPHENSON, N. and VINCENT, D. (Eds) (1975) *Teaching and Understanding Drama*, NFER.
10 DAVIES, H. (1975) 'Drama: Aims and objectives' (Parts 1 and 2), in *Information for Drama*, winter 1975 and spring 1976.
11 HOETKER, *op. cit.*
12 GRIFFITHS, D. (1970) *The History and Role of the Drama Adviser*, unpublished thesis for Institute of Education, University of Durham.
13 O'NEILL, C., LAMBERT, A., LINNELL, R. and WARR-WOOD, J. (1977) *Drama Guidelines*, Heinemann Educational Books in association with London Drama.
14 MCGREGOR, L. (1977) 'Assessing drama. Some implications', in *Educational Review*, 29, 4, pp. 267–72.
15 Quoted in DEVERALL, J. (1975) 'Drama: Subject and service' (Part 2), in *Young Drama*, June, p. 56.
16 ELLIOTT, J. (1977) 'Conditions of public accountability', in *Cambridge Journal of Education*, 7, 2, pp. 100–4.
17 ELLIOTT, J. (1976) 'Preparing teachers for classroom accountability', in *Education for Teaching*, 100, Summer, pp. 49–50.
18 BAKER, W. (1970) 'Explain to a headmaster who knows nothing about educational drama why you think it should be taught as a basic subject throughout the school', in 't', magazine of the Drama Department, Alsager College of Education, pp. 7–8.
19 BOLTON, G. (1976) 'Drama teaching. A personal statement', in *Insight*, Summer, BCTA.
20 PICK, J. (1973) 'Five fallacies in drama', in *Young Drama*, February, pp. 6–11.

10 Reflections on the Initial Training of Drama Teachers: Past, Present and Future

John Norman

The papers presented so far in this collection have debated the nature, practices and evaluation of drama in schools. In this paper, John Norman focusses the debate on the initial training of teachers. He presents a bleak picture of the past, present and future of drama in education courses and, while he cites the negative influences of the dead hand of conventional academic practice, the demarcation of academic, educational and professional studies and the control exercised by universities and the CNAA, more significantly, he places moral responsibility on the tutors of these courses. He contends that there has been little, if any, change in the nature, style and orientation of teacher training for drama during the period of growth and decline of initial training courses, principally because tutors who in the main are not experienced classroom practitioners have not been interested in change. He criticizes both traditional theatre bound courses, with their emphasis on aesthetic, academic and personal development, and those which seem rooted in sociological theory for their lack of explicit commitment to preparing teachers to use drama effectively in schools; and, by inference, he links this with the failure to establish drama in education firmly on the school curriculum. For the future he proposes specialist and non-specialist courses which focus on enactive teaching and learning techniques across the curriculum, and which do not perpetuate the 'absurd' separation of subject and method work, and of theory from practice.

In one sense, writing an article about the pre-service training of drama teachers in 1982 is rather like sticking your finger in the dyke after the water has escaped. Quite simply, during recent years there has been the most amazing destruction of teacher training courses offering some form of drama as a major study at BEd or Certificate level. From the golden days of 1973 when 63 colleges ran BEd or Certificate drama courses, not including the various PGCE courses with a drama option, by the beginning of 1982 we had reached the stage where it was possible to take a BEd drama course in only eight polytechnics or colleges of higher education, although many institutions still offer drama as a minor or optional course.

It would not be fair to suggest that drama has been the only victim of the cuts, closures, amalgamations and rationalizations which successive govern- ments have imposed on teacher education. With one or two notable subject exceptions, every aspect of teacher education has been affected, as small and caring institutions have been replaced by ever larger and less efficient ones. Vision and innovation have been replaced by cynical pragmatism, in which flexibility of response to ever-changing fads and fancies is the key to survival, especially if it comes with an expensive machine attached. Dejected colleagues stagger towards their crockful of Crombie and shake their heads over the latest DES projections which confidently predict no further jobs for new primary teachers before 1990. In the light of this projection, one wonders how we can justify training any teachers at all and, indeed, it is increasingly difficult to spend three years training young people of quality and caring when the chances of most of them ever practising their craft are just about nil. School rolls fall, class sizes rise, behaviourism and functionalism gain strength – in short, teacher education in general and drama training in particular have probably reached an all-time low.

Yet paradoxically, while opportunities for drama training diminish and school posts and support services are under great pressure, there has been an undoubted growth of interest in the potential of drama in education (DIE). National associations are flourishing, especially those which represent the interests of practising teachers organized at local level. There has been a spate of new books on educational drama which, whatever their quality, are a useful indicator of current interest, since publishers are not noted for their philanthro- pic support of lost causes. At least three significant journals are being produced and a wide variety of conferences continue to attract support, particularly if they address themselves to serious educational issues rather than pandering to the teachers' tendency to seek easy answers which merely maintain current practice. Similarly, many forms of in-service education for drama teaching, short, long part-time and award-bearing courses have continued to develop. In the case of the few one-year full-time Advanced and MA courses where recruitment has decreased, it is not for lack of interest but rather because of the difficulty of obtaining secondment. From some experience of these various activities, it is hard to escape the impression that a growing number of teachers want to explore the possibilities of DIE. Many who have had some form of specialist pre-service training have come to recognize the partial nature of that training and many others who did not encounter drama in their training at all are seeking new and active approaches to learning appropriate to an in- creasingly restive and questioning school population. In this chapter I explore the challenge which the paradox of a decrease in training opportunities and an increase in teacher interest implies, in the belief that if suitably radical answers can be found, despite the gloom of the current situation, all may yet not be lost.

While not wishing to present a historical survey of the nature and develop- ment of initial training courses, it is useful to reflect on past influences on the current context. Although no standard course has ever been devised, it is possible to discern some general trends. The 'average' BEd or Certificate drama major course includes many of the following elements: the history of drama and theatre, the study of dramatic literature, practical and skills work in theatre arts, speech and communication skills, technical and design aspects of theatre, the historical development of DIE, theatre in education (TIE), use of DIE, provision and resources for drama and the nature and practice of DIE. Even these general headings are problematic, since they are likely to mean very different things to different people. Hodgson, writing in 1972, worrying about the increasing academic demands of the universities in validating BEd courses and the enormous disparity between courses, outlined what he saw as the four basic essentials for a drama major course:[1]

1 the extension of personal and individual qualities and powers of expression;
2 the development of particular teaching skills where movement, noise and space are involved;
3 the acquisition of a growing fund of material and an expanding appreciation of its qualities;
4 an understanding of the different uses of drama to avoid a confusion of aims and values.

These elements may reasonably be seen as aims, but one wonders for what. There is a sense here of a course which, while broadly relating to training for teaching, is as much concerned with what he called 'a different kind of training and education which has parity of esteem with that of the universities'.

Similar concerns emerge from the aims of a CNAA validated BEd drama major course of which I have some direct personal knowledge. The aims of the course read as follows:

During the course a student:
1 Is encouraged within the course group context to gain increased perceptions of his culture and to articulate these perceptions.
2 Experiences and investigates some of the ways people make representations of their view of reality which they present to themselves and others using various media; and attempts to situate these processes in their historical, social and cultural context.
3 Is encouraged to regard his personal development and professional training as a unified process over a broad area of study.
4 Participates in group work which is wide ranging and refers to specific personal action in the social and political sphere.
5 Is encouraged to think of the preceding points as providing a continuing and developing experience of the course as a whole as opposed to a series of finite and contained studies.

From these aims, prospective students could be forgiven for thinking they were applying for a sociology and cultural studies course. There is no mention of any explicit commitment to preparing teachers to use drama effectively in schools or indeed any kind of teaching process or even practical drama work. However, these aims, while wholly flabby in every respect, do include some interesting notions of culture, social perspective and the unity of theory and practice which would, I suspect, not be found in many similar course descriptions. Of the 24 units which comprised this course, only three were explicitly concerned with DIE, while perhaps four others had some link with children or teaching. The remainder were concerned with communications and society, Brecht, naturalism, modern English dramatists, group work studies and practical theatre projects. Although there was some commitment to group practical work, it was possible for a student to pass this course without ever having taught drama in any school, either on official teaching practice or on placement arising from the major study area.

It would be very easy for those who believe in a vocational and professional orientation for teacher training to be wholly dismissive of such a course. However, it could be seen to represent a significant development from the majority of 'theatre-bound' BEd courses, in that it seeks to give students a wider perspective on the nature of drama in a social context. To be simply dismissive, too, is to miss the point, as there is a large complex of factors related to the development of these drama courses which needs to be understood.

To summarize, the large number of BEd drama major courses which developed between 1966 and 1974 may be characterized as follows: three/ four-year courses in the study of drama and theatre with some stress on the cultural, aesthetic and literary tradition associated with the form. Students were encouraged to develop the various skills of the medium of theatre and some understanding and experience of informal approaches to doing drama were offered, such as improvisation, theatre games and group playmaking. Such concern as there was for the teaching of drama was largely informed by the work of E.J. Burton, Peter Slade, Brian Way and Richard Courtney, and the justification for the inclusion of such work in the school curriculum concerned itself with personal development exemplified by confidence, self-expression, linguistic competence, imagination, concentration and movement skills and with initiation into the rich world of dramatic and theatrical culture, in the hope of producing, if not an active theatre-making generation, then at least a theatre-going public. The aims of these courses seem to be a strange compromise between a concern for the personal development of the student as an end in itself and the requirements of a quasi-academic university-style course in the study of drama.

This generalized account of the 'average' BEd drama course is gleaned from the reading of many syllabuses, from personal experience of training and from talking to drama teachers all over the country. There may well be notable exceptions to this view, but they are few and far between. Talk to any group of drama teachers trained in this period (or subsequently) and you will find it hard to discover any who believe their training prepared them in any very particular way for the business of teaching drama. It is, however, interesting to note that many will admit to having enjoyed their courses hugely and look back with some nostalgia to those heady days of personal growth before drama became so very serious.

Many of the ideas expressed in the courses of this period still prevail and yet as long ago as 1971 serious criticism of the style of drama teaching was voiced by Dorothy Heathcote[2] and that stream of criticism has continued ever since. Heathcote commented on the tendency to teach conventional drama areas and expressed the view that 'many teachers emerge with the skill to teach 5% of the school population, when they could emerge capable of teaching 95%. It is not their youth or inexperience which holds them back. It is the bias which we give to their training. Many teachers of drama emerge with too little academic background to their work and also too little experience of thinking and talking with precision about their job.' She went on to imply that the teaching of DIE requires the synthesizing of a variety of skills and understandings which could not be drawn from courses in conventional theatre alone. Under the heading 'A Possible New Curriculum', she proposed an experimental course which included elements of the exploration of myth and legend, dramatic forms, group dynamics, anthropology and play, motivations in learning, personal values and teacher types, signs and symbols, non-verbal signals and a variety of teacher skills concerned with questioning, focussing, raising tension and classifying action. I cannot comment on the reaction to such a proposal from those involved in teacher training, but there is little evidence that such suggestions were taken up then or are being taken up now. Clearly, the implications of such a proposal are wide-reaching, but most important is the vision of a style of drama teaching underlying this proposal which was radically different from practice in teaching and training current in 1972.

McGregor, Tate and Robinson in 1976 made various comments on the initial training of drama teachers.[3] They proposed that any drama teacher should have a knowledge of the drama process and its application in a wide variety of situations, be aware of the effects of their decision-making, sensitive to learning opportunities as they arise and able to emphasize particular aspects of the process in practice. Also the teacher should be able to create and devise learning structures, take roles and relate activities to the needs of the child's development. These elements, plus some understanding of the social, political and educational context of drama teaching, are seen as providing a basic set of aims. Their comments, drawn from the experience of the Schools Council Project: Drama 10–16, Sharpless[4] and the Training Conference,[5] indicate that 'although many courses contain some "method work", there is evidence that in a number of courses, practical training for the classroom is not considered to be of paramount importance' and that 'many courses in drama which relied heavily on the teaching of literary and traditional theatre skills are not necessarily appropriate for the preparation of those who are to teach drama in schools.' They identified the problem of those submitting courses with a large practical element to CNAA – that they believed that such courses were in danger of being rejected. They suggested that CNAA did not take this view and recommended that every initial training course for the training of drama teachers should contain a compulsory unit of DIE.

It is important to note that these comments arose from a view of 'drama as a learning medium', which cannot be held to have been generally accepted at the time. Ironically enough, in what was in some ways a radical and important study, their final comments on training serve to indicate the extent to which they had wholly failed to understand the seriousness of the problem as they unwittingly offered solace to the vast majority of incompetent and reactionary trainers of drama teachers. They suggest that 'a way must be found to use the practical skills of drama within both the subject teaching area and the method work, as well as providing students with the ability to use these in the school experience' and 'training should contain two interrelating elements: learning to use the process themselves at their own levels and having direct experience of classroom work and what it entails.' Further, they ask, 'How much importance and time is given to both practical and academic aspects of training?' and finally, 'however good an initial course may be, the quality of teaching is usually developed through experience in the classroom', a view supported by Male,[6] whom they quote as saying, 'The newly qualified teacher has seldom absorbed and balanced these experiences to the extent that they enable him to commence teaching in an organized and competent manner ... by virtue of the nature of initial training, experience of relating work to the total learning pattern cannot be given.' Thus, without so much as a sign of regret, they totally miss an important opportunity to make radical proposals. By framing their recommendations in terms of existing structures and beliefs in teacher education, such as the absurd separation of subject and method work, the clear distinction between theory and practice and the overwhelmingly held view that it is not really possible to produce teachers who on day one of their teaching careers can actually promote learning effectively, they fail to identify the underlying causes of so much of the chaos that is teacher education. Further, they seem to offer support to the old myth of the desirability of doing drama at the students' own level, the very myth which had supported so much of the theatre-based activity of existing courses. Finally, the idea of one unit of compulsory DIE is absurd. All courses contain one unit. The problem is that they do not contain 20 units in a radically different school-focussed integrated training course which sees practice as theory in action and pursues understandings arising from any relevant source in the solution of real teaching problems.

Since the early seventies then, there has been much criticism of initial training courses in drama, some of it radically constructive, some less thoughtful but always representing a changing view of DIE from that espoused by the early courses. During this time, we have seen the spectacular rise and fall of the BEd drama course and, more importantly, an enormous growth in understanding of the potential and practice of what Bolton has called 'Type D Drama'[7] that is, drama for understanding or drama as a learning medium. What evidence is there that this fund of new insights has been applied to the training of drama teachers or the practice of classroom drama? O'Hara has recently published the results of his enquiry into BEd drama courses, which makes fascinating, if distressing, reading.[8] He set out to research the views of heads of drama departments responsible for the running of BEd courses and explored course objectives and course content, structure and emphasis, as well as collecting reactions to a variety of statements about the nature and practice of DIE. Subjects were asked for information on the basis of actual and preferred course descriptions and asked to indicate the importance of specific items. I will refer to some of his findings in the following analysis of the complex of factors which have influenced the development, or lack of it, in BEd major drama courses since about 1968.

It is my contention that there has been little, if any, change in the nature, style and emphasis of teacher training for drama during the whole period of growth and decline of such courses. Further, an opportunity to establish the practice of DIE on a sound and undeniable basis in the school curriculum has been missed. This opportunity will not arise again in the foreseeable future, indeed, more probably it will never arise. The factors which have influenced this situation seem to fall into three distinct categories:

1   the ideology and prevailing practice of teacher education institutions;
2   the background, attitudes and perceptions of those teaching drama courses;
3   the mediocrity, confusion and lack of insight which characterizes so much of the practice and discussion of DIE.

In commenting on these factors, I shall draw on personal experience and observation rather than any substantiating evidence. Since my comments arise from a set of personal values and perspectives on the nature of schooling and DIE, the reader who shares my views will identify with what I am saying. No amount of substantiation will influence those who hold different perspectives.

1   Since the move towards an all-graduate profession and the introduction of the BEd degrees, there can be no doubting the influence of the dead hand of conventional academic practice in teacher education. A rigid control of curriculum, teaching style and objectives has been exercised through the validation process either by universities or by CNAA and by the various institutions themselves, who have used the threat of non-validation, with its many implications for employment and status, as a means of controlling any hint of radical departure from established practice. A rigid demarcation of academic, educational and professional studies has been maintained, even though in recent years component areas have been required to demonstrate interrelations which are mostly fictitious and wholly cosmetic. Theory and practice remain separate notions, the latter being of distinctly low status, requiring only three

blocks of school practice time in most three-year courses. Teaching style remains largely instructional, with occasional concessions to seminar or workshop-style activity. Academic courses are wholly content-centred, educational courses focus mostly on very conventional perspectives, eschewing any mention of radical or challenging sources and professional studies vary from the ludicrous to the pathetic.

A grossly distorted description? I think not. I have yet to see any evidence of integrated courses which challenge the student to develop a coherent philosophical framework through the exploration of contentious issues such as values, ideology and the nature of knowledge which, allied to the practice of teaching skills, provide a sound base for satisfactory and innovatory future practice. The traditional odium which surrounds the idea of vocational training dies hard, as do the entrenched attitudes of teaching staff who jealously guard established territory. Those developments which have occurred more recently, such as the removal of major course studies for the primary student are highly supportable, but they have been tacked on to existing departmental practices where institutionalized intransigence remains paramount. Broadly, I believe that such teachers as are produced with vision, flair and an impressive range of teaching skills, styles and registers emerge in spite of their training, largely through outstanding personal qualities.

2   In such a context, it is not surprising that there has been little significant development in the nature and practice of drama courses from those described earlier. O'Hara's results, which are worthy of detailed study, show that all the literary and theatrical units of study and practical work remain in the ascendency in BEd courses. Respondents would increase students' contacts with dramatic literature and production skills, but would also not decrease the existing emphasis on the development and history of drama and theatre. In a preferred situation, greater attention would be paid to aims and objectives and the place of DIE in the curriculum, along with the skills of the drama teacher. However, work on development through drama, TIE and theories of DIE are seen as being less important than the headings mentioned above. The report concludes that the emphasis on academic studies is not supported by teaching staff who agree that, as presently constructed, BEd drama courses are not the most suitable form of training for drama teachers because not enough time or emphasis is placed on the pedagogy of drama teaching. He suggests: 'BEd Drama courses, it would seem, represent unsatisfactory compromises between lecturers' philosophy on training drama teachers and the requirements of the validating bodies'.

Further:

> The present emphasis on academic studies of theatre and literature is seriously limiting the possibility of students taking BEd drama courses developing a coherent conceptual framework of understanding which would guide their eventual practice in schools ... under prevailing

structures the aim that students would develop a personal philosophy of drama teaching through their main course programme cannot be fulfilled satisfactorily.

One unfortunate aspect of this research is that it gives no indication of what the respondents meant by 'drama in education', which term can disguise a plethora of diverse practice.

I cannot but sympathize with the view that the pressure of validating bodies and the present structures of teacher education make it difficult to alter the fundamental orientations of a course. However, such pleading has to be viewed with some suspicion since I believe that change is possible, even if to a limited extent. Can it really be possible that all attempts at radical or even minor course change have been thwarted by external influences? I suggest that the reasons for this intransigence, at a time when much more complex understandings of the learning potential of DIE have become available is in fact much more fundamental. Quite simply, the nature and practice of BEd major drama courses have not changed because the majority of those teaching the courses have not had the slightest interest in making changes.

As O'Hara indicates, the majority of such lecturers, especially those in positions of power, were and are holders of BA and MA degrees, and most have had on average only two years of teaching experience and that mostly in grammar and comprehensive schools. I submit that they have perceived themselves as teachers of drama and theatre with some commitment to practical exploration, rather than as teachers of DIE teachers. Even where attempts have been made to reorient courses, the low status of drama within the academic firmament has discouraged anything even remotely risky for fear of institutional reprisals. It is interesting to note the number of such teachers who, with audible sighs of relief, have sought refuge in the currently greener pastures of creative arts courses. These courses, which may be seen as some kind of pragmatic response to the rundown of BEd drama courses, are often uncannily like the old BEd Drama courses, exemplifying notions of personal development and liberation through the practice of the arts. It should be remembered that many such teachers had previously spent their whole careers apparently committed to the training of drama teachers and, by implication, the development of drama in schools. With a few very special exceptions, both during the 'golden years' of expansion and latterly as the world of higher education and training has undergone cataclysmic surgery, these very teachers have blithely continued doing more of the same. In 1971, in response to an article of mine,[9] an experienced teacher trainer wrote to me to protest that it was far too easy to blame the college of education staff, but the conclusion that they have much to answer for is inescapable. I submit that much of what has happened to the training of drama teachers has been done to us by others in the face of a complete lack of any serious effort on the part of the drama trainers to create a coherent educational base for their practice or to come up with any radical course proposals. The period of expansion and the period of change represented opportunities to break the mould of established practice, but while Rome burned about their ears, the trainers merely fiddled. The irrelevance, intellectual barrenness and lack of vision, indeed the deliberate rejection of a new view of DIE and its application in schools which characterized so many of the BEd drama courses has created a legacy for those who follow. It is a legacy we could well have done without!

3 Broadly then, the world of drama teachers who have had some form of specialist training seems divisible into those most concerned with 'outer form' and those concerned with 'inner meaning'. I make this statement in the belief that the orientation of initial training bears some relationship to subsequent views and practice of DIE. Bolton has suggested a rough categorization of dramatic activity into four types or orientations:[10] Type A – Exercise; Type B – Dramatic Playing; Type C – Theatre; and Type D – Drama for understanding. Since college courses have been principally concerned with types A–C, that is, with 'outer form', it is not surprising that when drama teachers meet, those whose primary interest is in 'drama for understanding' tend to find themselves in conflict with the majority whose perception of DIE is drawn from their initial training. What is at stake here is not some minor difference of activity style. Indeed, explicit in the pursuit of drama for understanding will be elements of many other types of drama. Rather, what is at stake is *a fundamental difference of ideology about the nature, function and values of drama in the school context*. Given the trends in the most recent literature of educational drama, it would be understandable to believe that this deep ideological division no longer exists. However, my experience leads me to suggest otherwise, and a brief glance at the content of in-service courses, conference programmes and much current practice would tend to confirm this impression. Thus the content of initial drama courses and the teacher education context, whose teaching style and format does not encourage the questioning of established educational values, combine with the drama teachers' perception of low-status work to produce a retreat into familiar practice. From such a position, the implications of the theory and practice of drama for understanding, which focus on teaching values, ideology and broader questions about the curriculum and its evaluation, can be very threatening indeed. Since most of the teachers who might now be moving into teacher training (if there were opportunities) were themselves trained in the 1960s and 1970s, it cannot be assumed that there would be substantial change. Sadly, we have seen so much of the energy which might have gone into establishing a secure base for the practice of drama spent in defending fixed positions. One cannot but feel that drama teachers have been and continue to be their own worst enemies.

I have spent some time on the three principal sets of factors which have affected the development of initial training for drama teaching because it seems to me vital to understand what has happened. I do not believe that the placing of blame is a worthwhile exercise in itself but, if we are to identify strategies for future development, we must both learn from the past and endeavour not to repeat it. It is also appropriate to make explicit the values and assumptions which underpin the comments I have made.

1   That the style of DIE most appropriate to the needs of children in schools is drama for understanding, defined as follows: 'DIE is an enactive learning process deriving from our common empathetic tendency. It is a collaborative medium accessible to individuals of all aptitudes and abilities, the aim of which is to explore past, present and future experience, our own and other people's, in an attempt to make sense of the world in which we live. The unique features of this activity are (a) the taking of roles, and (b) the motive power of feeling engagement.' Implicit in this definition are the beliefs that education should harness natural energies and spring from total models of human action rather than focus on the wholly cognitive; that there is no given truth, reality is socially constructed, experience must be explored and the learners' right to make sense of experience in a secure and non-competitive context must be protected.

2   That the starting point for devising any course of training for drama teachers must be some sort of vision of the kind of world we want our children to live in and thus the kinds of teaching and learning that best serve such needs. Educators cannot go on making decisions on grounds of social and economic functionalism.

3   That the teaching and learning style of such courses must reflect the implicit and procedural values of DIE and must strive, above all else, to help students create for themselves a secure conceptual framework which supports all future strategic decision-making. This process will entail, as a starting point and central fixing throughout the course, constant reference to the question, 'What kind of teacher do you want to be?'

4   That the implications of this kind of drama concerning knowledge, the role of teacher and pupil and the problem of evaluation must be explored by students and understood in terms of future practice in the real-world context of schooling.

5   That this view of DIE and the training process associated with it may be seen as problematic within the 'message system' of teacher education. Indeed, it may well be that the conventional context of teacher education is inappropriate to the training of drama teachers.

6   That the effective training of pre-service teachers is both possible and desirable and that a professional and vocational orientation to initial training is wholly honourable and necessary. I have never been able to understand the widely held view that several years of torment in the classroom learning to be a teacher is the appropriate consequence of an initial training course, especially when it is possible to prevent such pain. Naturally, experience creates confirmation and development, but if young teachers have not been helped to equip themselves with a

secure conceptual framework and the drive and skills to reflect productively on practice, there can be no more destructive evidence of the
absolute inadequacy of initial training. While these comments are
specifically related to the training of drama teachers, they also apply
fully to the training of other secondary specialists and primary
teachers. However, there is a sense in which training for drama
teaching is more problematic both because of the unpredictable nature
of the teaching process and because of the range and diversity of
current practice. I would suggest that so much of in-service work for
drama teachers is in a sense remedial. Many of these courses are about
views of drama, learning mechanisms, skills, strategies and evaluation,
all of which should be part of initial training. That any student should
leave initial training without a very clear grasp of fundamental questions about education and a range of specific drama teaching skills is
wholly lamentable.

These are the principle assumptions and values which inform my view of
teacher education in general and drama training in practicular. Other assumptions about prevailing traditions and practice are implicit in previous comments.

Thus far I have attempted to examine the past and present situation on the
initial training of drama teachers. If my analysis is even partially accurate, it
becomes clear that there are no simple answers for the future. Simply to
propose a new kind of course within the existing BEd structure, which is itself
in doubt and undergoing radical change, would be wholly inadequate. What is
needed are proposals which take account of the lessons to be learnt from the
history of DIE and the current realities of teacher education. Such proposals
might be seen to fall into two main categories: (1) those for the training of
specialist drama teachers; and (2) those for the inclusion of some element of
DIE in the training of all primary and secondary teachers.

Let us explore the second category first. There have always been minor and
optional courses in drama in existing BEd structures, usually first-year courses
which were scaled down versions of the major study. In my experience of such
courses, 150 hours is the minimum time needed to equip primary and middle
school students with an appropriate conceptual understanding and planning,
teaching and evaluating skills gained through practical teaching projects.
This experience enables them to enhance their teaching strategies across
the primary curriculum, both in the direct use of drama techniques and in
the development of the general teaching skills such as questioning and
elicitation.

Nationally we have seen the demise of the BEd major drama course and
where any kind of replacement has occurred, as in my own institution, the
move towards a more general training for primary and middle school students
is apparent. Thus a major drama course which accounted for one-third of the
students' time (approximately 700 hours across three years) and a minor drama

course (approximately 180 hours across two years) have been replaced by an arts in education course comprising music, drama and art. The description of this course and its content, although taken from my personal experience in one institution, may be seen to represent a national pattern. Students choose one elective focus which involves up to 70 hours in Years 2 and 3 and also take additional studies in the two other areas of 16 hours each, plus some common sessions on approaches to the arts in education. In theory this course has merit, but in reality the absurd time allowance and the extreme difficulty of finding common ground between art, music and drama and the staff that teach them mean very little of value can be achieved. This course wholly exemplifies the institutional pressures, myopic decision-making and radically diverse arts practice which has been described elsewhere. It is a classic illustration of the results of attempts to recruit, and to please the DES. It enshrines a principle, but in so doing destroys the very processes which support the possibility of training primary and middle school teachers to higher levels of general competence across the curriculum. It should be remembered that this development, if indeed it can be so dignified, has been forced on a drama department with a proven record of running relevant and challenging courses wholly oriented towards classroom practice; a department staffed by teachers with substantial school experience who are still willing and able to teach children and who are welcome in local schools which have experienced the quality of student drama teaching projects; and a staff all of whom have higher degrees in education and could reasonably claim a sound grasp of most aspects of teaching and learning theory; in short, a staff who in their thinking and practice might reasonably be seen to exemplify an approach to teacher training which transcends the absurd departmental demarcations and prepares students to be active and thoughtful teachers of children. Is it surprising that such staff, in attempting to support the principle of introducing more general courses for all students, have at the same time sought to avoid the total destruction of the best elements of the old major course structure? This opposition has been viewed as intransigence, when in fact it is no more than an attempt to avoid a situation in which both the baby and the bathwater have been thrown away.

Despite the justifiable anger which has perhaps crept into the foregoing description, I still believe that a general introductory course in DIE for all primary and middle school students on BEd courses is both desirable and achievable, given certain minimum conditions. I make this proposal on the sad but realistic assumption that no radical change in the broad pattern of teacher training towards enquiry-based, school-focussed and integrated courses will ever occur because of all the professional, political, economic and perceptual constraints explored above. The proposal represents a normative functionalist compromise which would fit into existing patterns. It is worthwhile simply because experience with students leads me to believe that those who have tasted something of a DIE course and explored the resulting implications about the nature of learning and knowledge and the role of the teacher and pupil emerge immeasurably better teachers who are motivated to learn more about DIE in subsequent teaching and in-service learning.

The minimum conditions for such a course would be 180 hours spread across Years 1 and 2 with absolutely no institutionalized links with arts activities such as art, music or dance which might reasonably be grouped into an expressive arts course. Whatever tired administrators may believe, no similarities can be assumed between art and music on the one hand and DIE on the other, as these activities are currently taught. While not denying the obvious similarities of symbolic meaning-making activity, DIE moves towards process and learning intention, while art and music are mostly concerned with product and expressive activity. The course should be entitled 'Enactive Learning Techniques across the Curriculum', should relate carefully to aspects of supporting educational study and draw topic material from other course areas in social and environmental studies, moral and religious studies and reading and the language arts. It needs to be presented as a professional study area and demonstrate its application in practical teaching and research projects with other subject staff. The aims, content, pedagogy and evaluation procedures of this course would be as follows.

Aim: To provide an introductory course in DIE which assists students towards a coherent theoretical framework in support of future classroom practice.

Objectives: Students who complete this course should be able to:

1   demonstrate an understanding of the nature and procedural features of DIE;
2   utilize an awareness of the creative learning process involved in DIE and its relationship to developmental theory, with special reference to play, cognition, affect and language development;
3   develop a variety of teaching skills and strategies for the effective promotion of learning through DIE across the whole curriculum;
4   devise and execute DIE teaching in a variety of different contexts.

Outline content blocks

Year 1 (60 hours, blocks not of equal weight, nor necessarily in sequence)

(a) An introduction to the background and historical context of DIE through the literature of selected pioneers (Way, Bolton, Heathcote)
(b) An introduction to the fundamental features of DIE as a learning activity – the enactive concept, role-taking, groupwork and interaction
(c) An introduction to the procedural features of DIE – listening, sharing, problem-solving, decision-making, etc.
(d) An exploration of games as metaphor and as starting points for drama
(e) An exploration of two basic working approaches:
     (1) progressive groupwork
     (2) whole group drama

Year 2 (120 hours, arising from the work of Year 1 and drawing on students' own teaching experience)

(a) Starting points and stimuli: visual, aural, literary, mythic and historical – the isolation of contexts appropriate to children's needs and developmental stages which are rich in potential learning areas

(b) Teacher skills and strategies: teaching in role, person in role, role register, role dissonance, questioning, building belief, focussing issues, reflection and resolution, group working skills

(c) Planning for drama: the expressive objective, open and closed planning, structure and progression, flexibility, the isolation of meaning, 'play for teacher and play for children', 'dropping to the universal'

(d) Evaluating drama process and learning outcomes: skills of observation and analysis, illuminative approaches to evaluation as an indicator of current learning and future practice

(e) Justifying drama in the curriculum: consideration of the role, status and values of DIE in relation to the whole curriculum and society – exploration of personal values and structures for school-based curriculum development through drama.

Pedagogy: Throughout this course, teaching and learning will be enquiry-based and involve practical exploration of problems and skills, groupwork and practical planning and the observation and analysis of teaching in action on tape and in schools. Practical work is designed to improve the students' creative confidence in the medium, provide concrete experience and practical insights into all elements of content and be appropriate to the values of DIE in action. Opportunities for group teaching and reflection are also included.

Practical projects: In addition to the practical elements listed for each year, the course would include one practical teaching project which experience has shown is vitally necessary to provide a focus of problem-solving and decision-making and to offer a common experience for reference and demonstration of drama in action. It also provides an opportunity for the enhancement of group identity which improves subsequent group working.

Year 1: Whole-group DIE project which is group devised and offers a structured intensive experience to groups of children. Using some theatrical techniques for context and belief building, clearly defined roles and moving from closed start to open-ended resolution. More of a TIE programme in format but with no given resolution. (Examples previously used include 'Pity Me Mine Disaster' – children as miners in structured setting, oppressed by overseers who are subsequently trapped; dilemma concerns taking personal risks to save others, especially those who have been less than caring of us.) This project would be executed at least four times with different groups of children, each for approximately two hours. Repetition allows for reflection and refinement of structure and response.

Year 2: School-based group teaching (in addition to normal teaching practice). Involves choice of school and class, division of students into teaching groups of two or three, preliminary observation visit, planning of first lesson by whole student group, first lesson taught by course leader. After each lesson reflection with class teacher and planning for next session – subsequent sessions taught by student groups who may begin a new theme or continue from the previous week as appropriate. This approach, although time consuming, provides continuity of contact with children and opportunities for planning precisely as knowledge of the class is gained. All students observe and evaluate all lessons. *Assessment:* It would be appropriate to courses of this length and level to generate some five assignments which might be ordered as follows:

three course work essays of 2000–3000 words which focus on the following topics: (1) conceptual framework for the practice of DIE; (2) planning, skills and strategies in the teaching of DIE; (3) the role of DIE across the curriculum.

All essay work should include substantive reference material and relevant practical examples.

Two practical assignments as detailed to be assessed on the three elements of (1) planning and preparation; (2) execution of teaching; (3) evaluation of teacher action and learning outcomes through the submission of a 1500-word piece. These three elements could be weighted as required but must include a proportion of grade for preparation and teaching. All assignments to be moderated and each to represent 20 per cent. This assessment requires students to demonstrate competence in all objectives at a level appropriate to an introductory course of this length.

I have dealt in some detail with this course outline because it seems to provide a base model for all courses which would be designated non-specialist. The deliberate exclusion of many aspects of more traditional drama courses such as dramatic literature, theatre history and technical and theatre skills is inevitable. There is, however, an opportunity to consider the relevant application of theatre skills in solving problems associated with the practical teaching projects. Aspects of playmaking and theatre for younger children, which may have a place in the repertoire of the first and middle school teacher, could be offered separately as option courses. It is also inevitable than an introductory course of this level cannot deal adequately with questions concerning drama and theatre, symbolism, groupwork studies, approaches to evaluation, and knowledge and ideology which would be central to any major drama course. However, students will at least be aware of these problems as they are encountered in action in workshops and practical projects.

PGCE courses, both primary and secondary, tend to be organized on a similar pattern to the old BEd, that is, with education and professional studies, teaching practice and main and second method courses. These courses, so beloved of the DES planners because they are cheap to run and easily adjusted to changing requirements, would seem to offer some potential as a context for the training of specialist drama teachers, but in reality they cannot be regarded as more than non-specialist courses. Two particular problems affect these courses. In my experience graduate students of a specific academic discipline have spent little time reflecting upon the nature of their own educational experience and tend to hold fairly traditional views of education, largely informed by their own school experience. Thus they need considerable time to reorient, if indeed many ever do, to thinking about the processes of schooling. Their knowledge of schooling tends to be wholly content-centred and new approaches to education, let alone education through drama, come as something of a shock not lessened by their first experience of the average comprehensive school. Combine this problem with the obvious time constraints, and the limitations of PGCE courses in DIE begin to appear. One especially worrying trend in PGCE secondary courses is for teaching practice to be in the first two terms to avoid clashes with school and public summer exams. The result is that students have been examined in the practice of teaching before they have experienced the bulk of their method courses. Thus students can hardly be expected to cope with teaching drama in difficult secondary schools where they are expected to operate as specialist teachers. Quite apart from the obvious conclusions to be drawn about the real intentions of PGCE teacher training, the net result is a high drop-out rate, retreat to main subject teaching and the retrenchment of views, which is a dreadful waste of some highly capable and committed young teachers. There are, of course, many exceptions to this gloomy view who will succeed in teaching despite the inadequacy of their training, but postgraduate courses in drama can never be appropriate for the training of specialist secondary drama teachers. The constant irony of this situation is reinforced time and time again as graduate students are appointed to specialist drama posts in preference to BEd major drama students.

If and when PGCE teacher training courses begin to be taken seriously they could be a context for specialist drama training, but in the meantime the introductory level course described appears most appropriate – better to train students to function effectively in classroom teaching. Theatre skills related to school play work and CSE teaching can be pursued in subsequent in-service training.

All of which brings us to the thorny problem of training the specialist drama teacher – to which there are no simple solutions. It is not in devising appropriate courses that the problem lies, but rather in conceiving appropriate contexts in which such courses could be operated. In the past specialist drama teachers have been drawn from BEd major drama courses, university courses of the literary dramatic tradition followed by a PGCE year or, as in my own case, from duopartite courses split between specialist drama schools and colleges of education. This last model, while equipping students with a good range of practical theatre skills, was woefully short on relevant educational application and deeply immersed in the 'speech and drama' tradition. Similarly, the university drama departments have never shown the slightest tendency towards much other than the academic study of dramatic literature and obscure fourteenth-century stage machinery. It is unlikely that an overnight conversion to vocationally oriented courses in the educational application of drama will occur. Better, I think, to let sleeping dons lie.

Of the major existing routes to qualification as a specialist drama teacher only the BEd in colleges of higher education and polytechnics remains to be discussed I think I have made it clear that, in my view, BEd courses do not nor did manage to produce specialist drama teachers who were academically, practically and educationally secure in all aspects of practice. Nor can I believe that there is any opportunity for innovation at a time of further decrease in general provision. Although there is some evidence of a gradual breakdown of departmental intransigence, a factor which may aid the development of the non-specialist courses I have outlined, I can see no real movement towards integrated school-focussed courses. Such courses, taught by a core team, assessed on the basis of teaching problems solved, and designed to be neither subject- nor education-studies-centred, would be the minimum conditions for the training of teachers in what are, after all, synthetic professional disciplines whether it be drama in education or science in education. Merely to resurrect the old-style major courses for secondary specialist teachers cannot be desirable. Thus what is logically the most appropriate context for specialist training seems to offer little scope for furture developments.

What new possibilities do exist for specialist drama training and, indeed, is it even desirable? While it is desirable for all primary and secondary teachers to have had some non-specialist training, there is still a vital role for the specialist drama teacher, especially in secondary and further education, but not excluding primary education. Briefly, five principal functions might be defined.

1   *Classroom drama teaching* – offering school students significant learning opportunities through the practice of drama and associated activities, extended in some schools into CSE and O-level work in drama or theatre arts.

2   *Developing theatre projects* – initiating theatre work arising, where possible, from classroom work in styles and formats appropriate to the needs of young people, that is, large-cast ensemble work, project theatre devised from improvisation, research, documentary, small group TIE and children's theatre projects in the service of others; training opportunities in theatre and skills – all to be available to students of all abilities and ages on the basis of choice.

3   *Providing a bridge into the community* – through the development of outward-looking theatre work and projects performed by students creating links with special interest groups such as senior citizens, luncheon clubs, YOP schemes, church groups, etc. Developing cooperative enterprises with PTAs for events and opportunities for sharing through drama and theatre with all sections of local communities. As social and educational needs change, a major section of concern will be the role of the school in the local context, and such developments can be spearheaded by the drama teacher.

4   *Fulfilling an in-service role* – the drama teacher is uniquely qualified to make accessible to other colleagues the teaching and learning methodo-

logies implicit in DIE, including roleplay and simulation techniques. By linking team-taught projects and creating opportunities for colleagues to observe drama teaching, use materials and the resource of the teacher as, for example, person-in-role, a valuable contribution can be made to the enhancement of teaching styles in a school. This process requires considerable diplomacy and secure practice.

5   *Operating as an agent of curriculum change* (linked to 4) – drama teachers, through the practice of their art and through involvement in staff working parties, have a significant role to play in the consideration of curriculum and pedagogy in any school system. Isolationist policies and unprofessional practice do little to promote the status of drama or drama teachers.

All of these functions must be viewed in the light of the implicit and procedural values of DIE detailed earlier and clearly indicate the need for a very demanding and wide-ranging course of specialist training. However, the one orientation common to all these functions and so noticeably missing from many courses which concentrated on the study of drama or the doing of drama or both is that of *the teacher as enabler providing opportunities through many aspects of theatre and drama for others to learn about and explore significant dimensions of experience.* There may be, as I have experienced personally, great dangers in the central focus on enabling to the exclusion of the other elements of using and understanding the medium, with the result that students have no real grasp of what is essentially dramatic. Naturally it is a matter of emphasis towards the enabling orientation which should distinguish any specialist training course for teachers or other drama workers.

I do not intend here to provide a detailed outline of a specialist course beyond that implied by my previous comments and the broad headings suggested for the non-specialist course. Clearly those content headings would have to be expanded to include aspects of theatre and drama skills, cultural studies of symbolic activity, ideology and education, groupwork studies, drama and theatre in the non-school context, management and organizational skills in drama and theatre experience, approaches to text, play-making skills, assessment in examination work, role theory, gaming and simulation, integrated arts approaches and many of the details of Heathcote's proposed syllabus. Similarly, practical work to include theatre pieces, TIE and drama projects in a community context would be included in addition to the classroom-based teaching projects. However, the distinguishing feature of such a course would be the pedagogical style and the enabling orientation.

My co-editor has proposed a conceptual model for the training of drama teachers which offers a helpful insight into the framework for such a course, which I would wholly support.[11] However, it is interesting to note that he takes no account of the context within which such courses could be run and avoids the issue of balance in content in using the phrase, under 'the learning needs of students', 'knowledge of skills in drama'. This phrase could mean almost anything, and yet the issue of content balance is critical. Time spent in the exploration of nineteenth-century Romanticism and dramatic literature, for example, is time wasted. However, his chapter aptly supports the central enabling orientation and the pedagogical values appropriate to the teaching of DIE.

I have explored some current contexts for specialist drama training and concluded that they offer little hope as settings for new courses and developments. There are, however, two suggestions worth making which take account of recent developments in society, education and drama. The first concerns the recent growth of BA courses in creative arts of which there are currently seven operating in polytechnics and colleges of higher education. These courses are well subscribed and evidently moving beyond the pragmatic reasons for their birth and the academic stagnation of their infancy. There is no common course pattern and I cannot wholly support the uneasy alliance of incompatible areas of arts activity. However, in the course of which I have some knowledge, the best traditions of liberal arts work are combined with an emphasis on innovative practice and sharp critical perspectives. More importantly, the recent resubmission, particularly in the drama strand, shows a marked reorientation towards training the arts worker as animateur and enabler, capable of initiating drama activity in a variety of social contexts. I cannot pretend that words written in submissions represent the reality of practice, but should such a course continue to develop in that direction and provide students with significant skills in enabling through the arts, it could well offer a new context for the training of the specialist drama teacher. This possibility, of course, implies the redefinition of the concept of drama teacher to include working both in and out of school. It challenges the prevailing assumptions that teachers must be trained in educational studies towards context-specific teaching tasks. However, I cannot see why a student trained in the enabling orientation, which would include many aspects of current traditional training but towards the solution of real teaching problems, would not emerge capable of operating in a variety of contexts, especially if those wishing to teach in schools undertook a further PGCE course. Thus, after a period of foundation studies, operation in the medium of drama and theatre and general arts activities, options could be offered in specific directions, one of which could be school-based work. Realistically, this is more plausible than the notion of a course equipping students to operate in any context simply because of the problems and constraints of assessment. There are, I think, some possibilities here towards the training of a multi-purpose drama specialist, but a note of warning is essential. It should be remembered that many of those teaching on creative arts courses demonstrated in their BEd days a marked resistance to radical change. It may well be that nothing has really changed and that the old liberal arts drama course in whatever disguise is destined to live forever. Nevertheless, an innovation of this kind is surely worthy of exploration. It has many advantages, such as much more time than compartmentalized BEd courses, an established structure, usually good resources and possibly some staff with radical views of new approaches to learning and education who are not entrenched in the deep ruts of academic educational disciplines. Clearly such courses could never be validated as conferring qualified teacher status *per se*, but either through the PGCE course or the option system such developments might be possible.

Finally, it may be that the most potentially exciting prospect is a wholly new concept course of three years to honours entitled 'BA in Drama for Learning and Leisure'. Ideally such a course should be based in a university or institute of education which has greater control over its own validation. Such a course for the full-time training of the enabling drama worker would aim to produce specialists capable of multi-context operation and be a single-topic degree not organized as a module with other combined arts subjects. I am convinced that such a course would recruit from those who wish to fulfil the growing need for drama workers in non-school situations as have been described. Clearly the problem of qualified teacher or professional worker status remains paramount, but in the event it may be that various postgraduate one-year courses would provide the answer.

These two proposals, which I have only lightly sketched, may seem to be clutching at straws, but as the situation stands, only radical solutions will suffice. Unless new contexts are conceived and new courses proposed, the current need for and interest in the learning potential of DIE will never be satisfied. There is a body of knowledge, skills and practitioners available who hold the key to some crucial aspects of educational and social change. Alone they can do little, but with the informed and determined support of the various professional organizations who might well develop real policies for pre-service training and the many teachers searching for new approaches to the demanding educational climate of the eighties, all may not yet be lost. Indeed, the prevailing tide of education for social conformity may yet be turned.

Notes

1 HODGSON, J. (1972) 'What's it all for?', in *Drama in Education*, I, The Annual Survey, Pitmans.
2 HEATHCOTE, D. (1972) 'Training needs for the future', in *ibid.* 1.
3 MCGREGOR., TATE, M. and ROBINSON, K. (1977) *Learning through Drama*, Heinemann Educational Books.
4 SHARPLESS, S. (1975) *The Training of Drama Teachers*, unpublished MA dissertation, University of Sussex.
5 MCGREGOR, L., TATE, M. and ROBINSON, K. 'Report of the initial training conference', Schools Council Drama Project.
6 MALE, D. (1977) 'Some thoughts on initial training', quoted in MCGREGOR *et al.*, *op. cit.*, see note 3.
7 BOLTON, G. (1980) *Towards a Theory of Drama in Education*, Longmans.
8 O'HARA, J. (1981) 'To whom it concerns', a report on BEd drama courses, in *Speech and Drama*, autumn.
9 NORMAN, J.L. (1971) 'The secondary specialist', in *Speech and Drama*, autumn.

10 BOLTON, *op. cit.*
11 DAY, C.W. (1981) 'A conceptual model for the training of drama teachers', in *Speech and Drama*, autumn.

11 The In-Service Education of Drama Teachers

Chris Havell

In this chapter the author provides a rare insight into the phases through which drama teachers on a part-time in-service course pass. He identifies similar concerns which he categorizes into (1) those concerned with the medium and (2) those concerned with the teacher's roles. In discussing the medium, we are reminded of the issues raised in O'Neill's chapter – drama as subject and method; in discussing the problem of handling the 'living through' experience, Havell echoes the points raised by Bolton concerning the difficulties in creating a balance between the play for the child and the play for the teacher; and in discussing classroom constraints, there is a link with Watkins' notion of authority for the pupil. This chapter is particularly valuable as an example of how we may begin to look for more effective ways of reflecting on the relationships in the classroom between the child, the teacher and the drama.

Teachers learn naturally, and the purpose of in-service courses for teachers is primarily to enhance that learning process which is normally constrained by time, energy and institutional demands. Teachers expect that in-service education will directly or indirectly contribute to improvement in their classroom practice.

The purpose of this chapter is to raise issues concerning the phases through which a drama teacher passes. These issues have been derived from teachers involved in two-year part-time drama in education courses. They have reported that within their development a series of changing concerns can be identified; and as the same concerns are regularly featured, then it can be argued that every teacher's development has some pattern to it. Though the stages of development are unique to each teacher, by identifying the nature of these stages we may be able to clarify the kind of support that in-service education can offer.

Teachers' Needs

For the purpose of our analysis, it is necessary to categorize the concerns of the drama teacher into what he understands about (1) the medium of drama, and (2) his role in the lesson in relation to what children are learning.

1.   *The Medium of Drama*

Usually the teacher's first concern about the medium is to establish what the nature of drama in education is. For example, confusions can arise about whether drama is a subject or method; whether theatrical skills have any place in the drama lesson; whether mime and dance should be included in a drama syllabus, etc. When a teacher is trapped into this kind of thinking then it is unlikely that he will be able to perceive what experience he is really aiming to give the children and how each aspect of drama can be used appropriately to improve the quality of that experience.

A typical development at this stage of a teacher's thinking is the growing awareness of the concept of *'living through'* an experience in drama as distinct from a 'recreated' experience. The term 'living through' has been widely adopted to represent those moments in drama when the response by the participants has not been pre-planned and so incorporates an important feature of real life. A 'recreated' experience is one that has involved some previous planning, even rehearsing. It may be defined as 'playmaking' in which the children discuss what roles to adopt and decide how they should react to each other prior to acting out the situation. Both can be valid educational experiences, though the 'living through' mode offers more potential for spontaneity.

Perhaps it is this notion of spontaneously 'living through' in dramatic activity that first confirms the teacher's impression that creative drama may be the means of achieving specific educational goals. Teachers are often impressed by children's inventiveness when under pressure in a 'living through' drama and value the releasing effect that a role has, for example, on children who rarely contribute.

At this early stage of his thinking, a teacher may value drama because it enables him to create opportunities, for example, for the class to work cooperatively, for all kinds of decisions to be made, for children to be challenged to use different kinds of language and for the drama to stimulate work in other areas of the curriculum. It seems that teachers appreciate how drama can contribute to a child's development in these ways, before they develop an awareness of its fuller educational potential.

2.   *The Teacher's Role*

(a) *Building belief.*   An increasing awareness of the prerequisites for any 'living through' drama experience usually accompanies this appreciation of what drama can achieve. Teachers and children soon become frustrated with drama that has a plot but not much else, with a set of stereotyped characters who have little connection with the people playing them, and with those lessons in which belief is minimal. They begin to recognize that it is necessary to select those aspects that participants can relate to because they will have some relevant experience to draw upon. So that a group of pilgrims become people who have had to make sacrifices in order to make the journey, and it is the feeling of having to give up something now in the hope of future satisfaction that will be the experience the participants will build upon. As teachers become more experienced in this selection process they can help children to operate this principle for themselves. Understanding the need to select what is central to the experience solves the problems of superficiality more effectively than many usual teaching aids such as darkened rooms, spotlights, dressing up materials and props. The teachers also find their responsibility lies in focussing the story on specific moments so that the acting-out can begin at a concrete level.

In the limited space of a junior school classroom, a group of war-painted Indian warriors and their families solemnly ate their last meal around the fire before going into battle against the guns of the white men. As the meat was ceremoniously carved and distributed they spoke of other occasions they had sat around their fire to celebrate happy and unhappy times, and of their hopes of seeing the flames again. Gradually the fire began to symbolize peace and 'times of plenty' and, as it burnt out, the death of the tribe. In this example the quality of the children's belief had been greatly influenced by the teacher's own belief in her role as the eldest woman in the tribe. Many teachers adopt roles so that they can operate within the drama, and yet the failure to use these roles to convey their own belief often detracts from the usefulness of this strategy.

(b) *Building significance.* As the nature of drama is clarified by the teacher, and the children's involvement in lessons is achieved, a new set of concerns emerge which are typified in the statement, 'in my lessons I want drama to happen more often and last longer.' Teachers begin to question the value of their drama work, not by dismissing what is being achieved, but by suspecting that they should be able to harness more of its potential.

One of the first steps towards the realization of this potential is the recognition by the teacher that in his selection of a focus he may well be opening up a way for the children to find what was significant to a particular group of people at a particular time. In the lesson described above, those primary schoolchildren clearly wanted a battle in their drama. Without denying them that experience, the teacher helped them first to explore what they were defending and possibly sacrificing by going into battle. She held them at the brink of the action so that they could savour its significance. In doing this she was also testing their commitment to their fight because, unless a group is committed to the decisions it takes, there is no way the teacher can pressure them into facing the implications and consequences of their actions.

Drama can be more than just a series of events if the teacher can find a way to help a group to 'stay with a moment'.

At this phase in their thinking, teachers may fall into the trap of finding the significance for the children and then, unwittingly, leading them to do a play about it, when, in fact, the children have already begun to find a different area of significance for themselves. Once the teacher is aware that the theme may change as the drama proceeds, then he is more likely to use his interventions to supply a means for further exploration. In one drama lesson, to enable the class to explore the potential of a meeting between a group of aliens from outer space and a group of Earth's inhabitants, the teacher announced that he was bringing in a special instrument that would help them to find out what was happening inside the space craft. The children were able to use the instrument to find out what this invasion meant to them. By supplying this idea for them, the potential tension within the drama, in this case the first emergence of the aliens, was heightened. As Heathcote is quoted as saying, 'If the thinking is right, then the feeling will be right.'

The excitement of experiencing dramatic tension may mean that the children are ready to reflect on their actions in such a way that they will really learn something new about themselves. It may not be until these moments that a teacher discovers that he will have to learn a new set of skills if children are to reflect on their drama at a personal and thematic level. If, with his help, the children are able to see beyond the context of the story and begin to recognize the universality of the events, then the teacher can feel that he is harnessing the full potential of drama as a means of education.

Classroom Constraints

These broad outlines of what the teacher needs to develop in his drama teaching do not satisfactorily explain the disturbance he may go through during the process of this development. It is a fact of life that the acquisition of teaching skills is a very public affair as the teacher encounters groups of children. The trauma of losing all sense of direction during a lesson is not confined to probationary teachers.

(a) *Social order and the need for structure*.   Probably the first and most widely experienced concern about the practice of teaching is the need to maintain social order. Problems in improving practice appear to stem from an apparent conflict between the need to keep ultimate control through playing a dominating role and the growing awareness of the learning opportunities created by a less dominant role. In this sense, a drama teacher's development is the journey he takes to increase his range of teaching registers while at the same time maintaining social order. At the beginning of his career, he may function as a teacher who determines outcomes for the children, and later may spend much of his time trying to find ways of enabling children to shape their own learning

It is only when a mutually secure relationship has been established with a class that teachers begin to experiment with their teaching and to move towards a more open approach.

(b) *Adopting a following role.* This open approach will undoubtedly involve the teacher adopting a following role at some time in a lesson. A teacher is in a following role when he is in the position of having temporarily handed over to the children certain responsibilities for the direction of the lesson. The term 'following role' may give a false impression of the teacher's function. There must never be a total abdication of responsibility. For instance, it is unlikely that drama will be achieved if a teacher asks a class, 'What do you want to make up a play about?', without having planned what his responsibility will be after that point. Many teachers, in pursuit of their ideal, discard their own experience, knowledge and skills and risk everything by doing nothing in the name of following the children's ideas. Teachers have to learn to differentiate between what children want and what they need; and since needs will differ, so will the teacher's contribution to the development of the drama. For example, there are times when a teacher may contribute an idea, a particular piece of information; or he may play a leading or following role. He may even stand outside the drama and observe, and this in itself may be a significant contribution.

In-Service Education

The need

The content of the drama course will consist of learning about the subject itself and the skills necessary to teach it. As Bolton states, 'If we ask what the teacher must know then the answer might be that it is a mixture of the interaction which takes place between the child, the teacher and the subject drama.'[1]

Since every drama lesson contains a complex mixture of relationships between the medium, the teacher and the child, effective teaching involves balancing and unbalancing these. For instance, the teacher who sets out to explore the confrontation between a farmer (the teacher in role) and a group of schoolchildren (her class) who take an illegal short cut across her fields on the way to school, may well see the potential dramatic tension of the situation. If, however, the children ignore the farmer's threats to report them, and break down her gates (and the teacher is unable to exploit this new situation), then it is likely that the drama is over. Afterwards the teacher may examine her relationship with the group and wonder whether they were exploiting the vulnerability of the one against the many or were exploiting the vulnerability of the teacher in role, or both. She may examine the lack of any significance in the drama for the children and decide that a farmer burying a dead animal that had strayed as a result of the broken gates would have enabled the group to bring a more personal commitment to the work. She may examine what was happened to the class in previous lessons and discover that they needed preparation for the drama that approached the subject more obliquely. The teacher may need to shrug and forgive herself for not achieving very much; but if the mistakes of this lesson are repeated then she is faced with the choice of finding time to explore what is going wrong or returning to the kind of lesson she can confidently handle. She will need support and guidance if she chooses to interpret what is happening in her teaching, because it is through precise analytical reflection that teachers recognize the root causes of their concerns, which can produce a complete overhaul of attitude, thinking and practice.

Very little research has been done on the journey that takes a drama teacher from a beginner to an advanced stage of development, or why some teachers appear to stop developing their teaching skills. As each journey is bound to be unique, there may be resistance to categorization anyway. A teacher's learning arises from the identification and confrontation of a problem which causes him to engage in a pattern of action which moves through a cycle of planning, action, reflection, and further planning, action, etc. Time for reflection is at a premium in teaching with its constant demands for instant decisions. Unless teachers are involved in an in-service scheme, it is unlikely that they will receive help in recognizing how their teaching is or how it is changing and what new skills are being demanded of them.

The provision

Until the late sixties, the provision for a sustained period of in-service training was only offered by a handful of higher education establishments. The Universities of Durham and Newcastle, the Rose Bruford College, and the Central School of Speech and Drama all ran Diploma courses in educational drama. Except for Durham, which offered a two-year part-time course with one term's full-time study, they were all full-time one-year courses for seconded teachers. At a national level, short residential courses were organized by the DES. At a local level, Drama Advisers were providing support through school visits, evening meetings and occasional weekend and holiday courses. The lone Adviser had little chance of following up a teacher's attendance on in-service training by working with him. Throughout the sixties the number of Drama Advisers steadily increased and there was a corresponding increase in the provision of in-service courses. In order to improve the quality of the training, many Advisers managed to persuade their Authorities to provide teams of advisory teachers who could be timetabled to work regularly with teachers in their classrooms. The immediate result of these teams was to improve the effectiveness of the evening workshop sessions as the advisory teachers could help the teacher apply the new skills in the classroom.

Perhaps it was as much in response to teachers' demands for recognition of their attendance on local in-service courses as the desire to coordinate the different schemes that prompted some of the Advisers to approach the Drama Board to validate courses and to organize examination procedures. The Drama Board had 20 years' experience of promoting and validating nationally recognized courses designed to improve the quality of amateur theatre work. By undertaking to validate courses concerned with the practice of educational drama, the Board was venturing into new territory. Amid a great deal of scepticism about the possibility of examining drama teaching, the first course leading to an Associateship of the Drama Board (Education), usually known as the ADB(Ed) Certificate, was started in 1968. Sixty-four part-time courses were validated by the Drama Board between then and 1981 and advanced level Diploma courses were established in 1973. These involved part-time attendance; the Certificate and Diploma were equivalent to four terms' full-time study and, as they were generally tutored by members of an advisory staff, featured periods of follow-up work in the classroom. The part-time period of training for those teachers interested in pursuing the Diploma (an advanced course for those who have completed the Certificate) could take up to four years.

The underlying philosophy of all the courses was that the drama teacher should be receptive to the children's ideas and be prepared to work within their logic. When examiners asked, 'Does the teacher understand the *nature of a play as a spontaneous activity?*', they were indicating that the teacher must realize where the roots of drama lie. It was the Drama Board's policy to offer only an outline syllabus so that courses could be tailored to suit the 'needs and work of the students on the course and the local conditions.'[2]

From the section on *criteria for assessment* came the question, 'Are the children given increased chances for choice and implementation of choice?' The examiners clearly required a teacher to use and develop ideas which came from the group which, they emphasized, could only happen when a 'relaxed and uninhibited relationship has been established.' Reasons for referral or failure were listed as 'too much reliance on material that answers all the questions . . . and an unwillingness to relinquish the traditional role of teacher as the one who instructs and controls.' The message is that in drama the teacher has to negotiate both the content and the process of learning with his pupils.

In 1981 the life of the Drama Board came to an end and, at the request of DES, the Royal Society of Arts took over its functions. The Society took the opportunity to review the syllabi and examining procedures and the result is a content more explicitly grounded in education. Validating and administrative procedures are now standardized. Yet the strengths of the previous guidelines have been maintained. For example, it is still emphasized that the teacher must recognize that many aspects of drama appear in education and that each will be appropriate for different age groups. It is understood that there can be different levels of involvement in drama, ranging from playing at being people in a situation to a level at which the participants appear to be living as if they were in the situation. The syllabus continually stresses that educational goals must ultimately guide planning and assessment.

RSA students, like those of the Drama Board before it, frequently comment on how they have experienced many ideas for starting drama and have been provided with useful devices for control in drama. They recognize the more far-reaching results of the course as it has so often clarified their thinking about drama. They also report on the mutually supportive nature of group learning.

The Certificate, now as then, is awarded as recognition that a teacher 'has mastered the basic principles of drama in education and is capable of applying them to classroom practice.'[3] The Certificate holder must, therefore, possess an understanding of what is needed to make creative drama happen, what to look for once it is happening, and how to assess what has happened in terms of its value to a particular group of children.

The RSA Diploma Course covers a further two years of a teacher's classroom experience and retains many features of the Certificate course. Under the guidance, observation and support of the course tutors, the skills acquired at Certificate level are developed. A teacher often needs this further period to evaluate the strengths and weaknesses of his drama teaching and so clarify his understanding of the process of drama as education.

The significant difference between the Diploma and Certificate courses is the degree to which the advanced level student – in theory and practice – is expected to be explicit about his various educational values, goals and objectives for a particular lesson and to assess outcomes in terms of a wide range of teaching skills and learning areas. An important feature of the Diploma course is the experience of observing other teachers with classes and their sharing analyses with the teachers, the children and other observers. These exercises in observing the teaching and learning processes in drama work are supported by relevant educational theories so that the student is equipped to analyze his own lessons critically and knowledgeably long after the course is over.

The syllabus emphasizes that the course should enable teachers to develop an understanding of drama in a wider educational context. Whilst the Certificate student is expected to use drama with a class and assess its value for those children, the Diploma student is expected to recognize its value in general terms as part of the curriculum and to generalize about its value with different age groups. Therefore, another important feature of the course is that teachers are given the opportunity to teach in a variety of institutions.

The assumption in expecting teachers to understand drama as education is that they will be more able to use strategies that consistently provide drama experiences that engage children intellectually and emotionally. At Diploma level the teacher must have clarified the nature of his responsibility within the drama process and he must be aware of, and be able to use, a variety of strategies.

Although full-time courses inevitably operate differently and will effect change in teaching in a different way, the RSA courses have four central features which may be applied to all in-service education for drama teachers: (1) the syllabus is designed to reflect the interests of teachers at different stages of their development; (2) the courses aim to effect long-term change in classroom practice by accelerating the natural process of development of teaching skills; (3) the courses provide opportunities for a teacher to view his work in a wider perspective by helping him to formulate a theoretical framework for his teaching; and (4) the unique feature of the RSA courses is the provision of help with the transfer of skills from the course to the classroom through school-based tutorial support.

At the beginning of this chapter it was suggested that it may be possible to clarify the kind of support in-service education can offer when it is concerned with classroom practice. The basic principles that emerge are that a course initiates a period of close scrutiny for the teacher of what is happening in his classroom, and that throughout this period he will need the support of course tutors and other students. In the model presented here, this support is provided by regular meetings involving practical work, lectures and discussions. Whatever form this support takes, the task will be to help a teacher to recognize what he is aiming to do in his work, how far he is achieving these aims, and what he can aim to do in the future. During his career, a teacher has relatively little contact with in-service education and so he must emerge from a course having clarified the areas of teaching he still needs to develop and how to innovate and monitor change for himself.

Notes

1   Taken from GAVIN BOLTON's opening remarks at a Drama Board Conference on the Diploma in Education, January 1979.
2   The Drama Board (1980) *Regulations and Syllabus for the Certificate of Associate of the Drama Board (Education)*, p. 15.
3   *Ibid.*, p. 15.

12 The Role of the Drama Advisory Teacher

Kathy Joyce

This chapter is at once optimistic and pessimistic. It reveals how the provision of advisory teachers/teams of teachers by LEAs can ensure immensely important moral and intellectual support for classroom teachers. At the same time, however, it poses questions as to the adequacy of the level of support provided. Drama is a minority area of the curriculum in most schools, and in times of economic hardship it suffers proportionately more than the more established disciplines. LEAs will only regard it as a priority if they are convinced – by teachers – that learning through drama should be an essential part of every child's curriculum.

The role of the advisory teacher is multi-faceted, coming into contact with children and teachers in a range of situations, often both in and out of the school environment. It is in this continued working contact with both teachers and children that the essence of the role, and its uniqueness, exists.

Though job descriptions and even titles of advisory teachers vary in different LEAs, some common factors are usually in evidence, for example:

1 most advisory teachers are immediately responsible to an adviser or officer, rather than to the Chief Education Officer;
2 most advisory teachers are based at centres of some kind and not at the Education Offices for the area;
3 the majority of advisory teachers are paid on Burnham rates, often at scale two or three level, and are, therefore, entitled to normal school holidays;
4 regardless of their responsibility or expertise, advisory teachers are on a low rung of the LEA hierarchical ladder.

Advisory teachers are usually recruited direct from the classroom situation. They often view the advisory teacher role as an exciting opportunity for widening experience; teaching a variety of age groups; working as part of a team; or generally offering more flexibility than is usually possible in the school situation. Though most advisory teachers are employed as components of a team, headed by an adviser, there are as many patterns of work and organization as there are teams in existence. Such patterns are usually imposed initially by whoever is responsible for setting up the team, often the Drama Adviser, but then evolve over the years to meet the changing needs of the area and developing interests and expertise within the team. Below are very brief details of just a few possible organizational forms.

Sample Patterns of Team Organization

1 A team of six advisory teachers employed as drama specialists in secondary schools for three days each week and working together as a team for the other two days. This work as a team would mainly consist of devising and presenting some form of theatre work, in primary and secondary schools.

2 A team of four advisory teachers, each acting as an area adviser, being responsible, within the overall responsibility of the Drama Adviser, for the development of schools' drama and in-service courses within the limited area. The team may meet together on one day each week or sometimes for longer periods, to prepare theatre or drama projects, or devise joint in-service courses.

3 A team of four advisory teachers based in a drama centre, working with classes or groups of children in the centre to provide a complementary experience to that of the school drama lesson. The team will also be responsible for in-service courses for teachers and maybe other groups, such as youth leaders.

4 A team of four advisory teachers based for half the week in a drama centre and working for the remainder in schools. The in-service element is the basis of all the work, and the teachers are always involved actively, or in planning and discussion. The team may also undertake in-service courses, youth theatre and drama club work and occasional children's theatre presentations.

5 A team of two or three advisory teachers working, mainly individually, alongside the class teacher or drama teacher in school. The team will also be involved in some in-service work.

These descriptions are by no means comprehensive but all advisory teachers who are team members would probably recognize some aspects of their work in one or more of the examples. Having illustrated very briefly a range of organizational patterns, it might be helpful to focus on the range of work undertaken by one particular team.

This team is composed of four advisory teachers, based at a drama centre. They work under the guidance of a Drama Adviser who instituted the team to assist in promoting the quantity and quality of drama work in the area.

In-service is the basis of most work, though the work in schools is more directed to meet the needs of the teacher. The work in the centre is more slanted towards providing an experience for the children which the school could not easily provide.

For two-and-a-half days each week, the advisory teachers work individually (sometimes in twos) alongside teachers in schools. Half a day is devoted to team discussion and planning, and the remaining two days are spent with children and their teachers, in the drama centre. At some time in the year, perhaps for half a term, the team will devise a children's theatre or theatre-in-education programme which they will present in schools.

Apart from the work during the normal school day, team members will be involved in in-service courses or meetings on one or two evenings each week. Individuals may also be involved in the evening with youth theatre groups or drama clubs. There may also be ongoing commitments to Saturday morning drama clubs and occasional involvement in holiday or weekend in-service courses or projects with children or young people.

It will be evident from the indication of the extent of the advisory teacher role that, although very interesting, it is also extremely demanding. Genuine commitment is essential to fulfil a role which often exacts long and difficult working hours while providing minimal extrinsic rewards. Advisory teachers are, on the whole, inadequately paid for the work they do and have few fringe benefits, such as time in lieu of evening or weekend work.

Some of the particular skills necessary for a successful advisory teacher are obvious: teaching ability, backed by experience; sound knowledge of drama in education and awareness of recent developments; an ability to adapt and respond flexibly to a situation; ability to work well as a team member and relate easily to others. It is immediately apparent that those are skills important to any teacher of drama, but the particular challenges or the advisory teacher role demand such skills, and many others, in even greater measure.

The work in the drama centre provides its own particular challenges by affording opportunities for the team to work together in a manner not often possible in schools. The scope of such work is enormous: freedom from practical restraints normally imposed by the school situation; space; time; number of teachers; facilities and materials available all combine to create a potentially ideal learning and teaching situation.

The advisory teacher's work in schools is often the most difficult and crucial, especially in the initial years of a team when much of the work is likely to be innovatory, even pioneering! Not being perceived as 'entitled' to the respect usually accorded to the Adviser's role, the advisory teacher must earn respect and credibility. This may sometimes be difficult, particularly with some heads and teachers who have extreme misconceptions of drama in education and make demands which conflict with the ideology of the advisory teacher. The infant headteacher who timetables the advisory teacher for six lessons in a single morning, because 'twenty minutes is the ideal time for an infant lesson', has somehow to be persuaded that the arrangement is unsatisfactory. The heads and teachers who regularly use the advisory teacher on a supply basis, because a teacher is absent, or has something important to attend to, must be tactfully corrected.

When the whole purpose of the work with the children is to introduce the teacher to the use of drama techniques, the ongoing interest and cooperation of the teacher is essential. On the occasions when the advisory teacher's services are engaged by the head and inflicted on unwilling teachers – 'Let's try drama – he's no good at anything else' (a direct quote) – a difficult task becomes almost impossible. The unwilling teacher usually finds some reason to absent himself from the lesson or demonstrates his resentment overtly, perhaps by marking books of interrupting the lesson in a generally destructive manner.

Not all such interruptions are meant to be destructive, however. The teacher who intervenes to tell the children to put their hands up if they wish to speak, or to reprimand a child, may be reflecting his school's adherence to particular standards of behaviour which may not figure as priorities for the advisory teacher. Such considerations constitute a very real problem for advisory teachers, namely, that of adapting to the organizating and general atmosphere of different schools and staffrooms. The undefinable ethos of a school, indiscernible perhaps to the casual visitor, may influence considerably the kind and quality of the drama work the advisory teacher feels able to initiate. I remember the rewarding times spent in some schools (often infant schools) where I have felt free to teach at risk, experimenting and exploring creatively with the children. These were also usually the schools were the classteachers were most interested and the drama most integrated into the general curriculum. In such circumstances we all learnt together. In another type of school where the accent was on order and the children accustomed to a generally repressive regime, I often felt equally repressed by the general atmosphere. Drama in such schools usually evoked one of two responses: either an apparent inability on the children's part to cope with work demanding any degree of initiative, or an overexuberant response to a less directive teaching approach. The attitude of the classteacher coupled with the children's expectations of the teacher role made the task of the advisory teacher apparently hopeless.

Although it is often possible to generalize about the ethos of a school, the atmosphere and organization within each classroom may vary tremendously. The advisory teacher must, without compromising his own basic philosophy, be able to adapt to a variety of circumstances and people within a short time, striking an instant working relationship with each class and individual teacher.

I have concentrated particularly upon a specific in-service strategy, one amongst many and not necessarily the most successful method of advisory teacher deployment. It is, however, a strategy which has been used by many teams, especially in their early states of development, and which serves to pinpoint many of the problems inherent in the advisory teacher's role. However, one must not lose sight of the rewarding aspects of the work, or the very positive, valuable and unique contribution advisory teachers may make in developing all aspects of drama within an LEA.

Apart from the intrinsic value of projects undertaken in schools or a centre, it is often because of such initial contact with an advisory teacher that teachers who would not otherwise have considered applying for a drama course become interested enough to attend. The title 'Drama' in an LEA in-service course booklet may have threatening connotations for many teachers, for whom the link with an advisory teacher forms a bridging security. Advisory teachers possess great potential for forming working relationships with teachers which may stimulate them to seek opportunities for furthering their knowledge and experience. Such personal contact must be at the heart of advisory work and cannot be overestimated.

This is not to suggest that the adviser's role precludes the formation of good working relationships with teachers, rather that there are greater initial hurdles to be overcome. The advisor's status and inspectional connotations often create barriers and his administrative responsibilities, requiring frequent attendance at meetings, limit the time available for school visits. A survey conducted in one Authority revealed that advisers spent only 25 per cent of their time in schools and colleges. Advisory teachers, allowing for planning sessions, still spend approximately 90 per cent of their time with children and teachers, partly in situations such as classrooms and staffrooms where advisers are not always able to penetrate.

Such factors serve to illustrate the complementary nature of the Adviser and advisory teacher roles. The advisory teacher is not a replacement, but a valuable supplement and practical extension of the Adviser's role. The low status of advisory teachers will probably apportion them, therefore drama, a very small slice of the economic cake unless there is a supportive Drama Adviser, with all the status the role implies, to pressurize the Authority. The very existence of an advisory team is probably due to the effort and planning of the Drama Adviser, and generally suggests a developing subject area. Continuing development, though, requires money, resources and staffing. Without an Adviser to negotiate at Education Office and headteacher level, it is likely that the team will lack essential support.

The other aspect of the Adviser's support for his team exists in their shared working relationship. The Adviser who establishes a team must recognize the responsibility he has assumed. The Adviser/team relationship needs to develop as a partnership with equally important contributions and responsbilities on each side. The roles are complementary. The Adviser will have an administrative overview of the area; the team, a detailed knowledge of individual schools and teachers. A mutually supportive working relationship enables the combination of knowledge and experience which is the basis for further development.

Also important to an advisory teacher is the supportiveness within the team itself, if the potential of the work is to be fully realized. The hybrid nature of the role, in which exists its very strength and uniqueness, is also its greatest problem. The advisory teacher has one foot in both advisory and teaching camps, yet belongs to neither. The existence of the team provides a professional structure which serves as a reference point for the individual. The opportunity to identify with others sharing the same role alleviates the potential insecurity of the advisory teacher's position.

Unfortunately, there are some advisory teachers who have been employed by an LEA specifically instead of an Adviser and without the support of a team. Such people, fulfilling the function, as far as possible, of a cut-price Drama Adviser, often epitomize all the problems of the advisory teacher post, whilst enjoying few of the advantages. Without a support Drama Adviser, the advisory teacher becomes encumbered with necessary administration and is forced to sacrifice some of the teacher contact time so vital to the role. Without an accompanying team, the range of work must necessarily be curtailed and decisions taken to limit the responsibility assumed. Without reference to a team or specialist Adviser, vital decisions must be made regarding advisory strategy and in-service work.

Although he is accorded a great deal of responsibility and the total burden of promoting drama in the Authority, his position is often ill-defined and his responsibility does not include the authority necessary to carry out the task. Often a drama advisory teacher plays no part in interviewing candidates for drama posts, though he alone has the necessary specialist knowledge of the subject. Similarly, he is often excluded from policy decision-making regarding his subject and must rely on others to relay his feelings and present his case. Given that the decision-makers may have no concept of drama, other than as the school play, the chances for the advisory teacher to affect policy are slim. This will probably result in very limited spending power and little expansion in staffing or facilities, ultimately inhibiting the development of drama in the area.

In many ways, the role of such an advisory teacher, working in isolation, parallels almost exactly the position of the drama specialist in school. Both are fighting similar battles for subject recognition, better timetabling and facilities – on the same front and against the same odds. The position of the advisory teacher in the LEA hierarchy, whilst making him more accessible to teachers, often renders him impotent in the political areas where they need most support. His advice and assistance with the actual teaching may be invaluable, for therein lies the strength of his role, but in the competitive political arena, he is no match for his more strategically placed adversaries.

It is possible in the present economic and educational climate that more Authorities may resort to the 'cut-price' advisory system. Already there are examples of areas where Drama Advisers have left and not been replaced. Such areas may suffer a complete loss of the drama advisory service or a limited service run by one, or a team, of advisory teachers. If this pattern became widespread, coupled with general educational contraction, the outlook for advisory teachers would be bleak. The increasing difficulty in obtaining posts back in schools, especially after several years out of the normal classroom situation, together with the decline of promotion prospects to full advisory posts, may result in a generation of advisory teachers trapped in increasingly frustrating job situations. Such situations are already very evident amongst the teaching population and underline the obvious link between the future of the advisory teacher and the future prospects of drama in education on the school curriculum. The immediate future does not look very promising.

What, then, are the possible avenues for future development of the advisory teacher role? There seems to be several alternatives.

1 The *status quo* may be preserved with a variety of combinations and patterns nationally evident.
2 Advisory teachers may gradually 'replace' Drama Advisers.
3 Advisory teachers may gradually be phased out or redeployed.
4 Advisory teachers may be used to replace the specialist role in secondary schools, working in a consultative capacity throughout the disciplines of a group of schools.
5 The advisory element may be phased out and the role become peripatetic.
6 The advisory teacher role may be limited to drama centre work with the children, the advisory aspect being gradually phased out.

Such possibilities and many others which come to mind are mere conjecture. It would, though, be a very retrograde step if the advisory teachers who have contributed so much to the national development of drama were to become extinct.

On the more positive side, however, there have been some encouraging developments in the last five years, following the publication of the Schools Council Drama Project (10–16).[1] In the wake of dissemination courses for the project, held in a variety of centres throughout the country, many drama associations were formed at local level and the National Association for the Teaching of Drama emerged as a coordinating body. Such organizations are of inestimable value, not least politically, arising as they do from the grass roots of the profession. At local level, an assocation may make three main contributions. First, it may extend in-service opportunities, maybe reaching a wider range of teachers than those already involved. Secondly, the publicity of such a group may create interest at all levels of the LEA. Thirdly, the association has powerful potential as a local pressure group. Teacher-power should not be underestimated.

Advisory teachers, in their ambiguous position, have a close relationship with teachers which affords every opportunity to harness their spirit and commitment. They are also closely linked to the Drama Adviser (where one exists) and his ideals. If all of those who believe in the value of drama in education can demonstrate their solidarity in shared objectives, its chances of survival and development must be multiplied. Together, those who work at classroom level must seek to influence those whose classroom days are distant – or future generations may be the losers.

Kathy Joyce

Note

1 McGregor, L., Tate, M. and Robinson, K. (1977) *Learning through Drama*, Heinemann Educational Books.

Contributors

Gavin Bolton is a Senior Lecturer in Drama at the Institute of Education, University of Durham. He is author of *Towards a Theory of Drama in Education* (Longman, 1980), has a second book in preparation and has published many papers on aspects of drama in education. He has lectured extensively in Britain and abroad and is particularly known for his determination to establish a sound conceptual base for drama teaching and his willingness to teach practical lessons with children. He is a RSA Drama Committee member and national examiner, member of the Drama in Education Committee of IATA and President of the National Association for Drama and Education and Children's Theatre (NADECT).

Haydn Davies is a Lecturer in Drama at Jordanhill College of Education, Glasgow. He began his teaching career in 1955 in a primary school in South Wales, and has taught in secondary schools, further education and now teacher training. Alongside his teaching commitment in pre-service and in-service work, he is engaged in a research project on discussion in secondary school classrooms. He is interested in guidance and counselling and had a paper published on this aspect of the curriculum in *Education in the North*, 18, 1981.

Christopher Day is Head of the In-Service Unit, School of Education, University of Nottingham. He was previously Associate Professor of Drama and Curriculum at the University of Calgary; he has been a Drama Adviser for the London Borough of Barking. He has lectured in drama and curriculum at a number of Canadian universities, is the author of several articles on educational drama, a book (*Drama for Middle and Upper Schools*, Batsford, 1975) and a monograph, *Classroom-Based In-Service Teacher Education: The Development and Evaluation of a Client-Centred Model* (University of Sussex Press, 1981). He is Vice-President of NADECT, a RSA Drama Committee member and national examiner, and sometime editor of *Outlook*.

Chris Havell is Course Tutor for North-East London region's in-service Diploma in Education course based at Having Technical College. He has taught in primary and secondary schools and worked as a member of the ILEA Drama Advisory Team. He is a RSA Drama Committee member.

Desmond Hogan is a Reader in Education at the University of Sussex. He has had many years' experience of teaching both in England and abroad. where he was head of the first comprehensive school in Nigeria. While coordinator of the Humanities Faculty at Walworth School he became interested in the use of role-play and simulations in support of curriculum innovation. He is Director of Studies and Deputy Director of the MA in curriculum evaluation, planning and management in the context of national development at Sussex, and is the British representative on the Council of Europe Working Party on the use of educational technology in lifelong education.

Kathy Joyce is Curriculum Development Leader for Drama in Manchester LEA. She is a contributor of articles on drama and theatre in education to journals and two recent collections. A RSA drama examiner and sometime member of NADA Executive, she has led many courses and workshops throughout Britain.

Lyn McGregor is a freelance consultant and journalist. Previously leader of the Schools Council Drama Project (10–16), co-author of *Learning through Drama* (Heinemann Educational Books, 1977), author of *Developments in Drama Teaching* (Open Books, 1976), she is currently completing doctoral research specializing in the management of creative change in industry. She is the founder chairperson of NATD.

John Norman is a Senior Lecturer in Drama in Education at Newcastle Polytechnic. He was previously Director of Outreach Youth and Community Arts Team at the Cockpit Arts Workshop. He is author/editor of *Drama in Education – A Curriculum for Change* (Kemble Press, 1982) and contributor to drama and youth service journals and the *TES*. He has lectured extensively in Britain and abroad, is a RSA Drama Committee member, national examiner and Director of Fairfield House Conference Centre which specializes in arts education courses.

Cecily O'Neill is a Drama Warden of the ILEA Advisory Service. She is co-author of *Drama Guidelines* (Heinemann, 1976) and *Drama Structures* (Hutchinson, 1982), author of many articles and reviews in journals and the *TES* and is co-editing a collection of the writings of Dorothy Heathcote. She is well-known in Britain and abroad and has extensive experience of leading courses and workshops with a particular emphasis on in-service education for teachers.

Ken Robinson is Director of the Arts Eduction Project. He was a team member of the Schools Council Drama Project (10–16) and co-author of *Learning through Drama* (Heinemann Educational Books, 1977), editor of *Exploring Theatre and*

Education (Heinemann, 1981) and author of the Gulbenkian Foundation report, *The Arts in Schools* (1981). He has lectured extensively in Britain and abroad and contributed to many journals and books on drama, theatre and the arts in education.

Michael Vernon is a Senior Lecturer in Drama at Queen's University, Belfast. He was previously Lecturer in Drama at Edge Hill College of Higher Education and assistant editor of *Teaching Drama*, to which he contributed many articles and reviews. He has extensive experience of running courses and workshops with special emphasis on the place of theatre and dramatic literature in classroom drama.

Brian Watkins is head of the Department of Curriculum Studies and Post-graduate Teacher Training at Birminghan Polytechnic. He is a RSA Drama Committee member, a member of the Postgraduate Initial Teacher Training Board and of the Drama and Theatre Board of the CNAA, and is a former Vice-Chairman of the Regional Arts Association of the West Midlands. He was Arts Consultant to the Education Department of the Provincial Government of Manitoba and remains a Consultant to the Prairie Theatre Exchange in Winnipeg. He has lectured and examined at a number of British and Canadian universities, is a reviewer for the BBC programme, 'Kaleidoscope', and has written several books and articles for British, Canadian and Australian maga-zines. His most recent publications have included a chapter in *Making Language Work* and the book, *Drama and Education* (Batsford, 1982).

Author Index

Subject Index